RALPH RI...

John Miller has worked closely with Sir John Gielgud, recording his memoirs for radio and television, and on the two subsequent books, *An Actor and His Time* and *Shakespeare – Hit or Miss?* He has worked for the BBC, UNESCO and TVS, and is now a freelance writer and broadcaster. His TV series *Eye on the White House* won a Gold Medal and the Grand Award at the New York International Film and Television Festival. He devised and produced *The Norfolk Connection*, an historical entertainment on the Dukes of Norfolk and their relations with the Crown, which is regularly performed at festivals with a National Theatre cast.

To Mu Richardson without whose unstinting generosity this book would have been much less complete

RALPH RICHARDSON

THE AUTHORIZED BIOGRAPHY

With a foreword by Sir John Gielgud

JOHN MILLER

PAN BOOKS

First published 1995 by Sidgwick & Jackson

This edition published 1996 by Pan Books
an imprint of Macmillan Publishers Ltd
25 Eccleston Place
London SW1W 9NF
and Basingstoke

Associated companies throughout the world

ISBN 0 330 34780 2

1 3 5 7 9 8 6 4 2

A CIP catalogue record for this book is available from
the British Library

Typeset by CentraCet Limited, Cambridge
Printed and bound in Great Britain by
Mackays of Chatham PLC, Chatham, Kent

CONTENTS

FOREWORD

Sir John Gielgud

He was my friend, faithful and just to me,
But Brutus says he was ambitious . . .

BUT RALPH was not, I think, a predominantly ambitious man, except in his lifelong determination to perfect his art. He was never satisfied with a single one of his performances, but would go on working to improve what would seem to me a perfect interpretation, however often repeated, until the very last time he came to play it.

Besides cherishing our long years of work together in the theatre, where he was such an inspiring and generous partner, I grew to love him in private life as a great gentleman, a rare spirit, fair and balanced, devotedly loyal and tolerant and, as a companion, bursting with vitality, curiosity and humour.

A consummate craftsman, endlessly painstaking in every detail where his work was concerned, he was something of a perfectionist in many fields outside the theatre. He read voraciously. Two or three different books – a novel, a classic, a biography, a thriller – would, during a long run, be propped up on shelves and tables for him to peruse during his waits in the dressing-room. His beautiful houses were filled with furniture, ornaments and pictures which reflected his unerring individual taste.

He loved to discuss his motor-bikes and cars, his clocks and pets, to argue about films and plays he had been to see. He never cared for gossip, and would avoid, if possible, giving adverse criticism of other players, though he could tell a good actor at a glance and shrewdly sum up an indifferent one equally quickly. He was a wonderful influence in a company, punctual, concentrated and completely professional, patient and courteous in delays and crises, critical (and intensely self-critical) and never malicious, taking his own time to consider questions and answering them patiently, with grace and wisdom.

On the very few occasions when I saw him in a rage, he suddenly showed formidable strength, but the mood would quickly pass, and he never harboured grudges.

When we first acted together at the Old Vic in 1930, I little thought that we might be friends. At first we were inclined to circle round each other like suspicious dogs. In our opening production I played Hotspur to his Prince Hal, and was relieved, though somewhat surprised, to discover that he was as reluctant as I to engage in the swordplay demanded in the later under-rehearsed scenes at Shrewsbury. On the first night I was amazed at his whispered instructions – surely, I thought, the audience must hear them too – 'Now you hit me, cocky. Now I hit you.'

A few weeks later, as we moved into rehearsals for *The Tempest*, I rather hesitatingly ventured to suggest to him a private session for examining one of our scenes together, and he immediately agreed with the greatest modesty and good humour. This was, as he has often said himself, the beginning of a friendship that was to last for fifty years.

There are many things about me that he must have found deeply unsympathetic, but his sensitive generosity never faltered. When we ventured into the avant-garde together in *Home* and *No Man's Land* we both felt we were paddling dangerously in uncharted seas, but our shared success in both plays was a lively encouragement as well as a refreshing challenge after the more conventional ups and downs of our past careers.

I think he was fundamentally a shy man, and in his later years he cultivated a certain delightfully eccentric vagueness, especially when he was cornered by strangers or failed to greet someone he had not noticed. Once, when an understudy whom he had never seen before went on for one of the two supporting parts in *No Man's Land*, Ralph absentmindedly congratulated the stagehand who happened to be standing near him after the curtain fell.

But actually he was intensely observant and extremely farseeing. He warmed immediately to a sympathetic author, or a new director whom he had decided to trust – Lindsay Anderson, for instance, Peter Hall and, I am proud to say, myself. He was never jealous or spiteful, never bitter, and never attempted to blame anyone but himself after his occasional failures, instead always eager to set to work on the next venture, fighting his gradual difficulties in learning a complicated new text by writing it out in huge letters with coloured chalks and pinning it on boards all round his study walls.

He could give delightfully comic advice. 'How many clubs do you belong to, Ralph?' I once asked him. 'Three,' he replied, 'but you know, you should never go to the same club more than once a week.' 'Aren't your subscription bills rather heavy?' 'Oh, I just write out a banker's order.'

How sadly I miss his cheerful voice on the telephone, telling me of a new book he had just finished reading (a copy would arrive by the next post), and his patience with my chattering tongue. When we appeared together on talk-shows in America, his pauses and slowness would make me nervous and, fearing to bore the listeners, I would break into a torrent of anecdote which I kept trying to control lest he should think I was trying to steal the show. But he would cap my gabble brilliantly with a look or a short comment, well-considered, which threw the ball back into his own court with unerring skill and deftness. When I was directing him in a play he learned most cleverly how to make use of the few good suggestions I made at a rehearsal and discard the many bad ones.

One of the few arguments I ever had with him was over his first entrance in *The School for Scandal*, as Sir Peter Teazle. Ralph argued every day, and we could not begin to rehearse the scene. 'Should I have a newspaper in my hand? A walking-stick? Or be taking snuff perhaps?' At last, one morning he leaned across the footlights and said, 'You know, Johnny, I prayed to God last night to tell me how to come on in this opening scene. And this morning God answered, "Do what it says in the text, just come on."'

The loss of a most dear friend is only equalled by the loss of a great man of the English theatre. His Falstaff, Peer Gynt, the drunken actor in *Eden End*, Borkman in *Early Days*, all these superb performances, as well as those in plays and films when we have appeared together, are unforgettable memories for me and will always remain so. I hope the happiness of his married life and the great successes and popularity which he achieved, especially in his later years, consoled and gratified him after the long struggle he won so patiently in the early days of his career.

I wrote the above article for the *Observer* soon after Ralph's untimely death. Reading it again, I do not feel inclined to alter it, and I am proud that John Miller has asked me to let him use it as a foreword to his very accurate and delightful book, in which he has gathered from critics, friends and colleagues such a wealth of history and anecdote to commemorate a superb artist, an endearing human being, as well as a cherished and never to be forgotten friend.

John Gielgud

1985

ACKNOWLEDGEMENTS

IT WAS listening to Sir John Gielgud's wonderful stories about his old friend over the years that inspired me to begin this book, and his great interest and support have encouraged me to complete it. He also kindly introduced me to Lady Richardson, who agreed that this should be the authorized biography, generously made available her husband's early diaries, and gave her consent to those friends who sought her permission before agreeing to answer my questions; I am deeply indebted to her for her patience over many months.

That so many extremely busy people – actors, writers, directors, and production staff of all kinds – made time in their full schedules to talk or correspond with me about Sir Ralph is sufficient tribute to the high regard in which he is still held by them all, twelve years after his death. I am very grateful to all of them: the late Lindsay Anderson; Frith Banbury; Felix Barker; Keith Baxter; Diana Boddington; the late Gary Bond; Michael and Judy Bryant; Gillian Cadell; Selina Cadell; the late Simon Cadell; Phyllis Calvert; Judy Campbell; Peter Copley; Tom Courtenay; Michael Denison and Dulcie Gray; Alan Dobie; Laurence and Mary Evans; Richard Eyre; Edward Fox; Michael Frayn; Christopher Fry; Michael Gambon; Patrick Garland; Derek Glynne; Sir Alec Guinness; Sir Peter Hall; Edward Hardwicke; Katharine Hepburn; Nicky Henson; Jocelyn Herbert; Charlton Heston;

Dame Wendy Hiller; Richard Hoggart; Sir Anthony Hopkins; the late Sir Michael Hordern; Peter Howell; Hugh Hudson; Angela Huth; Martin Jarvis; Michael Jayston; Barbara Jefford; Ben Kingsley; Anna Massey; Daniel Massey; Michael Meyer; Robin Midgley; Christopher Morahan; Paul Moriarty; Frank Muir; John Neville; Tarquin Olivier; Anthony Page; Harold Pinter; Piers Plowright; John Powell; Tristram Powell; Joyce Redman; Max Reinhardt; Paul Scofield; Ned Sherrin; Donald Sinden; Sir Georg and Lady Solti; David Storey; Jane Suffling; Dorothy Tutin; John Tydeman; Sir Peter Ustinov; Gladys Varney; John Wells; Michael White; Michael Williams; Penelope Wilton; Peter Wood; and Irene Worth.

For invaluable assistance in my research I am indebted to Barry Norman and his colleagues at the Theatre Museum; Gwyniver Jones at the BBC Written Archives Centre; the late Marguerite Fawdry of Pollock's Toy Theatres; David Blagbrough at the British Council; Meg Clarke at Hudson Films; Joan Wimbleton and her team at Alresford Public Library; the Royal Society of Arts; the British Film Institute; the Dean of Westminster Abbey; the Chancellor of Oxford University; Christina Foyle; Richard Bannerman; Clive Bradley; John Cain; Clive Francis; John Irving; Jim Moir; Jean Orba; Thalia Verganelis; and Richard Wade.

Without John Ling's help and instruction in the mysteries of the word-processor, and my wife Aileen's tenacity in deciphering my scrawl, and her constant encouragement, I doubt that this manuscript would ever have reached a state fit for my publishers. The latter have, as always, taken great care over its production, for which my grateful thanks go to Ingrid Connell, Helen Dore, Neil Lang and Glen Saville.

Any faults that may remain must, of course, be my responsibility, and I shall be very happy if all the above feel at the end that I have succeeded in doing justice to the memory of one of the great figures of this century.

INTRODUCTION

SIR RALPH RICHARDSON eluded me in his lifetime, when I sought to persuade him to undertake the same autobiographical exercise on BBC Radio that Sir John Gielgud embarked on in 1978 under the title *An Actor and His Time*, which we later turned into a book. We corresponded over a period of some months, and spoke several times on the telephone, and he was always most charming and courteous, but took refuge in saying, 'Oh, I can't talk like Johnny', an assertion to which he gave the lie whenever he did tell theatre stories to the chosen few. But it became apparent to me, as to all his other would-be interviewers, that he had no intention of talking on the record even briefly, let alone at length, about his work or his life. This explains why, unlike the other two members of the great triumvirate, Gielgud and Olivier, so little has been written about Richardson, and even less by him.

But the more I talked to theatre people in the years following his death in 1983, the more I became intrigued by the combination of his eccentric personality off-stage and his spellbinding presence on it. Which of those legendary stories about him were true, and which were apocryphal? What distinguished him from his great contemporaries, and why did he excel in such different roles from them? How did he reconcile his often lacerating self-criticism with his supreme command of certain parts?

Sir John gave me sufficient clues to make me think I could find the answers, aided by the expert witness of all those who worked with Sir Ralph down the years. To my delight, all the key figures agreed to share their memories, and their names are listed in full in the Acknowledgements. Several actor-friends remarked as I began my quest, 'You are going to have fun researching Ralph's story,' and they could not have been more prescient. I spent many long hours in fascinating and often hilarious conversations, in many different locations, with what reads like a *Who's Who* of the English-speaking theatre and the other acting media. Many of them said to me afterwards how much they had enjoyed recalling their experiences with Ralph – 'It's helped to bring him back.' They all remembered him with affection, and laughter, and when we talked of his end, with tears.

Usually we parted with the injunction, 'You must talk to so-and-so, I'll give you their address and telephone number,' until I reached the stage where I was able to answer, 'I already have,' and then I knew I had completed the circuit.

I have tried wherever possible to quote Ralph directly, from the original source or from first-hand report, to ensure I captured the authentic tone of that unique voice. Some stories which I had always believed must be apocryphal turned out to be true, and vice versa.

One example of the former will suffice here. It really is true that Ralph took his pet mouse on tour, and exercised it in the street at night. In Oxford he was walking in the gutter to protect it and stop it scurrying out under a car, when his slow progress caused a passing police-car to stop.

'Can we help you, sir?'

'No, no, I'm taking my mouse for a walk.'

When the patrolmen recognized him, and saw that this

was no less than the truth, they said, 'Shall we put our torch on, sir, the better to conduct him?'

So for fifty yards or so, Oxford High Street was occupied by a little procession of policeman with torch, mouse in its own little follow-spot, with Sir Ralph Richardson bringing up the rear. When he thought it had had enough exercise, he picked up his mouse, put it in his pocket, thanked the police and returned to his hotel.

Such stories about him in both his life and his work have become famous, and are in fact more often truth than legend. It is hard to disagree with his own description of his chosen career. He liked to quote one of his favourite painters, Turner, who sat through a debate on painting at the Royal Academy of Art without uttering a word, and when asked for his opinion by an admirer as he left, merely said, 'It's a rum go, painting.' Ralph then added, 'That is so true about acting: it's a rum go, acting!'

John Miller

1995.

PROLOGUE

THE DATE is 29 January 1980. The stage is the Olivier at the National Theatre. The royal guest is Princess Margaret. The occasion is the *Evening Standard* Drama Awards. Because this is the twenty-fifth year of the Awards there is to be an extra award for twenty-five years of outstanding service to the theatre. The man presenting it has a distinguished record of more than twice that length. The cue for his entrance comes from Diana Rigg, co-hosting the event with Alec McCowen: 'This is a very special award, and it requires someone very special to present it – Sir Ralph Richardson.'

Sir Ralph rises from his aisle seat in the fifth row, as if surprised to hear his name called; across the aisle the editor of the *Standard*, Charles Wintour, also rises, and whispers a couple of words in his ear. As Sir Ralph walks up the steps on to the stage the packed audience erupts with applause and cheers. When he reaches the microphone he looks around and with a characteristic gesture puts his cupped hand to his mouth. When the applause dies he begins.

Your Royal Highness, ladies and lords [first laugh], I must tell you this is rather a tricky little job [second laugh]. Now I want to tell you why. Mr Wintour said to me, 'Richardson, you go up on the stage.'

I said, 'Yes.'

He said, 'You make an announcement.'

I said, 'Yes.'

He said, 'But for goodness' sake don't let the cat out of the bag.' [Laughter.] Wintour said, 'Richardson, if you say anything you'll ruin everything.' [Laughter and applause.]

Well, let's do the announcement first, because that's fairly easy. The announcement is about the Special Reward – Award. [His hasty correction gets a huge laugh.] Award/reward, it's all the same. [Laughter.]

This award is not an award for a single year's achievement, it is an award for the achievement of twenty-five years, it is an award in celebration of the twenty-fifth birthday of the *Evening Standard* Drama Awards. All right, all clear? [Laughter. He frowns at the audience in mock-reproof and holds up his hand.] No, I haven't begun yet, this is the tricky bit. [Laughter. He closes his eyes and wags his finger at himself.]

I must remember – Richardson, *do not let the cat out of the bag* [with equal and deliberate emphasis on those nine monosyllables]. *The cat* is, to this very moment, I believe, to almost everyone in this theatre still a secret. It is a secret that will be revealed very shortly [laughter], in a very, very special way.

Now, who is going to get this reward? [Laughter.] The *cat* in the *bag* is going to. [Laughter and applause.] And of course this is a theatre cat. [Laughter.]

This cat lapped up its first saucer of milk twenty-five years ago [laughter], in the little Arts Theatre in Newport Street. This cat went on to other, larger theatres, and it did some splendid things, and it is doing them still. You might think that's a long time in the life of a cat [laughter], but cats lead nine lives.

This cat sat on many mats. [Laughter.] This cat in its life also went ratting. [Laughter.] I must stop, I'm getting terribly near to ruining the whole thing. [Laughter.]

I now have the honour of inviting Her Royal Highness Princess Margaret to release this splendid cat out of the bag. [Laughter and prolonged applause.]

For ten minutes he has cast the Richardson spell over this professional audience, convulsing them more with each repetition of 'cat' or 'bag', and dropping only one hint as to the identity of the recipient. The Princess has enjoyed it as much as anyone, and raises a laugh herself with her heartfelt 'Oh, Sir Ralph, you've kept us all on tenterhooks.' She then announces that the award goes to Sir Peter Hall, whose own improvised speech has to begin by echoing the Richardson imagery: 'Your Royal Highness, this cat really didn't know.'

He is clearly moved by the introduction of the man who has become a father-figure to him, and pays tribute to 'a performance that I would be foolish to try and top'. The laughter and applause is now for both men, but also in recognition of a brilliant demonstration by one of the great actors of this century of his sublime comic timing and gift for surprise. On the page, this verbatim report cannot possibly convey fully the Richardson magic that transformed these words into a performance that entranced those present. Just as he did with Shakespeare or Pinter, he left everyone wondering whether these comic effects were planned or improvised, and kept them in eager anticipation of just what he might say or do next. A decade and a half later many actors in that audience still talk of that vintage performance in awed tones, even though few of them can now remember either the date or the subject of Sir Ralph's mysterious and hilarious encomium.

The image he chose was a particularly apt one, because if ever there was an actor who was determined never to let the cat out of the bag, it was Ralph Richardson. Not only did he excel in the art that conceals art, but he rarely talked about acting, and was the despair of interviewers. He invariably turned the tables and interviewed them instead, and deflected all probing questions with such skill that the conversation was usually over before his hearers realized what he had done, or how he had evaded answering.

He never wrote more than a fragment of his own memoirs, and worried when other actors embarked on the exercise. Donald Sinden was a little discomposed to answer the telephone only to hear that unmistakable greeting: 'Hello, cocky, I hear you're writing a book about yourself and the acting. Don't tell them how it's done!'

Finding out how he did it has been rather like constructing a jigsaw out of the memories of his friends and colleagues in which the main picture keeps shifting its outline. His own public explanations often seemed designed to obscure as much as they revealed.

> No one can show, no one can really act what the audience sees a great actor do. He doesn't in point of fact do it. He suggests it to you and you do the work in your own imagination. This is complete contact with the deep imaginative subconscious inside the mind of the beholder.[1]

His own imagination was a vivid one, as is well attested by all who knew him and worked with him – actors, writers, designers and directors – an imagination which imbued him with a self-confidence that made him peerless in certain parts, but paradoxically also inflicted sudden shafts of self-doubt that could paralyse him in rehearsal, and occasionally even in performance.

He had many enthusiasms outside the world of acting – cars, motor-bikes, clocks, machinery of any kind, animals, painting and, perhaps above all, books. By the end of his life he must have been one of the best-read people in the country; he had read all of Dickens, all of Trollope, all of Joseph

Conrad and Henry James, and much else besides. Nicky Henson asserts that everyone at the National Theatre fondly believed that Sir Ralph was one of the few people to have read the whole of the *Encyclopaedia Britannica* from cover to cover.

This would have been in character, as part of that never-ending self-education process he seems to have felt necessary from the difficult days of his childhood, which were so different from those of most of his generation, and help to explain why he grew up to become not just one of our very greatest actors, but also one of the most extraordinary characters ever to grace the acting profession.

CHAPTER ONE

1902—1920

THE RICHARDSON family had no theatrical blood in their veins. For generations they had been leather manufacturers in the north-east of England. Ralph's grandfather David Richardson was successful in business and a good amateur painter; his wife Catherine came from the Fry chocolate-manufacturing dynasty. They were both devout Quakers. Their son Arthur was born in 1865, and was the first Richardson to choose a career in the arts instead of in industry. It was while Arthur was studying art in Paris that he met Lydia Russell, a fellow-student who became his wife. She was a devout Roman Catholic, and Ralph was brought up in that faith.

It may have been the onset of parental responsibilities, with the arrival of his first son Christopher, that decided Arthur Richardson, in 1893 at the age of twenty-eight, to accept the post of senior art master at Cheltenham Ladies' College, which he held for the next eighteen years. The second son was christened Ambrose, and the growing family moved to three different addresses in fairly quick succession, all in Tivoli Road in Cheltenham. The last house, an imposing rented villa, was named Langsyne, and it was here that Ralph David Richardson was born on 19 December 1902.

Many years later he unveiled a plaque on the wall of his birthplace, but his memories of it were rather hazy, as he left it at the age of four, or rather, he was taken away from it by his mother; in Ralph's own romantic phrase, she 'eloped with him', leaving his two older brothers with their father. The immediate cause of the quarrel that provoked her departure seems trivial enough — whilst her husband was away she had the wallpaper in his study renewed in a design he detested, and when he remonstrated with her she decided to leave him. Ralph was never told of any deeper disagreements that must have preceded her move. There was no divorce, but husband and wife never set eyes on each other again. It was another fourteen years before Ralph met his father again, so that, as he put it, 'I was a mother's boy until I was eighteen.'

In those early years they had to live on a weekly allowance of £2.10s. from her deserted husband, which even at Edwardian prices left precious little for luxuries. One of the very few she indulged in was her own headed notepaper, which helped to impress tradesmen and Ralph's schoolmasters too when she sent in sick notes for him later.

Their first home on their own was in a bungalow on the beach at Shoreham-by-Sea in Sussex. 'Bungalow' seems a very pedestrian word to describe what sounds like a creation of Dickens's pen. It was converted from two complete railway carriages set side by side, joined by a tin roof. There was a front door and a back door, and about twenty side doors, all with brass handles and leather straps to raise and lower the windows. Illumination was by lamps and candles, and rain was collected from the tin roof in a water-butt and then boiled for drinking. It was an enormous change for a four-year-old.

Of course it was a kind of dreamland for a child. But I had very few companions. It happened that we didn't know anybody there, and I did spend a great deal of time walking about, climbing the groynes by myself.[1]

So Ralph did a lot of play-acting for his own amusement, falling dead and rolling over in the soft shingle. It was a trick that was to come in very useful, and his stage-falls electrified audiences on many occasions.

His search for companionship did not always turn out happily. For a while he found a friend in the daughter of the suffragette leader Mrs Pankhurst who lived nearby. But one day when they were playing together Ralph found an iron hoop that had come off a barrel and twirled it round and round on a stick until it flew off and struck the little girl on the head.

> Blood streamed down her face – she screamed – Mrs Pankhurst emerged from her bungalow. She could be very dramatic. She was then. 'You brute!' she stormed. 'You have killed my daughter!' It turned out to be a graze on the scalp. Many notes of apology were sent, but we were never allowed to play together again.[2]

Friendship with another famous figure of that time turned out more happily. Lydia's sister-in-law lived at Lancing, and Ralph and his mother paid her frequent happy visits. It was on one of these that he met her neighbour George Hacken-schmidt, the champion wrestler of the world, who conquered the little boy's fear of the sea by taking him shrimping, perched on his powerful shoulders as he ploughed through the waves.

> And then one of the most delicious dishes I can remember in my life. He gave them to his cook who made a huge omelette straightaway on a fire, put those shrimps right out of the net, and mussels and things, and stirred them all round. He said, 'Now how's that for going shrimping?'[3]

But Ralph's later gift for comradeship was very slow to blossom in his boyhood. He said that throughout his schooldays he made only three friends: George Pensotti, Cyril Shaw and George Loftus. He failed to impress his teachers, and was bored by all the school subjects. This cannot have been the fault of one particular school, because he went to a succession of Catholic teaching institutions in Shoreham, in Norwood near Crystal Palace, and in Brighton, as he and his mother seemed to move constantly from flats to small hotels and boarding-houses.

Ralph enjoyed being an altar boy at Brighton, but as he was a poor Latin scholar he 'winged' the middle parts of the Latin responses, sure of only the beginning and the end. This knack of sailing through and inventing confidently what he could not remember was to prove another useful trick.

Ralph's mother was a hypochondriac about her own health and even more worried about his: he always seemed to be catching things – mumps, scarlet fever and diphtheria. Because diphtheria was thought to have left him with a weak heart he was forbidden games at school. This was either a wrong diagnosis or he recovered completely, so that he was able to play tennis and squash very vigorously and competitively all his life.

But his mother's gloom about his health and his own aversion to school meant that he stayed at home quite a lot in his early teens, often confined to bed. His diary entries for 1917 are revealing of his interests and state of mind towards the end of his schooldays. They show his original approach to spelling, an individuality he never lost; and also the beginnings of his great respect for literature – the birthdays of Shakespeare and Dickens are carefully entered in a different ink, presumably at the beginning of the year so he should not forget them.

JANUARY 26. I ran away from Were and came home as Were was such a rotten place, it was called St Edmund's College.

JANUARY 27. I went back to Xaverain College Queen's Park where I had been before — as a boarder. I liked it much better than at St Edmund's.

FEBRUARY 7. Chas: Dickens b. 1812.
Mother came to see me.

APRIL 24. Shakespeare b. 1564.

There are several references over four days' entries to a bird he bought in Bond Street in Brighton. Eventually he decided to let it go because it was so wild.

APRIL 28. So I let Dick go and he flew away quite all right . . . I would very much like to have a mouse and cage but Mother won't let me.

APRIL 29. (Sunday). Went to Holy Communion and after at breakfast I got Mother to allow me to keep a mouse — joys. I started a little tin which I call a 'Mouse Box' for the saving of money for my mouse. In the morning Mother and I went to the West Pier. We watched some trick diving heard the band and Mother had my sillowett taken. After dinner Cyril came and stayed until tea time. Went across to Vespas in the evening. Cyril bought a catapult stem from me. The 'Mouse Fund' is now 5/2d. Nothing else worth recording.

MAY 5. I did not go to school today as I have been feeling unwell. I got up after breakfast and went out with Mother and bought some seed and a feeding bowl for my mouse. And then something which is a great disappointment to me happened. Mrs Beckett says she cannot allow a mouse to be kept in the house and the potty old thing thinks that he would smell. Just as if one mouse ever dose! I am very sorry and also am feeling very angry about it. I will keep the cage and all things for the time when we can leave here and can have another mouse. After dinner I went out for a minute and bought two new books by Rider Haggard *Eric Brighteyes* and *The Worlds Desire*. Stayed in the rest of the day, and did some little drawings.

MAY 8. School all day. I don't seem to be getting on very well, I do wish I did not learn Latin. Got my watch back from the watch makers it had something wrong with it.

JUNE 1. [A long entry about moving into a new flat at St Michael's Place. Ralph finally found a coloured buck mouse.] He only cost 6d, very cheep indeed for so large and hansome a mouse he is black and white piebald. He did not get on with his wives so he was no good for breeding purposes and therefore was so cheep. He is very strong, large and is of a good class and will I should think go very well alone in his cage. I can get paper shavings at Waterloo St, bran at Queens Road. I am very glad to have him. We are getting on very well with the housework and are much straighter.

He was thrilled to have a second-hand bike, spelt 'byke'.

JULY 3. Yesterday I had an accident on my bycycle and hurt my leg. So today as I cannot walk properly I stayed in bed with my leg.

JULY 17. [He cycled over to Lewes.] On my way home I met some German prisoners working in a field and I spoke with one who told me he had been captured at the Somme.

JULY 21. Went out in the morning doing odd things for Mother. I spend a large part of my time doing odd things. Mr Wheeler who I went to see gave me 1/-. My mouse is very well.

AUGUST 13. [He travelled up to Newcastle on his own by train and taxi.] On reaching Kings X the fare on the taxi was just 2/6 and I gave the driver a half-crown piece and was fumbling for some pennys for a tip the driver however did not think I was going to give him one and he said 'Well, aint y'er goin' to give me some think for meselfe?' He said this in a nasty tone and I answered him 'You can fish for your tip until you can be civil.'

AUGUST 14. [He visited the leather works with his Uncle Guilbert who was a partner there.] It was a fine place and I enjoyed going round and seeing the different things very much.

OCTOBER 27. [He burnt his foot when he upset a frying pan.] Today my foot does not seem to be very well. I stayed in all the time. Looking out of the window I espied a ship with many holes in her. She had been in the fighting I expect. Of cores this is the time of the Great War the 4th year it has been on. There seems to be no prospect of it ending and no one not only our great people seem to be quite at a loss to say when it will end. Khim is quite well and is not any the worse from yesterday [when he had escaped down a hole in the skirting-board]. I received some catalogues that I sent up for about bykes.

Most other boys of his age who bothered to keep a diary would have abandoned it at the end of the year, and opened a new one, but not Ralph. On the last page he tries to sum up the year as a whole, and what it has meant for him, before making a resounding new resolution for the future.

REVIEW OF THE YEAR

No great thing has happened during the year, no great turning point which might stand out high above the other events. Upon the whole I have had a very happy year though several little troubles with which life is beset have chanced. I am moreover rather surprised at the lack of adventures in the last year. I am still at school preparing for the great change from boyhood to manhood. Now many thoughts come into my

brain too many to get down, thoughts some merry some
sollemn so I think I had better close now. A new year dawns,
a new page in the book of life, let me try to fill it with good
deeds so as if it be the last page I may be fit to close the 'Book'
and meet the Great Unknown.

> Ralph David Richardson
> Age 15 written
> on the 31th day of
> December in the year
> > 1917.

The 'great change' Ralph was waiting for seemed to come
in 1919 at the initiative of his friend Cyril Shaw, who left
school and got a job in a Brighton insurance office. He did
well there and soon told Ralph there was a vacancy which he
could help him get. Ralph persuaded his mother that he was
not learning very much at school, and he got the job of office-
boy at ten shillings a week, which he thought was a princely
salary. His health immediately improved and he never missed
a day's work.

But this initial change proved illusory. Employer and
employee soon discovered that Ralph was not suited to
insurance work. He kept putting the cheques and the demand
letters in the wrong envelopes; and once he frightened the
manager, Mr Barry, nearly to death by appearing on the ledge
outside his window as he climbed around the top of the
building.

I thought one day when I was at work that it would be
amusing to traverse this ledge above the heads of the populace
below. Perhaps I wanted to show off, perhaps it was the purer
inspiration of adventure – the Alpine climber's audience is
sparse ... Mr Barry never commented on my odd behaviour

but I think he must have underlined in red ink a note that he had already in his mind: Richardson is not reliable.[4]

Then, out of the blue, came what Ralph always regarded as his greatest stroke of luck, which truly transformed his life. His grandmother bequeathed him £500 in her will. It seems that she was impressed by his strength of character as a small boy when he had refused to enter her house in Newcastle if he could not bring in his pet mouse, the first Kim, and had demanded the time of the next train back to Brighton. Her faith that he would put her bequest to good use was to prove justified, after one more false start.

Overwhelmed by his unexpected riches, Ralph went and knocked on Mr Barry's door.

'Sir, I have some very bad news for you.'

'Oh dear, not bad news again, Richardson?'

'No, no, I have grave news. I have to leave you, I have to give you notice, I've fallen into a great fortune and I shall have to leave you.'

'Oh, Richardson, thank God. I was afraid I'd have to give you the sack next Thursday.'[5]

Ralph decided to go to Brighton School of Art to see if he had the talent to become a painter. He worked hard in class, and when he took up painting again for pleasure he found he had profited from those early lessons, but at the time he felt his draughtsmanship and inspiration were much inferior to those of his fellow-students. The only classes he really enjoyed were in the book-binding department, a knowledge he was able to put to good use much later.

In despair at what he might do with his life, he suddenly had a blinding revelation of his future career. He would go on the stage. The performance that produced for Ralph 'the momentous and decisive moment that moved my compass was Sir Frank Benson as Hamlet'. Ralph knew the play quite well (he had read all of Shakespeare by the age of fourteen), but he had never seen it acted on the stage. When the Ghost said to Hamlet, 'Revenge my foul and most unnatural murder,' Benson scraped his sword along the stage where he was kneeling, producing what seemed the most wonderful noise to the suddenly stage-struck Richardson.

A piece of mime, a sound not in the text, something that never interfered with the text but in a wonderful way illuminated it, like a book of illustrations, yet something that could be done nowhere else but upon the stage. I suddenly realized what acting was and I thought: By Jove, that's the job for me, not books, and illustrate not by drawing or painting, but by acting![6]

CHAPTER TWO

1921–1930

RALPH'S SUDDEN revelation had come to him on a Saturday. The very next day he set off to find the man who ran a little theatre near his home in Brighton, with a semi-amateur company called The St Nicholas Players. His name was Frank Growcott, and although it was his day off Ralph tracked him down to his home in the Port Hall Road.

By a remarkable coincidence he was a pocket edition of Sir Frank Benson on whom he liked to model himself, and in whose company he had once been. I explained to Mr Growcott that I would like to become a member of his acting company. There was a silence. Growcott leaned against the door and looked me over.

'What acting have you done?' he asked me. I told him none.

'Then I don't see how, as an actor, you would be very useful to me,' he said pleasantly. This was an impasse.

'Mr Growcott,' I said cautiously, 'I might be able to pay you a small premium.' He stood bolt upright. 'Come inside.'[1]

Ralph inquired how long Growcott thought it would take to make a useful actor out of a total beginner such as he was. On being told three months he proposed that they make an agreement for six months. For the first three months Ralph would pay him ten shillings a week, for the second three months Growcott would pay him the same sum. After due thought Growcott asked him to bring the first month's premium to the theatre the next day and recite an audition piece. Ralph chose Falstaff's speech from *The Merry Wives of Windsor* about being dunked in the Thames, and presented himself promptly at 11.30 on Monday morning.

But no Growcott appeared. Ralph's growing impatience exploded when his prospective employer finally strolled in at 12.45 without a word of explanation or apology.

'Mr Growcott, you have kept me a long time waiting.'

Ralph never forgot his response. 'Young man, if you are going to get on in the theatre, you'll have to learn to wait.'

Nor did he forget his reaction to Ralph's first attempt at the fat knight. 'That is quite awful, it is shapeless, senseless, badly spoken, you don't even know it very well, and I can't think why you chose the piece you did, because you could never, never be any good as Falstaff.'[2]

His discouragement at these words ran so deep that over twenty-five years later it took all of Laurence Olivier's persuasive skills to overcome Ralph's conviction that the part was beyond him. But for now it was Ralph's unusual business arrangement that rescued him for the stage. As he gloomily picked up his copy of Shakespeare with his £2 tucked inside it he heard Growcott say casually, 'By the way, did you remember to bring that little premium? If you have, we might go and have a spot to celebrate, before getting down to work.'

He began work that very night, not on the stage but under it, creating the sound effects of a Zeppelin raid with two petrol tins on the end of a leather strap. The play was a wartime comedy written by Growcott and starring himself; he said he would cue the effects by stamping his foot. What he did not tell the stage-innocent Richardson was that to make up for his lack of inches the leading actor wore stage lifts in his shoes, and the eager new stage manager mistook the tap of those high heels for his cue, so the air raid erupted when the Zeppelins were miles away, and many pages before they were due to arrive as the climax of the last act. This made what Ralph admitted was 'rather a bumpy start for me – at the bottom of my profession in every sense of the word'.[3]

But he gradually made himself useful, learning about props, wardrobe, electric wiring, scene construction and scene painting. These chores can seem very boring and mundane to someone who only wants to act, but Ralph retained his interest in these technical skills acquired at the outset of his career; later colleagues were always surprised when they first worked with him to discover how very demanding and precise he was about the right props, the correct details of his costume and, in particular, the most effective lighting not just for him, but for the overall scenic effect. Ralph also acted as a kind of chauffeur, calling for Growcott before the show on his bicycle, when the actor-manager would mount the step behind him, and be whizzed down the hill to the theatre.

Soon Ralph actually stepped on to the stage as an actor, wearing the red and blue uniform of a gendarme in Balzac's *The Bishop's Candlesticks*, adapted and translated by the ubiquitous F. R. Growcott. The small company had to do much doubling of parts; Ralph played both Mr Bumble and Bill Sikes in *Oliver Twist*, and what would seem to be a rather more difficult pairing of Macduff and Banquo in *Macbeth*, though he never explained how he coped with the scene after Duncan's murder, when one of his two characters had to address the other. His first recorded notice was for Malvolio in *Twelfth Night*, when the local critic commended 'Mr Ralph Richardson, whose make-up was excellent, and who gave a thoughtful impression of the conceited steward'.

JOHN MILLER

For the first three months Ralph kept his side of the
contract, but thereafter 'I did not more than once in the moon
see the ten shillings a week we had agreed on. Each Saturday
night there was an argument which sometimes led to blows.
My first manager is the only one so far that I have actually
struck.'⁴ The last sentence of that recollection in 1960 reads
almost as a warning to other colleagues, some of whom feared
the violent expression of Ralph's frustrations, and in the case
of two distinguished actors actually experienced it.

At the end of his six months' contract the young actor
decided it was time to move on, to a larger stage and a more
demanding repertoire. In the 1920s there were still many
good touring companies, so he wrote to his first hero Benson,
to Sir John Martin-Harvey, to Ben Greet, and Charles Doran.
The first two never replied. Greet saw him, but had no
vacancy. So all his hopes rested on Doran, when he replied to
his letter, inviting him to come and see him in Eastbourne.
Ralph cycled over and Doran's dresser showed him to 'the
guv'nor's' dressing-room after the matinee of *The Merchant of
Venice*. He was wiping off his make-up as Shylock, and looked
up at his visitor framed in his mirror. 'Sit down, Richardson,
and tell me what you've been doing.'

He listened with interest and then asked to hear something. 'Stand over there,' he said, indicating the wall where
his street clothes were hanging next to his Shylock costume.
Ralph launched into 'Friends, Romans, countrymen . . .' and
as he warmed to his task his gestures became more sweeping. He thought he was doing rather well until he reached
'You all did see that on the Lupercal / I thrice presented him
with a kingly crown', when Doran burst out, "Stop it, man,
stop it!"

"I'm sorry, Mr Doran, wasn't it any good?"

"It's all right, it's all right, but you're trampling on my
trousers!"⁵

20

Fortunately Mark Antony's passionate oratory had damaged neither Doran's trousers nor Richardson's career prospects.

'I'm willing to take you on. What are your terms for a tour with me?'

'Mr Doran, sir, if I am to join your company, I am afraid you will have to pay me thirty shillings a week.'

'I'll give you a contract for £3 [then the Actors' Association minimum fee]. Go and fix it up with the manager.'

Other versions of this negotiation have Doran then saying that Richardson would have to give him ten shillings or a pound back. In any event Ralph was overjoyed as he pedalled back to Brighton and prepared to move to London for the first three weeks of rehearsal, when seven plays were to be rehearsed. Actors still had to provide a part of their costumes, and his instructions listed:

2 wigs – 1 juvenile, 1 scratch character.
2 court shoes – 1 russet, 1 black.
2 tights.
2 ballet shirts.

The company he joined had mostly toured with Doran before, and the young names yet to make their mark included Hilton Edwards, Norman Shelley, Earle Grey, Cecil Parker, Abraham Sofaer, Muriel Hewitt, and Don Woolfitt (as he then spelt his name). The new arrival found it difficult adapting to the method of acting practised here, and discovered that his experience in Growcott's tiny theatre had not equipped him to project himself in an auditorium of any size. There, he realized, they had all been soloists with no one in charge; here he was part of an orchestra. He feared he was not going to be able to strike the right notes as part of the ensemble. His Lorenzo in *The Merchant of Venice* seemed so feeble.

'Keep it up, Richardson, keep it up,' said Doran every time I
spoke. Bewildered, I shouted, I screamed and rushed about
the stage as if it had been on fire. I banged Solanio and
Salarino on the back as if they were choking. I spoke so fast I
felt my tongue must gabble out of my head. I laughed like a
tipsy hyena, But 'Oh, Richardson, do keep it up' was all the
response I got.[6]

At the end of the first week's tour in Lowestoft he nearly
despaired, but as the tour went on he gradually gained in
confidence until he could note in his diary with some
satisfaction, 'Doran hardly rages at me at all.' By December
1921 his performance had improved enough for the *Cork
Examiner* to note that 'Mr Ralph Richardson was an efficient
Lorenzo.' Not perhaps the wildest praise for the interpretation
of such a romantic part, but at least it was the first indication
of a growing competence on the stage. Soon he could afford to
exchange his push-bike for his first motor-bike. It was a
Rudge, with no clutch or gear-box, which had to be started
with a running push. 'You opened up, she was off like a
rocket, you leapt into the air and landed on the saddle – or
else.'[7]

He took advantage of the London rehearsals to observe the
theatrical stars of the day; Charles Hawtrey impressed him as
the best actor he had ever seen, and Mrs Patrick Campbell
spellbound and terrified him as Hedda Gabler when she threw
Lovborg's poems into the blazing stove. It is interesting that
he singled out two such very different players. Hawtrey excelled in light modern comedies, and he had a naturalistic style
that made him hugely popular with late-Victorian and Edwardian audiences, who were drawn by him rather than the plays
in which he starred, few of which would revive today, even as
period pieces. Mrs Patrick Campbell had a much wider range,
and made her reputation in the classics from Shakespeare to

Ibsen, mostly in tragic roles, although she had a great comic triumph with Eliza Doolittle in *Pygmalion*, which Shaw created with her in mind, despite her being really too old for the part. Ralph drew on both these acting traditions and styles, and later triumphed in both modern and classical parts.

Significantly – unlike Mrs Campbell – Hawtrey was never out of work, right up until his death in 1923, as the London audiences of the time preferred his lighter fare, and just after the First World War that preference was especially marked. In London only the Old Vic struggled to offer the great classical repertory as a matter of policy, and few 'fashionable' playgoers were drawn away from the West End to cross Waterloo Bridge in search of Shakespeare until the end of the 1920s.

The age of the great actor-managers who had dominated the English theatre was drawing to an end. Speculators had taken over much of the West End in the war, and major figures like Sir John Martin-Harvey, Sir Frank Benson and Ben Greet now spent much of their time touring the provinces in revivals of their earlier triumphs. Martin-Harvey was still playing Sydney Carton in *The Only Way*, an adaptation of *A Tale of Two Cities*, when he was quite an old man.

Charles Doran was not in their league himself, but he had a good company, and a challenging Shakespearean repertoire, which was an invaluable training-ground for the keen but inexperienced Richardson. As one tour succeeded another he graduated to leading parts like Orlando, Bottom and Cassio. It was as Cassio that he first struck a chord that was to resound again and again in his audiences, when his character was described as 'acted with great sympathy; one loved him drunk or sober'.

But his first markedly enthusiastic notice came in Dublin, when the audience at the Gaiety Theatre recalled him four times after Antony's speech in *Julius Caesar*. The performance was more controlled than the one in Doran's Eastbourne dressing-room, and the response correspondingly much warmer from the Irish reviewer:

> One of the finest performances of the night was the Mark Antony of Mr Ralph Richardson. Of course, the great test piece, if it may be so called, is the Oration over the body of the dead Caesar, and this was delivered by the artist with quite remarkable elocutionary effect. It had indeed this rare quality, that the actor seemed not to be giving utterance to a set speech, but rather to the spontaneous expression of his feelings, delivered in the most affecting tones of voice, and with gestures most natural.

The date was 15 February 1923, eighteen months after his limp debut with Doran's company. His persistence and determination to learn his craft had paid off. But so far he had only worn tights or togas on-stage, and he felt it was time for a change into trousers. This desire not to be limited to one style of playing set the pattern for his choice of plays throughout his career, as he moved from costume parts into modern dress and back again as a matter of deliberate policy on his part, rather than at the whim of casting agents or producers.

But at this stage he was still dependent on them. His two years' experience with Doran had been invaluable to him, but there were many actors seeking work, so he spent several dispiriting weeks tramping round the agents until one day he fetched up in the overcrowded waiting-room of Miss Connie's Agency. He feared this would be another fruitless visit, but the moment Miss Connie set eyes on him she called him into her office and said to her staff, 'Now here is a likely looking lad.' His spirits lifted, and thus began a relationship with

Constance Chapman that became a happy and productive one, especially when he subsequently embarked on his film career.

His first modern part was Henry in Sutton Vane's *Outward Bound*, and once again he felt ill-equipped for it. It was a well-written modern play, with about eight equal parts to carry the weight, and it was only now that Ralph realized how he had been helped by a powerful leading actor who had 'pulled the train along'. He was also at a loss to know what to do with his hands, without a sword or dagger to rest on, or a plumed hat to hold. But his greatest difficulty was maintaining concentration in continuous performances of a single play for six months, having grown used to an ever-changing repertory.

It was back into costume for his next part, Fainall in *The Way of the World*, produced by Nigel Playfair, which began its tour in August 1924. The date is more important for a major change in Ralph's private life. When he left Doran's company he found that what he missed most was the company of Muriel Hewitt, whom he called Kit. Her beauty and natural gracefulness were appealing to a man who was self-conscious about his looks and his clumsiness, and her slight stature and youthful vulnerability brought out his protective instincts. She was attracted by his kindness, his sense of humour and a maturity of character that made him seem older than his contemporaries. Doran had been her first employer, whom she had joined as a student. This was quite a common practice at the time, with benefits on both sides – the students enjoyed some early experience of the professional stage, and the management gained cheap labour. But these engagements were often of short duration, and Kit had no hesitation in leaving Doran to rejoin the man who now mattered most in her life. During the tour of *The Way of the World* she and Ralph were married – he was twenty-one, five years older than his bride. He had established a stability in his private life that he had never known since his mother had left home with him when he was only four years old. As a child he had not enjoyed their constant changes of residence, and as a young touring actor he hated the often dingy and spartan provincial lodgings. Soon he and Kit would be able to set up home together. The pleasure he took in creature comforts when he could afford them later in life is the more understandable in the knowledge of his earliest hardships.

Ralph and Kit's life together, off-stage and on, began very happily. For most of 1925 they were in Sir Barry Jackson's Birmingham Repertory Company, touring in *The Farmer's Wife*, in which they had a very effective scene together as the young farmer Richard Coaker and the flirtatious Petronell with whom he is in love.

In December they repaired to Jackson's own theatre in Station Street, Birmingham. A man of considerable private means, Sir Barry ran what was by then, and for many years after, the most exciting theatre in the country. His policy of combining new plays with original productions of the classics, including Shakespeare in modern dress, attracted attention well beyond the environs of Birmingham. His repertoire was often too adventurous for the local audiences, but many productions were mounted successfully in London, and profitable tours recouped the losses on those experiments too advanced for their time.

Jackson and his chief director, H. K. Ayliff, both had an unerring eye for promising talent, and between them over several decades they made the names of many of the most celebrated theatrical figures – from Cedric Hardwicke, Gwen Ffrangcon-Davies, John Gielgud, Laurence Olivier and Ralph Richardson in one generation, to Paul Scofield, Margaret Leighton and Peter Brook in the next.

Ralph's pleasure at joining the famous Birmingham Rep with Kit was a little dashed by his first part – Dick

Whittington in the annual *Christmas Party*. But 1926 brought greatly varied roles: Geoffrey Cassilis in St John Hankin's *The Cassilis Engagement*; Christoper Pegram in Lennox Robinson's *The Round Table*; Lane the butler in *The Importance of Being Earnest*; a Gentleman in Andreyev's *He Who Gets Slapped*; Robert Blanchard in Eden Phillpotts's *Devonshire Cream*; Albert Prosser in *Hobson's Choice*; Frank Taylor in Somerset Maugham's *The Land of Promise*; Dr Tudor Bevan in D. T. Davies's *The Barber and the Cow*; and, perhaps most notably, Dearth in J. M. Barrie's *Dear Brutus*, that character who is 'not so much a man as the relic of what had been a good one'. J. C. Trewin praised 'a performance that reached tragedy in the choked cry when he knew that his daughter was a mere wraith of Midsummer Night. Muriel Hewitt acted the dream-daughter, crying from the impalpable that is carrying her away, 'Come back; I don't want to be a might-have-been.'[8] The line is even more haunting now, in the knowledge of the illness that struck Kit the following year and soon cut tragically short her own very promising career. In their first couple of years with Barry Jackson she made a greater impact than her husband. Her modern-dress Ophelia cut an appealing figure (in the short skirts of that period) in the famous '*Hamlet* in plus-fours' that was the talk of London in 1925.

Ralph's London debut did not come until the following year. In July he played the Stranger in a Sunday night performance of *Oedipus at Colonus* at the Scala Theatre. But on 3 November 1926 he opened in a West End run that was to prove the longest he ever had. Eden Phillpotts's *Yellow Sands* ran for 613 performances at the Haymarket Theatre. This became for Ralph, as for many actors, his favourite theatre, and he trod its boards again and again in the next forty years, in many different productions. But what was happiest of all for him on this first occasion was that Kit was playing the juvenile lead. His own part was the small one of Arthur

Varwell, a romantic young man who finds red-heads irresistible; he was rather eclipsed by Frank Vosper, the star of the show, and by Cedric Hardwicke, who played the comic old man, Uncle Dick.

In each of his productions H. K. Ayliff had reinforced in Ralph the importance of detail, and impressed him by his own meticulous attention to every aspect of the production and the contribution of every actor in the cast, whatever the size of the part. The discipline of such an exceptionally long run was an invaluable experience, and Ralph learned a lot from it.

> I had a small part which was extremely tedious to play, I was on the stage for long periods of time with little to do but attend to the others. We played three matinees a week. I nearly went raving mad with boredom, but it was the making of me. Those years of grind formed the first thread of nervous tissue connecting what I had in my mind and what I was doing with my body.[9]

In the long scene of the reading of the will he sat next to the solicitor, played by H. O. Nicholson, and had nothing to do but listen. It was then that he perfected the stillness on stage and concentration of thought that became one of the most commanding features of his acting style. He described his technique best in a rare lecture on 'The Actor' to the Royal Society of Arts in 1952:

> In real life men's actions are often confused by the multitudes of thoughts and feelings that tangle the expression; but when the actor expresses a thought he endeavours to suppress all others that might cloud it. He will make no movement but those he has carefully selected to support and illustrate that one thought; in real life people fidget about, but the actor never fidgets, he only moves. First the actor must learn to

keep perfectly still; and then to make only those movements which have a bearing on what he has to express; that one thought. It is then that things begin to get difficult. It may now be necessary for him to introduce a second thought, and to hold that clear; then, with its own movement, even a third or a fourth.[10]

While he was learning these lessons on-stage nightly, and three afternoons a week, off-stage he and Kit were enjoying setting up home in their first flat after the discomforts of all those touring actor's 'digs', and going for spins in Ralph's pride and joy – the first model of the Austin 7 hp. An early trip in this new acquisition, not long before their move to London, had trembled on the brink of disaster. On the tour of *The Barber and the Cow* Ralph offered to give a junior member of the company, Laurence Olivier, a lift from Clacton-on-Sea to their next venue, Bridlington, mainly to show off his new car. Olivier had already shown rather too much interest in the newly married Muriel, and soon the two passengers were so busy talking and laughing that they failed to notice their driver's preoccupation with the needle registering the water temperature, which rose steadily to boiling-point as the little car struggled up a steep hill. As they crested the brow Ralph stopped the engine and jumped out to check the radiator, nearly scalding himself in the process of unscrewing the top. As the steam gushed out he suddenly found Olivier next to him, asking for a private word.

'What the devil is it, Laurence?'

'I wanted to ask, Ralph, if it was all right with you if I called Muriel Kit?'[11]

The relationship between the two men cooled as rapidly as the engine had overheated, at what Ralph regarded as a rather impudent request from a man fairly openly flirting with his wife. It was probably as well that their paths diverged for a while shortly afterwards, and the Richardsons moved to London.

Their friendship with Cedric Hardwicke got off to a much happier start, and continued so. Although he was the acknowledged leading man of the Birmingham Company, he never showed a trace of side, and was particularly kind to the young couple. Cedric shared Ralph's love of cars, and knowing that he envied him his front-wheel-drive Alvis, would often say, 'You know, Ralph, do you know what that car of mine wants? It wants a good, long, fast run. Could you spare the time over the weekend to take her out for me?'[12]

This generosity inspired a long-running and friendly four-wheel rivalry, until it reached a stage where the older man confessed to buying a new Bentley 'to avoid feeling under-privileged in the presence of Ralph Richardson'. Even Hardwicke was a bit bemused by what he saw as Ralph's various obsessions with rare and exotic makes.

> So long as there were no more than a half-dozen of his favourite brand in London, he was content. Let them begin to gain ever so slightly in popularity, then he started to find things amiss in their function or design, until he felt compelled to trade the fallen idol in against some new and more recherché line. He would have me take the wheel and pelt down the road as he yelled, 'Go on, faster, faster. You're not frightening me yet.'[13]

But for the moment he stuck with his treasured Austin 7, and only dreamed of the imposing vehicles he coveted.

Before *Yellow Sands* finished its long run a dark shadow appeared in their lives. Kit began to display disturbing signs of uncontrollable trembling and blinking, which were eventually diagnosed as encephalitis lethargica, more commonly known as 'sleeping sickness'. It was thought that the cause in her case was infected milk she drank in Croydon, but the epidemic was world-wide, claiming five million victims before it ended as mysteriously as it came, in 1927, the year that Kit caught the disease. Its final stages reduced those affected to a semi-conscious state, awake but neither speaking nor moving. It was some years before Kit succumbed to the full ravages of the virus, but gradually she weakened and needed more and more care, until Ralph could no longer manage alone, and she had to be taken into a succession of hospitals and nursing-homes.

Ralph concealed his worries about Kit's occasional early nervous attacks and never spoke of them publicly. In 1928, when *Yellow Sands* finally closed, he was cast in a much more challenging play – a revival at the Royal Court of Shaw's marathon *Back to Methuselah*. He was Pygmalion, described in the author's stage direction as 'a square-fingered youth with his face laid out in horizontal blocks, and a perpetual smile of eager benevolent interest in everything, and expectation of equal interest from everybody else'. (Interest in everything was certainly a characteristic of the actor playing him.)

It was a relatively minor part, but the *Times* reviewer remarked on his 'spirited' performance, and another critic predicted that 'the young actor who stands on the pedestal and makes that long biological speech about creating life synthetically is sure to be heard of in the future. I rather think he will be Sir Barry Jackson's next "discovery".'

Pygmalion is the dominant figure throughout his only scene, with the actor's bonus of falling dead at the end of it, the first time that Ralph had had the chance to utilize all that practice on the beach as a boy. An actor who shared the scene with him was Laurence Olivier as Martellus, and at the early rehearsals the atmosphere between them was so frosty that Olivier realized it was up to him to break the ice that had formed since his gaffe at Clacton. When they broke for lunch one day he invited Richardson to join him for a drink in the pub next door in Sloane Square; as they talked and joked the awkwardness between them thawed, and they took the first tentative steps towards a friendship that blossomed into one of the great professional partnerships of Ralph's life, although there were some tricky moments to come. Their different characters were revealed in their different modes of address to each other. Whilst Olivier called him 'Ralphie', Richardson never returned the familiarity with 'Larry', as everyone else did, but always addressed him by his full name, 'Laurence'. (This formality was reserved for Olivier; in his later, closer friendship with Gielgud, Ralph always called him 'Johnny'.)

They were together again at the Court in the next play, Tennyson's *Harold*, with Olivier in the title-role and Richardson in a supporting part as Gurth. St John Ervine considered that 'Laurence Olivier has the makings of a very considerable actor in him' and that the Gurth 'was a capital piece of acting'. But Tennyson was generally dismissed as a playwright.

After two plays that failed to enthuse the public, the third production at the Court was a riotous success. It was another of Barry Jackson's presentations of Shakespeare in modern dress – *The Taming of the Shrew*. It was played 'as a roaring farce. Petruchio comes to his wedding with Kate in a battered topper, a "fair isle" jersey, torn hunting breeches and a morning coat ... Tranio is a valet with a Cockney accent.' Ralph had a triumph as Tranio, and enjoyed playing 'chauffeur' to his master, driving his party home 'in a Harry Tate car with whirling wheels and comic scenery floating past'.

Another critic acclaimed it as 'a stroke of something like genius on this actor's part to bring the refinements of modern cockney to the speaking of Shakespeare's archaisms, and the idiosyncrasy that so refreshed the character was so cleverly sustained that one felt that Shakespeare would have enjoyed it too'. He praised Ayliff's production for turning the smaller parts into individuals, and for giving 'Mr Richardson the opportunity, which he took magnificently, to turn Tranio into a star'.

Ralph passed the secret of his success in this part to Peter Copley, when the latter was struggling with it at the Old Vic in 1947. After watching a late run-through he got hold of his friend afterwards.

> 'You're not very funny in this part, old chap, are you? I tell you what, I played it once in modern dress, and I played it as an outrageous Australian. I had all sorts of vulgar things, I had diamonds in my shirt-front studs, I put my feet up on the mantelpiece, it was outrageous, went far too far – reckless, extravagant.'[14]

Peter Copley's imagination boggled a bit at the thought of Ralph Richardson as 'an outrageous Australian', but it gave him the key to the character, and transformed his own performance – 'it worked absolutely like a bomb.'

Theatrical success is hardly ever a steady climb from one success to the next, and Ralph's progress was no exception. In the second half of 1928 he appeared in several unremarkable modern plays, and spent much of the following year touring South Africa with Gerald Lawrence's company in three costume parts, including Joseph Surface in *The School for Scandal*.

As 1930 dawned it did not seem at first that this year would be much different. In February he appeared in his first, and only, musical – *Silver Wings* at the Dominion. He felt rather out of it in this production, and was a little hurt by the manager's final instructions as they went on tour – 'For God's sake don't let Richardson sing' – because in the chorus in the line-up at the end the real singers like Harry Welchmann and Lupino Lane said, "If Richardson sings it absolutely mucks the whole thing up, it upsets our ears." 'So I pretended to sing

"Spread your wings and the morning is dawning in the sky", but nobody heard it.'[15]

After that short-lived experiment he was soon back in tights, this time at the Savoy Theatre in what was a famous, if flawed, production of *Othello*. The producer was Maurice Browne who played Iago, the great negro singer Paul Robeson was Othello, and the experienced Shakespearean Sybil Thorndike was Emilia. Ralph was Roderigo, and Desdemona was a rising young actress who as a schoolgirl had fallen in love with his Mark Antony when Doran's company visited Croydon — Peggy Ashcroft. She had briefly played opposite Ralph as his daughter in *Dear Brutus* at Birmingham, when she followed Muriel Hewitt into the part of Margaret; but it was as Desdemona that she shot to fame. She and Ralph would co-star many times in the coming years.

On paper this *Othello* should have been a major Shakespearean event. But it was under-directed, by Maurice Browne's wife Ellen Van Volkenburg, and under-lit.

The designer was James Pryde, who had worked on posters for Henry Irving, and an ominous note in the programme announced:

In order to retain, as far as possible, the quality of Mr Pryde's own paintings, no attempt has been made to light the scenes, particularly the exterior scenes, realistically; in the exterior scenes the lighting of the sky, for example, has been treated, not from the realistic point of view, but from the artist's.

This lofty approach provoked an acid response from James Agate: 'May I suggest that the first object of lighting a theatre is not to flatter a scene-painter but to give enough light to see the actors by.' This view was so ardently shared by Richardson that he carried a torch in his sleeve on the tour, to illuminate his own face as well as to find his way through the Stygian darkness of the set. At least the *Observer* critic managed to see enough of his performance to determine that 'Mr Ralph Richardson's Roderigo is a pretty snipe', although the *Daily Mail* dismissed both the Cassio (Max Montesole) and the Roderigo as poor.

It was a play that Ralph was not done with yet. He was to graduate to both the leading male roles before the decade was out, at the theatre which transformed him into a leading man and a major classical player, and where he went next – the Old Vic.

CHAPTER THREE

1930–1932

THE OLD VIC'S long struggle to bring Shakespeare to the masses in the early years of this century had received a major shot in the arm in 1929, when Harcourt Williams began his four-year term as producer by inviting John Gielgud and Martita Hunt to lead the company. Gielgud's brilliant success in several parts, especially Richard II and Hamlet, had brought theatre-goers flocking across the Thames in greater numbers than the Old Vic had ever seen before.

For his second season Williams was determined to bring in Ralph Richardson as well, with a view to his succeeding Gielgud as leading man when the latter returned to the West End. The low salaries that Lilian Baylis offered meant that few actors could afford to come to the Old Vic for more than a season or two.

Williams had been impressed by the vitality and humour of Richardson's Pygmalion. 'There was a dash of impertinence about him too; one felt that his wreath – though meticulously straight – might, at any moment, assume a slight tilt.' He had also seen his Tranio and felt that the rollicking fun of the production owed much to him. So he went to see him in his dressing-room at the Savoy during the run of *Othello*, and later only remembered that 'We laughed at each other more than perhaps was seemly in a business interview.' Surprisingly, given his experience with Doran, Ralph was a little doubtful about his usefulness in a round of Shakespearean parts but, more typically, was 'quite certain of his "bed-rock" terms'.

One of his reservations was about playing with John Gielgud, who had also initially queried with Williams the advisability of engaging Richardson. Neither actor knew much about the other's work, and both seemed to fear they might not get on. According to Gielgud, 'he thought that I was affected and conceited and wore unsuitably dandy clothes'. His opening gambit to Gielgud on the first day of rehearsals was, 'You've kept me out of more theatres than any other actor in London, I almost refused the engagement because of you.'

Gielgud roared with laughter, and thought this bluntness rather endearing. It was a quality that came to characterize their friendship and partnership for the next half-century, although it was not really cemented until the second play at the Old Vic. (They had in fact already appeared together two years earlier, in a Sunday-night production of *Prejudice* at the Arts Theatre, when Gielgud played Jacob Slovak and Richardson Hezekiah Brent, but they made very little impression on each other on that occasion.)

Richardson's debut at the Old Vic was as Prince Hal in *Henry IV, Part I*, with Gielgud as the fiery Hotspur. According to their producer, Ralph was so nervous that he brought in a bottle of champagne to give himself some Dutch courage. When he could not get it open he knocked the neck in desperation against the edge of the table, and it exploded like a Mills bomb all over the dressing-room, just as Williams came in to wish his new leading man luck.

The theatre was packed to overflowing for this first night of the new season, with all the standing-room taken. The crush was so great that several women fainted. On-stage, Hotspur and Hal were both anxious that their fight to the death should not lead to either of them needing medical attention afterwards, as Sir John Gielgud has recalled in his Foreword.

It was Hotspur who carried off the honours of the night, as well as, unusually and certainly incongruously, a bouquet of flowers clutched to his chain-mail. Prince Hal's notices were more mixed. One reviewer thought him 'vivacious, but a figure of modern comedy rather than of Shakespeare'; another praised his scenes in the Boar's Head but found 'his humour embarrassed his solemnity in his repentant preparations for heroism'; but the most encouraging said, 'Mr Ralph Richardson, though he could not, thanks to Shakespeare, help making the Prince a bit of a bounder, made him at any rate a royal one. His diction is excellent.' (Never again would anyone have to say, 'Keep it up, Richardson.')

The second production was *The Tempest*. Gielgud was Prospero, the first of his many assumptions of that part. Richardson was Caliban; he initially had some difficulty mastering the character of the monster, until Gielgud offered to stay behind after rehearsal and run through their scenes together. Rather reluctantly he agreed. It marked a crucial change in their relationship.

When everybody was gone he said, 'Now, come on, let's do our Caliban scene together.'

So I started, and then he said, 'Stop, you know, there's something about Caliban, he's much more unhappy than this, he's much more twisted. Try it this way.'

And I tried it that way, and he said, 'But don't you understand, this is so liberating for Caliban. I think if you come up the stairs this way and come round here it would help you, you'd immediately be in the key position for your first line. Why not try it like that?'

The scales fell off my eyes. I thought, 'This chap I don't

like is a great craftsman, he's a wonderful fellow, he knows an awful lot about his job.'[1]

'Craftsman' was always a term of praise in Ralph's lexicon, as he believed in taking endless pains himself in preparation for a part. A key element was his make-up, which he sketched out for Caliban, reminding critics of an 'ogre in a Japanese fairy-tale' or 'a Mongolian devil mask', who was 'more brute than demon, more clown than a freckled whelp hag-born, but becomes no scene better than the last, when he comes to distinguish sadly between the god and the drunkard in Stephano'.

Harcourt Williams's faith in the Richardson potential was proving well-founded; in his memoir *Four Years at the Old Vic* he commented that in *The Jealous Wife* his Sir Harry Beagle 'failed to attract the attention it deserved', but in the revival of Gielgud's Richard II 'Richardson was a fine foil as Boling-broke and lifted the whole production.' Williams knew how to cast to his strengths; as the *Times* critic noted next, 'Mr Ralph Richardson plays his best part as Enobarbus, in rhythm and in character continuously alive.'

Antony and Cleopatra had not been seen in London for twenty years, and the public's desire to see it extended the Old Vic run from the usual three weeks to four. Not all the critics were happy with the costumes in the Veronese style. James Agate devoted a sizeable part of his column in the *Sunday Times* to denouncing them, before turning his ire on Dorothy Green's Cleopatra and John Gielgud's bearded Antony; he ignored the other actors entirely. But the *Daily Telegraph* reviewer registered the enthusiasm of the very large audience, and picked out Enobarbus who 'gave an admirable display, notably in the soliloquy which gives to the third Act one of the many masterly Act-endings of Shakespeare in the words "I will seek some way to leave him."' John Gielgud still thinks he has never seen a better Enobarbus, Harcourt Williams thought it 'had everything – wit, true feeling, lyric beauty, tragedy', views endorsed by the *Morning Post* which bestowed the accolade 'among the first Shakespearean actors on the English stage'.

At the turn of the year Lilian Baylis realized her dream of opening her second theatre in the rebuilt Sadler's Wells, but for the Company it was more of a nightmare, with its acoustic difficulties, and confusion for both players and audiences about what was playing in which theatre. *Twelfth Night* was chosen for the opening on the actual date of the title, and Ralph's Sir Toby Belch was hailed by the *Times* reviewer for showing that he was no pot-house brawler but Olivia's kinsman and, prophetically, as 'a masterly portrait in the Falstaffian manner'. When he repeated it the following season, W. A. Darlington in the *Daily Telegraph* remarked on his 'ripe, rich and mellow Sir Toby, which I have seen before and would go many miles to see again', but he was dismissive of most of the rest of the cast.

Robert Speaight, who replaced Gielgud as Malvolio in the next season's revival, thought Ralph's performance was unequalled. 'Richardson has his own way of picking up the whole stage, putting it in his mouth, and chewing it very slowly, like a piece of ripe Stilton – and this is something which every good Toby must do.'[2]

Speaight was a perceptive observer of the actor's art, who wrote as well as he acted, and he gives a sharp insight into the technique of this most elusive of actors:

> Richardson builds up a part in what appears to be prosaic detail, until you suddenly realize that it is a little bit larger than life: and just as he will confer upon the best-tried briar the chic of a Corona, so you discover that the apparent homespun of his performance is really the finest tweed and has been cut in Savile Row.[3]

But the building of his next part was barely begun before it was demolished by the play's architect. Williams decided to leaven the Old Vic's Shakespearean diet with a lighter offering from Bernard Shaw. When he approached G.B.S. for permission to put on *Arms and the Man* he received one of those brief postcards from Ayot St Lawrence, dated 20 January: 'Would it help if I read the play to the company – or amuse them? It generally helps.'

While it was true that Shaw read his own lines brilliantly, his readings were often the despair of his hearers, who doubted if they could match his performance. The difficulty was compounded for Ralph, who as usual had prepared carefully for his first entrance; when he had escaped from the enemy and climbed in through the window he made a great thing of acting his exhaustion. Shaw took him quietly aside and told him he was sure he was going to be fine in the part.

> 'But you know there's one thing the matter with your Bluntschli. When you come in you're very upset, you spend a long time with your gasps and your pauses and your lack of breath and your dizziness and your tiredness; it's very well done, it's very well done indeed, but it doesn't suit my play. It's no good for me, it's no good for Bernard Shaw. You've got to go from line to line, quickly and swiftly, never stop the flow of the lines, never stop. It's one joke after another, it's a firecracker. Always reserve the acting for underneath the spoken word. It's a musical play, a knockabout musical comedy.'[4]

That taught Ralph a lot about the Shavian technique and paved the way for his success in other plays by that prolific author. The *Times* reviewer thought him well-cast as 'the chocolate soldier'; 'Bluntschli is obviously a man who can combine the domineering manners of a commercial traveller

JOHN MILLER

with the casual insolence of a soldier of fortune, and lo! there is
Mr Ralph Richardson to provide the domination and the
insolence.'

It was a mark of how much his reputation had grown
throughout the season that two of his severest critics had begun
to change their minds about him by the time *Much Ado About
Nothing* opened in March 1931. For W. A. Darlington, 'Mr
Ralph Richardson, who used to be a good low comedian and
not much else, has now developed into an actor of all-round
capacity, and plays Don Pedro with great authority.'

Even James Agate concluded that 'Mr Ralph Richardson,
made up to look like a baby lion or a good-tempered plate from
Buffon's *Natural History*, makes an exceedingly winning Prince
of Aragon,' and in his next part found him 'extremely moving
as Kent in *King Lear*'.

For the final play of the season Williams and Gielgud had
chosen to mark the latter's farewell from the Old Vic not with
the usual *Hamlet*, but with the actor's Everest. Some critics
hold that it is unactable, and Darlington christened this
attempt 'A Gallant Failure', softened by the expressed hope
that Gielgud would one day succeed as Lear, but he shared
Agate's admiration of Richardson's performance as Kent. So
did Gielgud, and the brilliance of their pairings at the Old Vic
evokes real regret that their later stage partnerships never saw
them together again in Shakespeare.

Despite the growing acclaim by critics and public alike for
Richardson's achievements in his first season at the Old Vic,
Harcourt Williams took some time to persuade him to inherit
Gielgud's mantle and return as leader of the Company in the
next.

His mood was diffident, I might almost say obstinate, and he
was doubtful of his ability to play such a wide range of parts.
He could not believe in the rich humour of his Sir Toby Belch,

the virility of his Kent, and the lyric beauty and tragic feeling
of his Enobarbus.[5]

This was not false modesty; he set such high standards for
himself that he was never completely satisfied with his performance. His perfectionist approach drove him to scale
heights that lesser actors could not reach, but even then he
measured his achievements against what he saw as the remaining distance to the summit. The self-doubt that surprised
Harcourt Williams here, when Ralph was making his reputation, never really left him; and would equally surprise a much
later successor at the Old Vic when it was home to the National
Theatre, Peter Hall, long after Ralph had been acclaimed as an
international star actor.

Having finally agreed to return for a second season at the
Old Vic, Ralph spent the summer interlude with the Malvern
Festival, and invited Harcourt Williams down to see the first
production, *Ralph Roister Doister*, directed by Richardson's
earlier mentor at Birmingham, H. K. Ayliff. Ernest Thesiger
was playing the title part, with Ralph as Matthew Merrygreek,
and they 'played into each other's hands with a skill that was a
delight to watch'.

During his visit Williams and Richardson discussed the
forthcoming Old Vic production of *King John*. One afternoon
the eager producer took all the small drawers out of his hotel
dressing-table and mocked-up a model of the planned set, with
all the coins out of their pockets representing the characters.
They were lying flat on the floor plotting the progress of the
play when a chambermaid walked in, took one startled glance
and fled.

Another interruption was more serious. Just before rehearsals began the 1931 financial crisis precipitated the country's
departure from the Gold Standard, prompting cries for econ-
omies all round, for which there was precious little room in

Lilian Baylis's budgets. Soon the rehearsal period was reduced from four weeks to three, which put increasing strain on a company already stretched, playing every night and two regular matinees for two weeks at the Old Vic, and one week at Sadler's Wells, plus LCC school matinees. Illness began to hit some of the less robust actors.

In the circumstances it was probably unwise to open the season with such a difficult play, for a company as yet unused to working together. Robert Speaight rather ruefully recognized that 'Richardson had the leading and I the title-role – for the leading part in *King John* is the Bastard.' They shared a dressing-room and rapidly became good friends; Speaight felt that this Faulconbridge supported much more than his own performance as the King, 'he bolstered the whole play with a superb panache'.

John Gielgud came to the first Wednesday matinee, and wrote Williams a mostly enthusiastic letter afterwards; his reservations did not apply to his recent partner. 'Ralph is wonderful – and he has developed and really strides the play like a god – but I've no need to tell you that.'

Ralph's next two parts were a little less godlike, but hugely enjoyed by actor and audiences. First he returned to *The Taming of the Shrew*, this time as Petruchio in a *commedia dell'arte* setting; then he appeared as Bottom in *A Midsummer Night's Dream*, much helped in the scenes with Titania by a mask of the ass's head that revealed his eyes, allowing much more expressiveness than usual. Robert Speaight thought it a wonderfully funny performance in those and earlier scenes, and the disenchantment at the end almost unbearable. 'There are performances upon which you know that Shakespeare smiles, and this was one of them.'

The critics smiled too. Agate, who disliked the Petruchio, enthused about Bottom: 'Shakespeare says he was "translated", and Mr Richardson translated him.' Darlington used the identical image, and the *Times* reviewer only spoilt an appreciative notice by crediting 'Mr *Frank* Richardson's Bottom', the last recorded occasion when the actor's first name was misremembered.

It is a big leap from Bottom the Weaver to the warrior-hero Henry V, and initially Ralph balked at it. Despite its good reception his Prince Hal had never satisfied him the year before, and he felt his lack of the matinee idol's romantic looks traditionally associated with the young King. In an attempt to escape from the expected rhetorical flourishes of the 'St Crispin's Day' speech he arranged some business of moving a pile of packing-cases from one side of the stage to the other during it. He escaped too far for the astringent James Agate.

> He talked while rendering assistance to the Army Service Corps of the day arranging their supplies, and having delivered the line 'God's will! I pray thee wish not one man more!' lent a hand with an orange-box before tackling 'By Jove, I am not covetous for gold.' This is to be too natural, for the speech is a firework and not to be tethered to joint-stools.

Elsewhere he applauded the attempt to show the man behind the public face by playing the text for what it was worth 'with sufficient panache' (a word that now begins to recur regularly in the actor's notices), 'and a sense of warm humanity'.

It was the quiet passages revealing that humanity which were most remarked upon, shifting the emphasis away from the thrilling exhortations to the troops that were the highpoint of Olivier's later wartime film. It was not that Richardson shied away from displaying physical bravery – his Petruchio dropped ten feet on to Kate from a balcony, and during the rehearsal period for *Henry V* he terrified his producer on a frosty November Sunday-evening walk in Kent, by climbing high into a dead oak tree oblivious of the risk of a fall.

But, in spite of his embarrassment with the heroics which some observers detected, the steel at the heart of his portrayal succeeded in showing a leader strong enough for C. B. Purdom, 'that if he had walked over Waterloo Bridge and down the Strand as he appeared on the stage, the whole of London would have followed him'.

The Old Vic at this time rarely had guest stars joining the regular company, but no one was likely to jib at making an exception for *The Knight of the Burning Pestle*. Both play and casting came to Harcourt Williams in a blinding flash, and this almost unknown play by Beaumont and Fletcher never looked back from the opening moment when a woman climbed out of the orchestra pit exclaiming: 'By your leave, gentlemen, I'm a stranger here; I was ne'er at one of these plays before.'

The roars of laughter and applause were for Sybil Thorndike, a favourite with Old Vic audiences ever since her earliest appearances there during the First World War. She played the Citizen's Wife in Lancashire dialect, and her co-star played his namesake Ralph, the Apprentice. She thought he was lovely, but he was still in awe of the first great star he had played with, in the Robeson *Othello*.

He knocked tentatively on her dressing-room door five minutes before curtain-up to wish her well. 'Come in, Ralph dear. Won't you have a bun? There isn't really time for introductions.'[6] She was entertaining a group of schoolgirls with a plate of buns just before the performance.

Her sense of fun, professionalism and bubbling enthusiasm for everything connected with the theatre made her a wonderful foil for Ralph in both classical and modern plays. He learned one other important lesson from her. 'Although Sybil's well-known warmth of heart is true indeed, she has a stiletto — a stiletto for fools, whom she does not suffer gladly. But she keeps it carefully concealed, as stilettos should always be.'[7] Their fans would have been amazed by the thought of either of these much-loved actors wielding such a lethal weapon, even in metaphor, but hapless directors who crossed Ralph felt they had been cut down by a weapon more the weight of a sabre.

After Ralph had romped through his partnership with Sybil 'with the resourcefulness of a music-hall comedian, culminating in his ascent heavenwards as a cross between an angelic vision and a slightly inebriated Ganymede', he faltered a little in his attempt at 'the noblest Roman'. Many of the cast of *Julius Caesar* were struggling to recover from flu, and Ralph's own voice was not at full strength, so it is not too surprising to read of 'a general lack of fire', or that Brutus 'for the most part spoke rather than seemed to feel his words'.

Other reactions ranged from praising his nobility without priggishness, and attractive air of vigorous wistfulness, to the downright 'Mr Ralph Richardson's Brutus was a great disappointment. His high-toned "chat" was sometimes so expressionless as to be merely dull.' It is doubtful if the actor was much mollified by the proffered comfort of the *Evening News* in its closing paragraph. 'However, the mood of the play was re-established by the dignity of the last scenes, in which the acting triumphed over a little mishap in which Brutus leaned against a massive pillar which immediately tottered and nearly fell.'

Even the producer felt he missed 'that metaphysical something in the character that Shakespeare was to develop more fully in Hamlet', and thought perhaps it was foreign to his scientific outlook.[8] Harcourt Williams had played the part of Caesar himself, as well as directing, and followed it by acting the title-role in John Drinkwater's *Abraham Lincoln*, directed by the author, with Ralph as a cigar-chomping General Grant. Lilian Baylis was fond of the play, but it created little stir.

Othello, however, did, even if the responses seemed positively contradictory. It is not unknown for Iago to steal both the play and the notices from Othello, and Richardson's exceptionally 'honest villain' did just that from Wilfred Walter. Agate was back in his perverse hypercritical vein; having proclaimed that Iago must possess a virtuosity unpossessed by any player since Kean, if he is to persuade the characters of his honesty and the audience of his villainy, he dismissed the latest interpreter who, 'growing more and more honest as the play proceeded, convinced us that he could not hurt a fly, which was very good Richardson, but indifferent Shakespeare'. Conversely, the *Times* reviewer thought this characterization the most original aspect of the whole production, and though 'he never stalked or hissed like a plain villain . . . we have seldom seen a man smile and smile and be a villain so adequately'.

The plausibility of Ralph's scenes was enhanced by the truthfulness of the playing of Edith Evans as his wife, who conveyed the whole background of Emilia's hidden life with Iago, throwing as much light on him as he did himself. In the revival of *Twelfth Night* which followed, she enchanted as Viola, and Ralph repeated his Sir Toby straight out of a Frans Hals painting. Although these two formidable players respected each other as actors, there was always a mutual wariness that was absent from the trust and rapport between Ralph and most of his other leading ladies. She seemed mistrustful of his eccentricity, which was already becoming apparent to his colleagues, though not as yet to the public at large.

Ralph was afflicted with serious throat problems soon after *Othello* opened, and at one matinee he could not continue after the disgracing of Cassio scene. Harcourt Williams had to tear the clothes from his back, and rush down the stairs with book in hand to finish the performance. Later Ralph had to relinquish the part to Alastair Sim.

Hamlet, as so often, brought the season to a close, but Richardson was not seeking to emulate Gielgud's success in that role; indeed Williams had had to offer it to both Robert Speaight and Robert Harris, in order to entice them into the

Company, and they alternated in the part. Ralph had the two small but effective parts of the Ghost and the Gravedigger. He wanted to get away from the usual sepulchral tones and death-like appearance of the former, an intention perceived, if not entirely approved, by the man from *The Times*: 'Mr Ralph Richardson's rather too human ghost is vocally impressive, which is no doubt the main consideration', although the knowledgeable noticed that his memory played a trick or two with the text on the opening night. No one records whether he advised Hamlet to scrape his sword on the stage like Benson on 'Revenge my foul and unnatural murder!'

The last night itself was *Twelfth Night*, a fitting farewell from Ralph's Sir Toby Belch, one of his most brilliant creations, to end a season in which that most perceptive observer, Richard Findlater, adjudged that Richardson had jumped from the third rank to the first rank as a Shakespearean player.

He would not tread the boards of the Old Vic again for another five years. He felt it was time for another change from Shakespeare, and in the intervening period he created his second reputation, as a most original creator of new roles by living writers.

CHAPTER FOUR

1932–1936

THE LAUNCH-PAD for the Richardson assault on the West End was the Malvern Festival. Sir Barry Jackson had started this event in 1929 to bring together, for days rather than hours, those with a real interest in both the history and the future of the theatre. The month of August was filled with a cycle of plays presented four times; lectures and informal talks were attended by authors, actors and audience. The work of Shaw was always prominent, and his unmistakable figure became a familiar sight in Malvern and on the rolling hills surrounding the town. Several of his plays were premiered there, including *The Apple Cart* and *Too True to Be Good*. Ralph repeated his visit of the previous August, opening with a revival of *Ralph Roister Doister* in which he again played Merrygreek, followed by Face in *The Alchemist*, a useful try-out for this part, which created more of an impact when he repeated it in 1947.

Malvern was set by the heels in his third characterization of the Festival – the title-role in *Oroonoko*, or *The Royal Slave*. This was an historical curiosity, a tragedy by Thomas Southerne, based on a novel by Mrs Aphra Behn, first produced in 1695, once played by Macready, and only rarely since. Its interest lies mostly in the fact that Oroonoko was the first 'noble savage' in a long line of such creations in the eighteenth

century, but the blacked-up Richardson blew life into this
rather two-dimensional figure, by a combination of 'grand
sincerity', 'repose and fire', and his now commanding vocal
range that was held up as a model for all young actors.

Harold Hobson was in the theatre for a Festival play not
featuring Richardson, and when the actor arrived in the stalls,
he observed him trying to conceal his embarrassment at the
cheering that broke out all over the house, from the audience
that had evidently admired his performance in *Oroonoko* the
previous evening. Harcourt Williams also saw Ralph's first
impersonation of a 'darkie' and thought that one day he would
make a good Othello.

But it was his fourth and final part of that brief Malvern
season that proved to be the herald of Richardson's emergence
as a leading man in the West End. The part, that of the
Sergeant, was better received than the play, Shaw's *Too True to
Be Good*, which as a dramatic vehicle lacked the appeal of *Arms
and the Man*. The *Times* critic lamented, 'Mr Shaw's present
work has, as a document, the interest, and as a play, the
tedium of an undigested notebook.' Neither the surrealistic
figure of the Microbe in Act I, nor the accurate representation
of T. E. Lawrence as Private Meek in Act II, caught the
audience's interest; then, in a short scene at the beginning of
Act III, the Sergeant quotes from *Pilgrim's Progress* and predicts
that 'London and Paris and Berlin and Rome and the rest of
them will be burned with fire from heaven all right in the
next war: that's certain. They're all Cities of Destruction.'

In singling out the actor in his *Sunday Times* column James
Agate used him to get in a dig at the author.

The piece was run-away-with, in vulgar parlance, by Mr
Ralph Richardson, who spoke the long speech of the sergeant
with a medieval forthrightness and a controlled passion
beyond all praise; the actor, taking his time from Bunyan,

affected us like a soldier coming into church from the open field. This was a grand performance and Mr Shaw will agree that it could only have been achieved by a Shakespeare-trained actor.

This was in September 1932, after the production had transferred to the New Theatre in London. But one actor's performance was not enough to save the play – it ran for just forty-seven performances. This set a pattern for Ralph Richardson's West End appearances in the rest of the decade that, could they have predicted it, would have dismayed the managements concerned more than the actor, for he enjoyed a succession of personal triumphs in a series of mostly short-lived plays.

He followed the Shaw with a brief run of Somerset Maugham's *For Services Rendered*, playing a disillusioned war hero driven to suicide. Flora Robson was his co-star in this, and also in the much less successful *Head-on Crash*. He had better notices in Clemence Dane's *Wild Decembers*, as the shy curate husband of Charlotte Brontë, who was played by the rising star Diana Wynyard. The scene in which she initially rejected the offering of his love was one of the most moving of the whole evening.

He was offered next the title role in Maugham's *Sheppey*, by John Gielgud who was directing it. Sheppey is a hairdresser's assistant who wins £8500 in an Irish sweepstake and decides to put into practice the Sermon on the Mount and give all he has to the poor. This infuriates his family, who try to have him declared insane. The director found it difficult to cast, finally settling on Angela Baddeley for the pretentious daughter, Eric Portman for her caddish lover, and Laura Cowie as the streetwalker who appears in the last scene as Death. Gielgud's confidence that his former Old Vic partner could carry off the saintly hero was not misplaced.

For Desmond MacCarthy Richardson revealed 'a rare understanding of human goodness, and a rare restraint in expressing it'. Rupert Hart-Davis felt he had been 'perfecting his acting towards its present excellence. He and the audience are now reaping the reward.' Ivor Brown too thought it 'superb in avoidance of the sentimental pitfalls, bluff, human, and continually a centrepiece that holds together the shifting values of the play'. Others admired 'a mellowness which fulfils the high expectations playgoers have long had of him', and acting 'which is so marvellously rich and tender that it puts the actor right in the front rank of our theatre at one blow'.

On the first night John Gielgud was on-stage as Richard of Bordeaux in the neighbouring New Theatre, and was dismayed when someone rushed across the passage between the stage doors of Wyndham's and the New, to tell him that the lighting had gone wrong in the final scene, when Death appears to the sleeping Sheppey. That may explain why Ivor Brown thought that 'Mr Gielgud's production could not save the Death episode.'

But Ralph had no reservations about his director.

Since *Sheppey* I have been lucky to have been produced in several plays by John Gielgud, and I have always found, maybe after small experiment, that I have ended up in a good position for my best speech and have faded mysteriously out of focus when not wanted, and I ask no more.[1]

Ralph stayed in the vein of fantasy for his next two stage assumptions. In December the Palladium featured him as Captain Hook and Mr Darling in Barrie's *Peter Pan*, and the *Daily Telegraph* critic almost grumbled that 'the worst of Mr Richardson is that when he is on-stage it is hard to look at anybody else' (as it got steadily harder fewer people complained of that quality in his stage presence).

That dual role was rather more fun than John MacGregor in James Bridie's *Marriage Is No Joke* at the Globe. The divinity student is reformed of his drinking by the publican's daughter he marries, and then goes off to the wars in Persia, rescues a princess and deserts to become Sultan of Jangalistan, returns to his wife, meets the princess again, now appearing at a local music-hall, and finally chooses to stay with his wife. It ran for just five nights.

Agate viewed it as a 'mistaken kindness of Sir Barry Jackson to put on this play' and was particularly put out that what he thought an appalling business was 'received by everybody else on the night of my visit with manifestations of extreme delight'. But he reserved his sharpest darts for the leading man – 'over Mr Ralph Richardson's performance I shall draw not one but many veils. It was as though, in penance for having accepted the part, he had divested himself of all hope of accomplishment.'

One accomplishment that the actor did study profitably, however, was the portrayal of the different gradations of drunkenness on the stage, the exhibition of which lay at the heart of his great success in his next part, Charles Appleby in *Eden End*. This was his first experience of J. B. Priestley, a partnership which greatly benefited both actor and author, and was to be repeated three times before the war, and once again after it. Priestley was now as well known and popular a dramatist as he was a novelist. The public adored his naturalistic comedies although the author himself preferred his time-plays, and those with a political message. Ralph was acclaimed for his performances right across the Priestley spectrum. The professional relationship between the two men blossomed into a close friendship, strengthened by their shared love of cars, pipe-smoking, and their membership of the Savile Club.

Eden End was the author's fifth play; for the actor this first Priestley role was a straightforwardly naturalistic one, and much the biggest box-office success, with the play running for six months. Richardson revelled in the part of the affable, heavy-drinking, jobbing actor, concealing his deficiencies in his public and private lives. When he entered, 'immediately a breeze of delighted expectancy ran through the audience like an electric current'. Ivor Brown observed that he did not pursue comedy, it proceeded from him – 'The third act has a tippling scene of some rare authenticity; there are no conventional violence and no comicalities, but the stiff, platitudinous gravity of minds befogged which, thus treated, is so much more amusing than hiccups and horseplay.' The *New Statesman* critic found Richardson uproariously funny in the drunk scene, and in the *Daily Telegraph* W. A. Darlington spotted that the part was ostensibly 'more on the surface – but how brilliant is the detail. And how utterly right is every intonation and gesture in the scene where he gets philosophic drunk.'

The flamboyant suits, the polka-dotted bow-tie, jaunty hat and curly pipe were all carefully chosen to create the image of this unreliable and larger-than-life character, and were based on Richardson's sharp observation:

> You know, when you're given a part, it's on paper, and you think, 'My goodness, what on earth does he look like? How does he speak?' And all day long you're thinking this problem over, and you're looking at people consciously or unconsciously and you're finding a little bit. 'My goodness, look at that man's eyes! Perhaps he looks like that.'[2]

Priestley's admiration for Ralph's performance as Charles Appleby led him to take a leaf out of the Richardson book of observation in his next play, by creating the title-role with him in mind. *Cornelius* was an allegory about the decline of capitalism, and it followed *Eden End* into the Duchess, one of the few small theatres that Ralph admitted to enjoying, as he normally came to prefer acting on a larger stage to a larger audience. The title-role was a much bigger part than Charles Appleby, the rather strange and lonely figure of a City aluminium broker desperately trying to stave off ruin, and he was praised again for 'that unique care in detail and that unique simplicity of approach which characterizes everything he does, a personality which fills the stage and lingers for long in the memory'.

But *Cornelius* did not linger long at the Duchess, coming off after only two months. This relative disappointment did not diminish the growing admiration of Priestley and Richardson for each other's work. Twenty-five years later the actor said:

> I have been favoured by much beautifully written English to speak on the stage, and perhaps my favourite is the dialogue of J. B. Priestley: his seemingly simple diction is rich in melody. The best shorter part I have ever had was that in *Eden End*. There I was given wonderful jokes all set to music – what more could one ask?[3]

The early demise of *Cornelius* left Ralph with an unexpected gap in engagements, which he filled by crossing the Atlantic to appear as Mercutio, with Katharine Cornell as Juliet, and his old colleague from the Robeson *Othello*, Maurice Evans, now playing Romeo. He cut a more imposing figure as Mercutio than he had as Roderigo, and enjoyed the part more than he did this first experience of Broadway. He had mixed feelings about Katharine Cornell: 'She couldn't play for nuts, but she had tremendous star quality. She was like a magnificent circus animal with a beautiful head and enormous eyes. There were moments when she ran across the stage that you *knew* she was Juliet.'

He learned a couple of lessons about star quality in New York. Another actor making his Broadway debut in this production was Tyrone Power, in the minor part of Benvolio. During it he received his first Hollywood offer, and asked Evans and Richardson for their advice. They both thought he needed much more acting experience before venturing into the celluloid jungle. Ralph said, 'He had superb looks but no technique. Anyhow, he wisely didn't listen to us, and he was a big star almost before I'd got back to England.'

His instincts were a bit sounder when he received an appeal for help from another younger actor. By a curious coincidence of dates, this was also the time of the famous Gielgud West End production of the play, when he and Olivier alternated Romeo and Mercutio. Olivier sought Ralph's advice on the right approach to the latter part. By then the American tour had reached Boston, from where Richardson counselled him:

> Be careful not to hurry the 'Mab' speech, as I did at first from over-anxiety to be bright. It is a speech that depends on detail, and if all the points are made will seem enormously brilliant, but if slightly rushed is just dull. The second scene plays itself. I play it with a sort of lazy humour and come on yawning and blowing pip-squeaks after the party – but don't forget the sudden delicacy of 'If love be blind, love cannot hit the mark'. The next scene you should do extremely well – here I am as rapid as can be – the real 'Mercutio' tremendously smart and as full of full-up light and life as I can make him. You should try to produce a different key every time you come on – and wear your clothes in a different way. I have a tremendous circular scarlet cloak of fine red flannelette; this I can do a great many things with.

Ever the practical man of the theatre, off-stage as well as

on, his final word of caution to an equally high-spirited friend seems only partly tongue-in-cheek:

> The greatest difficulty is to keep sober enough in the one hour twenty-five minutes' wait you have before the end to take your curtain-call without falling into an orchestra pit. This takes years of skill and cannot be over-estimated, as much of the effect of the poetic 'Mab' speech may be lost by such an incident.[4]

Ralph enjoyed a drink after the performance, as many of his colleagues have testified, but there is no suggestion of him ever being the worse for it on stage or off; indeed he was highly critical of actors who were undisciplined enough to let it affect their performance, and when necessary he would get rid of them. When he led the Old Vic Company at the end of the war he once fired a publicist on the spot, when he entered his dressing-room drunk.

After playing with an actress who rose to become one of the leading stars of the American theatre, Ralph returned home early in 1936 to join one of the established great ladies of the English stage in *Promise* by Henri Bernstein, translated from the French by H. M. Harwood. Madge Titheradge was his bullying wife, Thérèse Delbar, who dominated him and her two daughters, played by Ann Todd and Edna Best. The English critics did not think much of this import from across the Channel, but generally considered that it was saved by the quality of the acting. Ralph thought Madge was the greatest of all his leading ladies (or 'all but one' as he tactfully put it), and asserted that all who knew her loved her.

After three acts of tantrums and denunciations there was a scene of reconciliation with her ill-treated husband, when she opened the door and simply said his name, 'Emil.'

Madge made this moment superb. Her great eyes swelled with tears, the audience was breathless. I was on the stage alone before she entered for her magic moment. Now I have always been very sensitive about voices off-stage – and there was Madge off-stage, chattering, giggling, practically dancing. I would remonstrate afterwards.

'Oh, you poor lamb,' she would say, 'I'm so sorry, I'll be like a mouse.'

She was a mouse for the next night and the next, and then her gaiety and irrepressible high-jinks would simply bubble up and burst in a Vesuvius of laughter. It was useless to repress her, and she never failed her 'moment'.[5]

The way in which she achieved this 'moment' was clearly a lesson well learned, as his future audiences and reviewers would treasure similar 'moments' of sudden revelation in his own performances, although he never indulged in Madge Titheradge's antics in the wings. In his own much less showy part he surprised W. A. Darlington by his 'transmogrification of himself into a lean and doddering old gentleman', uttering wisdom 'in a shadow of his normal tones with a most impressive effect'.

The *Daily Telegraph* critic continued his enthusiasm for Ralph's genius for detail of characterization in his next notice, for *Bees on the Boatdeck*. The author of this 'farcical tragedy' was Priestley again, in his allegorical mode; the co-star was Olivier, and for the first time the programme bore the legend 'The play produced by Laurence Olivier and Ralph Richardson'. (They had first approached Basil Dean, but he had declined this particular challenge.)

It was set on a cargo steamer, moored with her furnaces drawn in an estuary in the West Country, marooned by the Depression. The Chief Engineer, Richardson, and the Second

Officer, Olivier, are visited by advocates of fascism and communism hoping to exploit their frustrations, but find them both incorruptible. To create the illusion of a ship on-stage they called in Laurence Irving, grandson of the first actor-knight, and this gifted film and theatre designer was surprised by the difference between the two actors' temperaments.

> My prognosis of their reaction to the nervous stresses of a first night was utterly confounded. Richardson's dreamy but decep-tive diffidence would, I foresaw, make him a prey to doubts and fears; Olivier's nervous system I judged to be as resilient as his physique. When the time came the captain was serene and confident; his mate lay on the sofa in his dressing-room as sick with apprehension as my mother had ever been.[6]

Olivier's forebodings were well founded – the play was not much liked by critics or audiences; some of the former found good words to say for the acting, but not Agate, in his most vitriolic form.

> Mr Ralph Richardson and Mr Laurence Olivier, having nothing to act, can only cover up poverty with fuss. And how poorly they do it! Mr Richardson is no more like a retired seaman than he is like a retired postman, which is odd in view of his magnificent naval officer in *For Services Rendered* . . . Mr Olivier is even less happy, for his Second Officer is no officer at all, but a young gentleman from behind the counter of a bank or stores.

Even the kindlier Harold Hobson admitted that it 'had become a doomed ship; and Olivier and Richardson went down with her after four weeks' struggle'. Hobson was nonplussed and rather disappointed that the West End audi-

ence had failed to support Richardson in a series of big parts
in fine plays by fine authors. Only *Eden End* could be construed
as a box-office success. Hobson's disappointment became
positive irritation when the actor at last hit the jackpot with
a play which in the critic's eyes had no artistic merit
whatsoever. *The Amazing Dr Clitterhouse* by Barré Lyndon
opened in August 1936 and ran for more than a year at the
Haymarket. It is a crime thriller in which the eponymous
doctor turns from studying crime to the practice of it, and
ends by committing murder himself. Ralph played the part
with 'breezy assurance', without really convincing many
people that he was capable of burglary and murder. Sydney
Carroll delighted in the idiosyncrasy he brought to the role:

> Observe the slippered, lop-sided glide with which he crosses a
> room, the lumbering, professional bedside manner, the confi-
> dent, authoritative air, the suggestion of surgical dexterity so
> applicable to the moon-ridden game of creep and grab, the
> ruler of a criminal gang, the deluder of Scotland Yard and the
> curse of the common Bobby.

It is no wonder that the Haymarket held such a favoured
place in Ralph's heart. Ten years before he had enjoyed his
long run there with Kit Hewitt in *Yellow Sands*; now in *The
Amazing Dr Clitterhouse* he met his future second wife, Meriel
Forbes. She was a member of the Forbes-Robertson theatrical
dynasty, whose greatest star was her great-uncle, Sir Johnston
Forbes-Robertson, one of the most acclaimed Hamlets of his
day. She was another graduate from the Birmingham Repertory Company, a few years after Ralph's time there, and by
the time they met she had established herself in the West End
through the combination of her beauty and her gift for
comedy. Ralph picked her out at the auditions to play Daisy,
the criminal's girlfriend, saying, 'I like that one.' He was

already exercising his rights as leading man to choose his stage partners, and his eye rarely failed him. He was immediately taken with Meriel's high spirits, and they formed a close friendship which later blossomed into love, and eventually led to their marriage in 1944.

The play clocked up 497 performances, and the leading man's 5 per cent of the box-office would have meant that he had at last achieved a substantial income, had he not already reached that state through his burgeoning film career. His success in this newer medium had come much more rapidly than in the theatre. He owed his start to Cedric Hardwicke, who got him an extra's job in the film *Dreyfus*, when he was very hard up in 1931, and then suggested him for his first speaking part two years later in *The Ghoul*, in which Hardwicke was already cast, with Boris Karloff playing the title-role.

Ralph always insisted that he had been given the best part.

> There was Karloff making up for hours in the dressing-room, having false teeth and strange eyes, took him hours, and I just walked in and they said, 'Oh, Richardson, we won't bother about you, you just put on your collar and on you go.'
>
> Being a parson I just had to put on my dog-collar. And where everyone was tremendously fraught I only came blandly in and said, 'Oh, your Ladyship, how kind of you to ask me to tea. Indeed, indeed I will have cucumber sandwiches. Oh, my Lady, how charming.'
>
> And all the time I was putting gunpowder under the house in order to blow it up. I struck a match at the end, it was the most dramatic thing I ever did, and the whole house exploded. I've never had a part like it since.[7]

That memory was recalled in a BBC radio interview as late as 1979, on *Desert Island Discs*, by which time the film had long been overshadowed by its many successors that ranked far higher in the estimation of others, but what comes unmistakably through that story is Richardson's lifelong love of pyrotechnics, which got him into serious trouble on more than one occasion.

After *The Ghoul* he played the Schoolmaster in *Friday the Thirteenth*, directed by Victor Saville, and within twelve months his first starring part in *The Return of Bulldog Drummond*. The same year he played in *Java Head* and, again at the suggestion of Cedric Hardwicke, the second lead in *The King of Paris*. Hardwicke, who played Sacha Guitry, delighted ever afterwards in reminding the producer, Herbert Wilcox, how sceptical he and the director, Jack Raymond, had been about Richardson's screen presence. He made a considerable impact in the unpromising part of a Parisian artisan and then, surprisingly for an actor who never counted a facility for foreign accents among his strengths, he was cast as another Frenchman, the master criminal Morelle, in *Bulldog Jack*. The audience had to glean his nationality from the dialogue of the other characters, since Ralph made no discernible attempt at a French accent; although, despite the hat and frizzy wig that gave him a passing resemblance to Harpo Marx, he managed to give a naturalistic performance that showed up Jack Hulbert's unconvincing 'mugging' in the title-role. But the film as a whole was dismissed by Agate as 'no end of rot'.

It was his next film *Things to Come*, released in 1936, that effectively established Ralph in his film career, by bringing him to the notice of Alexander Korda. H. G. Wells's *The Shape of Things to Come* had been published in 1933, and Korda's imagination had been fired by his prediction of a new Thirty Years War, to break out in 1940, and a manned flight to the moon in 2036. Korda and Wells collaborated on the film treatment of this futuristic epic, which cost the then huge sum of £300,000. It was Korda's most expensive production to date. Much of the acting was swamped by Vincent Korda's sets and the special effects, as the direction was entrusted to William Cameron Menzies, whose experience as an art director was of more help to the look of the film than to the work of the actors, who were left more or less to create their own characters.

This was an opportunity that Ralph seized with both hands, and his swaggering performance as the warlord was one of the most effective in the whole film. The hectoring style he adopted for the 'Boss' was both so convincing and so recognizable that Mussolini paid him the compliment of forbidding the screening of the film in Italy.

Korda was a volatile character, whose Hungarian charm was a major factor in helping him overcome difficulties that would have swamped a less determined man. He never realized his dream of heading a British film industry that could rival Hollywood, but for twenty years his efforts produced some notable films, and made stars out of the actors he put under contract. One of his great gifts was an eye for spotting new talent, another was for snapping up literary properties first, before other companies could take an option. His stable of actors, writers and directors was a roll-call of the most able talents working in Britain in the heyday of the film industry from the 1930s through to the 1950s; and one of the most consistently successful of these was Ralph Richardson, whom Korda had under contract from 1935 until his death in 1956.

Their relationship was as complicated as might be expected between two such complex characters, but Ralph was always grateful to his film patron for his early support, and stayed loyal to him in his later difficult years.

His manner to me was mostly one of ironic weariness. He gave me the impression that I slightly bored him – very likely I did – but at the same time he drew one towards him . . .

Though not so very much older than I am, I regarded him in a way as a father, and to me he was as generous as a prince.[8]

He sometimes found Korda maddening and exasperating when he wanted to discuss a problem, because of his darting mind and shifting moods, but it was never a lasting rage.

One would be left feeling like that for a while and then would realize that Alex had cast another aspect, more enlightened and more original and helpful to one's problem. Alex always understood. In all my moments with him I always sifted some gold.[9]

If Korda used his native charm single-mindedly to manipulate people, as many who worked for him ruefully recognized, Ralph for one never complained about the results. 'Alexander Korda was continually making people do things against their will but seldom against their interest.'[10]

Their next film was another adaptation by H. G. Wells of one of his own novels, *The Man Who Could Work Miracles*, a less convincing fantasy in which the gods indulge themselves by giving an unassuming little man the power to work miracles, and watch the havoc this wreaks in his life and others'. The special effects were the last word for their time, created by Ned Mann, whom Korda had brought over from Hollywood for *Things to Come*, but they were much less convincing than in the earlier film, and the back-projections today look very obvious. The film's only interest now lies in Ralph's performance as the peppery old retired Colonel Winstanley, almost unrecognizable under the wig and make-up, and barely remembered by the actor himself. 'I didn't connect myself with the Colonel at all. To me, the role was that of a total stranger. An actor plays so many parts. Mercifully, you forget them.'[11]

Even in this now very dated film his technique does not look old-fashioned, and reveals how quickly he learned the secret of playing for the camera. 'Acting on the screen is like acting under a microscope. The slightest movement becomes a gesture and therefore the discipline has to be very severe.'

He was always conscious that a film actor was much more at the mercy of other people than the stage actor, and made no secret of the fact that for that very reason his preference was for the theatre, but he never despised the medium, as both Gielgud and Olivier initially did, and he went on to make well over sixty films in his lifetime. As he once put it in one of his memorable one-liners, 'The film could be said to be a cage for an actor, but a cage in which they sometimes put a little gold.' That steady little stream of gold subsidized his much less remunerative stage work, and gave him the financial independence to pick and choose the most artistically rewarding parts, and to shape his own career as he wished.

CHAPTER FIVE

1937–1939

THE THREE years up to the outbreak of the Second World War saw Ralph in four plays, two triumphs and two failures; and seven films of varying success, several of which were memorable.

The first of these was *South Riding*, which Harold Hobson thought his best film of the decade, and although devotees of Winifred Holtby's novel thought the screen adaptation a travesty, it was a great success with audiences, especially in the USA. Discerning critics there, such as Shelley Hamilton, thought it 'an unusually real story of human beings in their private and public affairs in an English town, with an uncommon love element woven into important aspects of community life . . . Remarkably good acting in a good version of a good novel, with a strong appeal to intelligent audiences.'

Richardson was the landowner being driven towards bankruptcy by the costs of the medical bills for his mentally sick wife, played by Ann Todd, and torn by his love for the schoolteacher of Edna Best, who at the end persuades him not to shoot himself in his despair. His moving portrayal of a man caught up both in this private tragedy and in the public struggle at the local council between property exploiters and their victims, showed his gift for revealing deep emotions through the surface restraint with which he tries to conceal them.

By contrast, in *The Divorce of Lady X*, also made by Korda's London Films, he gave a light comic performance as Lord Mere, which stole the film from its nominal stars, Merle Oberon and Laurence Olivier. He nearly did the same playing the second lead in *The Citadel*, which starred Robert Donat as the doctor who loses his early idealism as he advances his career financially. MGM brought King Vidor over to direct it, for which the American received an Oscar nomination, and the film was popular with audiences on both sides of the Atlantic.

Richardson starred with Olivier again in *Q-Planes*, as Major Hammond, the unflappable and almost languid Secret Service agent tracing the disappearance of test-planes to a threatening foreign power, with Olivier as the dashing pilot-officer. Although the film was released in 1939 it was an adventure comedy, rather than deliberately inspirational like Leslie Howard's aviation film, *First of the Few*.

Ralph's last film before war broke out was the sweeping historical epic *The Four Feathers*, directed by Zoltan Korda, Alex's brother. A. E. W. Mason's novel was filmed five times between 1915 and 1955, but the 1939 version is deservedly the most famous. John Clements played Harry Faversham, who redeems himself of the charges of cowardice by saving the lives of his three former fellow-officers in the Sudan campaign, while disguised as a Singali native. Much of the exterior shooting was done on location in the Sudan, with exciting battle-scenes involving thousands of extras.

Ralph convincingly shows Captain Durrance going blind in the fierce African sun, and later coping with his sightlessness back in England. There is an in-joke for his Old Vic fans, when he tries to show that he is mastering Braille by reciting Caliban's speech, 'The Isle is full of noises', then says with a smile, 'But of course I knew that speech by heart.'

He was always a stickler for accuracy, but he lost out at

least once in this film to Korda. Clements and Richardson had been sent to one of the most expensive Savile Row tailors, to be fitted for the uniforms they would wear at the ball given by the retired General, played by C. Aubrey Smith, to mark his daughter's engagement to Harry Faversham, on the eve of the regiment's departure for Egypt. The scene was ready for shooting when Korda arrived on the set and stopped dead.

> 'What is this?'
>> 'This is the ball sequence.'
>> 'But what is this blue uniform?'
>> The military adviser said, 'But that's correct. This is a private house, not in the mess.'
>> 'But this is Technicolor!'[1]

The whole of the scene was postponed until the young officers could be dressed in red uniforms, to create a more striking effect on the screen; Ralph acquiesced on this occasion, but exerted his authority in later films to preserve his own strict adherence to re-creations of correct period or historical figures.

This rapid sequence of films over three years may have led cinema audiences to acknowledge him as a rising film star, but at the same time he was almost continually engaged in the theatre. If he wanted a change after his long run in a modern-dress thriller, he could hardly have found anything more of a contrast to *The Amazing Dr Clitterhouse* than the Hungarian fantasy in rhymed verse set in the fifteenth century, whose English title was *The Silent Knight*. Gilbert Miller gave it a lavish production, with sumptuous costumes and settings; Ivor Brown thought he overheard a whisper in the last act of 'Whaur are your Warner Brithers noo?'

Diana Wynyard looked stunning as the beautiful widow Zilia, courted by the knight, Peter Agardi. She grants him a kiss in return for a three-year vow of dumbness. When he refuses to be 'cured' by her later kiss she is condemned to be beheaded, and is saved at the final curtain when her executioner reveals himself as her bridegroom. Audiences clearly found this as nonsensical as it reads, and Ivor Brown put his finger on their disappointment: 'One does not employ Mr Ralph Richardson in order to have him speechless from the close of Act I, nor Miss Wynyard in order to have a lovely head removed from view at the second curtain.'

Or as Agate put it, lapsing into verse himself to crush this flimsy confection in a final quatrain,

> 'Why sate the audience something bored and glum?
> Plain stared the reason – the whole play was dumb!
> Nor Grimm nor Andersen wrote story sillier
> Than this of tongue-tied Peter and his Zilia.'

The play found few friends, but it was the cause of Ralph making one of the young actor playing his servant, and struggling to make his own name – Anthony Quayle. As *The Silent Knight* approached the end of its brief run, Ralph told him he was returning to the Old Vic to play Bottom and Othello: 'Good parts for you there, the Lovers in the *Dream* are no great shakes, but Cassio's a damn good part.'[2] Only a couple of days later, Tyrone Guthrie offered those very parts to Quayle, who had the good sense not to ask at whose instigation.

The *Dream* opened in December 1937 to universal delight. Oliver Messel created an exquisite Victorian setting, with fairies on wires, Mendelssohn's music was played by a full orchestra, and the impressive cast included Vivien Leigh as Titania, John Mills as Puck, and Robert Helpmann 'looking like some strange, sinister stag-beetle as Oberon'.[3] Writing half a century later, Quayle still remembered it as 'the greatest performance of Bottom that I shall ever see, absurd and sensitive, moonstruck but ever-hopeful'. Harcourt Williams thought it even better than his much-acclaimed 1931 performance.

The Queen brought the two young Princesses to a matinee, who were almost too enchanted by the supernatural elements in this, their first introduction to Shakespeare. The future Queen was so eager to see how the fairies flew that she hung out by her heels and nearly fell from the Royal Box.

The overall sure-footedness of the *Dream* was succeeded by the uncertainties and confusions that attended *Othello*, which opened in February 1938. When Guthrie had previously directed Olivier's *Hamlet* at the Old Vic he had been much influenced by an academic paper suggesting that the Prince was subconsciously in love with his mother. It was written by Freud's biographer, Dr Ernest Jones, and although most of the audience remained unaware of Hamlet's motivation, Guthrie and Olivier paid another visit to the psychoanalyst before rehearsals began. This time Jones came up with the theory that Iago's villainy is rooted in his frustrated homosexual love for the Moor.

The problem was that neither of them had the nerve to tell Ralph in rehearsal, knowing that he would have no truck with such an interpretation. As the first performance approached Olivier plucked up his courage. At the very last run-through on the morning of the opening night he waited until the end, when Iago is taken off to be tortured; as he passed Othello's prostrate body he stopped and bent over him, to the latter's surprise at this new move.

'What are you doing, cocky?'

Olivier paused and looked out into the auditorium for the director's support, in vain – Quayle professed that it was the only time he ever saw Guthrie turn tail.

'We thought, that is, Tony and I thought, that as I am
being taken away, it might be a good idea if I were to bend
over and give you a kiss.'

'Indeed? Then let me give you due warning that if you do
so, I will get straight up and walk off the stage.'[4]

No one doubted that he meant it.

If the two actors were not in accord on their relationship,
it is no surprise that the critics failed to perceive what had to
be concealed from the Moor. The *Times* reviewer noted that
'Mr Richardson is made to seem heavy by this gadfly about
him', and W. A. Darlington's emotions failed to stir.

> Casting about for reasons, I find that Othello seemed to have
> too much sense and Iago too little. Othello put up such a
> good fight against Iago's early insinuations that his ultimate
> rout seemed to be nothing but a break in morale. Iago's bluff
> heartiness serves him very well in company, but sat ill on him
> when he was left alone, at which times he seemed hard put to
> it to account to himself for the game he was playing. There
> was none of the zest in evil for its own sake which Iago must
> disclose.

Ralph's earlier assurances about the opportunities in his
old part were proved correct. Anthony Quayle's Cassio was
commended as 'excellent' and 'a sound piece of work'; but
unfortunately the leading lady was not. For the *Times* reviewer
Ralph was 'further handicapped by Desdemona, at once arch
in manner and lifeless in intonation, of whom it is best to say
– since Miss Curigwen Lewis has elsewhere shown merit – no
more than that she has been miscast'.

Most critics took no pleasure in what they saw as a
disappointing failure by the actor who had just excelled
himself on the same stage as Bottom. But Agate unleashed all
his bile:

The truth is that Nature, which has showered upon this actor the kindly gifts of the comedian, has unkindly refused him any tragic facilities whatsoever. His voice has not a tragic note in its whole gamut, all the accents being those of sweetest reasonableness. He cannot blaze. He saws away at his nether lip with the enthusiasm of a Queen's Hall fiddler or a maniac reducing a torso to its minimum. But nothing happens. Worse still, the result is faintly comic . . . But suppose we try keeping the performance and changing the part? If it were feasible to stage *Green Pastures*, what other English actor could approach Mr Richardson as De Lawd? And this without jot or tittle of alteration in his present make-up and present temper.

Harcourt Williams, who knew both play and player better than most, was also disappointed that his presentiment after seeing *Oroonoko* at Malvern had proved unfounded, but diagnosed a different cause for the failure: 'No one can show restraint in film work better than Ralph Richardson, but that particular virtue should be used with discretion in the theatre.'

Undoubtedly he was enjoying a consistently higher success rate at this time in the cinema than he was in the theatre. But he was never a man to play safe, and his last appearance on-stage before the war closed in was another piece of symbolism that tested the adventurousness of the West End audience. *Johnson over Jordan* was written specially for him by J. B. Priestley, and Basil Dean, who had directed *Cornelius*, returned to mount an imaginative production of this latest work from Priestley's pen, with specially composed music by the then relatively unknown Benjamin Britten.

Priestley divined early on that Richardson's special quality was the ability suddenly to take the character, and the audience, into another dimension:

a kind of Bully Bottom providing his own enchanted glade. For a while he may seem as commonplace as some familiar town, but then suddenly, above that town, a strange moon is rising. He can be a bank clerk, an insurance agent, a dentist, but very soon mysterious lights and shadows, tones of anguish and ecstasy, are discovered in banking, insurance and dentistry.[5]

This gift made him the playwright's favourite actor, and thirty-five years later Priestley tried to explain it further by dividing actors into two kinds – those who put themselves into parts, and those who take the parts into themselves.

Surprising as it may seem at first to many people, I feel strongly that Ralph Richardson belongs to the second group. He doesn't surrender to roles, completely identify with them; he gives them life by bringing them into himself, adding Richardsonism to them.[6]

Johnson over Jordan was a modern morality play that used Expressionistic techniques in a set that was largely symbolic, the main feature being two cycloramas, one behind the other and lit separately, to great effect at the end. The story moved backwards in time, until the third act when Johnson was seen after his death. It divided the critics, from those who thought it the author's greatest masterpiece at one extreme, to others who thought it his first failure at the other. Even the latter, however, agreed on the strength of the central performance, especially in the closing moments, which produced a standing ovation every night. Ivor Brown captured the emotional power most vividly:

I shall not easily forget the driving actuality of his blanched curiosity, his eye frenzied with apprehension, as he turns from the warmth of good earthly memories to the solitudes and immensities of everlastingness. Here was a real man and real acting . . . So Johnson goes to meet the timeless, spaceless mystery of things. Mr Richardson is here magnificent.

But after its first week at the New Theatre the play was failing to draw bookings, and Bronson Albery gave the joint management of Priestley and Dean the customary two weeks' notice. When the news spread the box-office was swamped, and the remaining performances were sold out, except, to Priestley's fury, in the front stalls, which prompted him to threaten to give up writing plays altogether. In an attempt to save *Johnson over Jordan* he put it on at the Saville at cheap prices, and Ralph waived part of his fees, but Basil Dean did not share their faith enough to put his own money into further rehearsals, even when he was entreated to do so. The play folded after only two and a half months.

The experience only strengthened Priestley's regard for Richardson, and ever afterwards he believed that in this play he had made outrageous demands on the actor's skill and endurance, without bringing him all the rewards he deserved. The final performance so wrung him that he could no longer see.

The end of this play, when Johnson said his farewell and then turned to go towards the glitter of stars, the blue-dark spaces, the unknown (and how Basil Dean contrived to suggest such cosmic depth, I have never understood) while Britten's finale sounded from the orchestra pit, moved most people any and every night. But this was the last night, the last farewell, the last glimpse of Johnson against that starry sky, the last sound of Britten's triumphant crescendo – never, never again – and I might be staring into a grave.[7]

When the play had come off Ralph told Harold Hobson that his own performance lacked understanding, to that critic's astonishment – 'rarely can an actor have so underestimated himself'. But the actor often said privately that it usually took him the first three months of a run before he was sufficiently set in the part to consider undertaking extra work in front of cameras or microphones during the daytime. His devotion to study of a role did not end on the opening night, and this was one of the reasons why some people, especially other performers, made a point of coming to see him more than once in the same play; and why actors who shared the stage with him invariably admired him even more at the end of a run than they did at the beginning.

Before the summer of 1939 was out the clouds of war had blacked out the London theatres, and Ralph was one of the first to don a new costume, this time a real uniform, as he offered his services to King and country, in whatever capacity the Lords of the Admiralty saw fit.

CHAPTER SIX

1940–1945

IT WAS an Army uniform that Ralph had worn in his last
film role in 1939, as Captain Durrance. The long-awaited
premiere of *The Four Feathers* was planned for 4 September.
When war was declared the day before, cinemas as well as
theatres were immediately plunged into darkness, the Korda
spectacular was put on the shelf, and its general release was
delayed until the war was over. The cinematic hiccup was not
uppermost in the actor's mind. He was much more concerned
with reporting for duty as a temporary Sub-Lieutenant in the
Royal Naval Volunteer Reserve.

His youthful passion for machines was now paying dividends. In 1935 he had risen into the air in his own Gypsy
Moth, but he was rather more cautious behind the joy-stick
than he was behind the wheel. He once invited his actress
friend Beatrix Lehmann for 'a little spin in the air' on their
Sunday off, and drove out of London at about 80 miles an
hour with her punching his arm, screaming, 'Slow down!' On
arrival at the airfield she tottered out of the car saying, '*Never*
do that to me again! *Much* too fast!' When the little aircraft
took off it gained height far too slowly for the nervous
passenger, who started screaming, 'For God's sake *go faster*!'[1]

By the time war broke out Ralph had logged 200 hours'
flying time. He admitted much later that they were cautious

hours, he did not fly in bad weather, nor did he fly on his instruments but followed landmarks on the ground. But the Fleet Air Arm was short of pilots and took him on, while other actor friends like Olivier and Hardwicke were marooned unhappily in Hollywood, to their frustration and the British public's incomprehension. They would have cheerfully broken their film contracts to come home and join up, but the British Embassy told them it was their patriotic duty to stay and try to counteract the American isolationists who wanted to stop any American support for the British war effort. This could hardly be announced publicly, so many in Britain were bitterly critical of Olivier and the others, whilst they fretted at the delay in joining their brother-actors in uniform.

Richardson was not quite sure what to expect when he reported for duty at RNAS Raven, at Eastleigh near Southampton, and was immediately summoned to meet the Commander.

> 'Ah, Richardson. I have a mission for you.' A mission! My heart went into my boots, or rather into my shoes, for my flying boots had not yet been issued to me. A mission! I thought he was going to send me into Germany dam-busting. Should I tell him how little flying I had done? I remained silent – but pale. The Commander's face grew grimmer still as he pushed some papers over to me.
>
> 'Take a look at these, Richardson. These are the butcher's bills, I want you to go down and see that man; I think we're overcharged.'[2]

His first actual flying mission seemed simple enough, flying a wireless telegraphist 200 miles straight up a north course, making just one turn, and coming straight back, so that a test could be made on the telegraphist's signals. But this pilot was used to making a turn every quarter of an hour or so to check his position, and was so nervous at this test of his navigational powers that he said, 'I nearly ate my map with fright.'

Much of his war service in the RNVR was routine and tedious to a man with such an imaginative temperament; the only other significant duty that stuck in his memory was his custody of 'the secret books'. These were the Admiralty instructions kept in the Captain's office and regularly amended and updated. Fortunately he shared this responsibility with an officer who had been a solicitor, L. A. Hart, whose legal mind mastered the intricate documentation; and Ralph mostly just filed under his guidance, staggering under the weight of the books, which were lead-covered so they could be sunk overboard in emergency, although Eastleigh is some miles from the sea.

When invasion scares came, alternative arrangements had to be made to meet the Admiralty warnings to make ready to throw the secret books overboard. Richardson and Hart would then carry them into a brick incinerator, and when the alarm passed carry them out again. Their fellows on the station regarded these activities as a barometer of the state of danger the country was in. Never a book was burnt, and Sub-Lieutenant Richardson privately believed that the best way to confuse the enemy would in fact have been to present them with the secret books to read.

He served at various stations in the south of England, and was at Lee-on-Solent in April 1941 to welcome Acting Sub-Lieutenant (A) Olivier, RNVR, to begin his training on British aircraft. Olivier had finally managed to extricate himself from Hollywood and, at Ralph's urging, had been taking flying lessons in America. Unfortunately he proved to be even less of a natural pilot than Richardson. The latter had picked up the nickname 'Pranger', but on Olivier's first day flying at Worthy Down near Winchester he wrecked one plane and damaged two others, when he was taxiing on the runway before he had even taken off.

The Admiralty clearly took the view that both men could do more valuable work for the morale of the nation, and less damage to its aircraft, by releasing them now and again for propaganda films and patriotic spectacles in the Albert Hall and elsewhere. Ralph's first appearance of this kind was in *The Lion Has Wings*, which Alexander Korda made as a demonstration that Britain would win the war. This was a rather curious hybrid of existing documentary footage and dramatized scenes involving Ralph as Wing Commander Richardson, Merle Oberon as his wife, and June Duprez as a pilot's sweetheart. Korda mobilized his forces on 2 September 1939, the day after the Germans invaded Poland, and within six weeks screened the show-copy to the amazed chiefs of the newly formed Ministry of Information. By the first week of November it was on general release. The total production costs amounted to only £30,000 as everyone worked for token fees, in the case of the actors about £5 each.

Korda's already close relationship with Richardson was cemented by a gesture of friendship not recorded elsewhere in the British film industry. The producer was initially taken aback to see the actor in his new guise.

'Ralph, what are you doing in this ridiculous uniform?'

'Well, I've joined up.'

'But you have pictures to make with me, how can you join up?'

'Well, I don't know, it's a tricky time, and I've got to do this just now.'

'Conn . . . ing . . . ham, what do we pay Ralph?'

David Cunynghame, who was Korda's production manager, told him the figure.

'I will give you half of that, till the end of the war.'

So Korda supplemented Richardson's meagre naval allowances throughout the war, and when they came together again afterwards Ralph thanked him and asked what he owed.

> 'This is a debt I must first of all quickly discharge.'
>
> 'Conn . . . ing . . . ham, bring me Conningham.'
>
> Cunynghame appeared at the side of the Hungarian again.
>
> 'What have we been giving Ralph? Forget it, Conningham, he does not owe us anything.'[3]

And Korda tore up the contract in front of the astonished actor, who was overwhelmed by this act of generosity at a particularly straitened time for him. It was not even as if the two of them had managed to collaborate during the war, apart from the narration on another propaganda film in 1943, *The Biter Bit*, only fourteen minutes long. Ralph's other wartime films could be counted on one hand, and included Thorold Dickinson's *The Next of Kin*; *The Silver Fleet*, in which he played a Dutch Resistance hero, Jaap Van Leyden; and as himself in a Ministry of Information film about the Fleet Air Arm, *The Volunteer*, made by the writer–director partnership of Emeric Pressburger and Michael Powell.

One of Anthony Quayle's sharpest wartime memories of Richardson was of sitting on a beach in Gibraltar with him when Ralph was making *The Volunteer* and suddenly being asked, 'What do you think, Tony, makes for success in an actor?'

While he was struggling for the answer, Ralph went on,

> 'I'll tell you, it's to be different from everyone else. Look at this beach. You see. They're all the same. Good, sound grey pebbles – all the same. Therefore not very interesting. Which catches the eye? It's that one, isn't it? Because it's green – different from all the others. That's how it is with acting.'[4]

Nineteen forty-two was the year in which Ralph was most nearly touched by death. His wife Kit had moved to a cottage in Wivelsfield, East Sussex, at the beginning of the war, with the couple who by that time had been caring for her for eleven years. On a visit to see her on his Harley Davidson motorcycle Ralph got into a speed wobble and came a nasty cropper. A local war-reserve policeman named Sinden (father of Donald) luckily came along shortly afterwards and summoned an ambulance to take the unconscious rider to hospital. He remained there for some weeks, and happily his wife was well enough at that time to visit him.

But later that year she began to complain of back-pains and increasing stiffness, and her doctor told her husband that she was now in the terminal stage of her illness. On the morning of 5 October 1942 she was found face-down in her pillow, having suffocated to death. She was buried on 8 October, in the churchyard at Wivelsfield. Her husband had inscribed on her headstone 'A LOVING WIFE, A CHARMING ACTRESS'. They had been married for just over eighteen years, and had not shared a stage together for the last fourteen of them.

The emotional strains of those last years reinforced Ralph's natural inclination to guard his privacy, and not even his closest friends could really tell what he must have been going through. Even years afterwards he would not go into any detail, merely saying that her disease was 'perhaps akin to polio', and that he was sure she was now in heaven.

He lost his mother too during the war years. Her hypochondria, already apparent in Ralph's childhood, had increased with age, until she retired to a series of nursing-homes, and she never ventured out to see her son act, even during his rise to fame in the 1930s.

The comradeship of service life mitigated Ralph's loneliness, but personal happiness only returned with his marriage to Meriel Forbes on 26 January 1944. This was also a fateful year on the professional front, as it marked his accession to the joint leadership of the Old Vic Company, which was first mooted early that year, and was up and running in performance by August.

Late in 1940 it had been decided that the Old Vic would have to move its operational base out of London to Burnley, in Lancashire, from where Tyrone Guthrie organized a series of regional tours of the classics. These were aided by the Council for the Encouragement of Music and the Arts, CEMA, the forerunner of the Arts Council of Great Britain. In the beginning almost its only client was the Old Vic Company; under its aegis Lewis Casson and Sybil Thorndike toured Wales with *Macbeth*, *Medea* and *Candida*, to hugely enthusiastic audiences. In 1942 the Old Vic Theatre in Waterloo Road fell prey to German bombs. By 1944, when it seemed the tide of war was turning, the management thought it time the Company returned to a full-time London base. Guthrie first approached Richardson to lead this comeback season, who refused to request his own release from the services, but said he would accept under two conditions. The first was that the governing board of the Old Vic should negotiate with the Admiralty on his behalf, the second was that he should not be sole leader of the Company. Originally he wanted Olivier and Gielgud, an intriguing prospect for theatregoers, but the latter gently turned down his old friend, telling him it was a recipe for disaster. 'You would have to spend your whole time as referee between Larry and me.'

So the third member of the triumvirate became John Burrell, who worked for Michel St Denis before becoming a BBC Radio drama producer. He had just worked with Guthrie and Ralph on an acclaimed radio production of *Peer Gynt*. (Dorothy Tutin heard it as a small girl, 'and for years imagined I'd actually seen him play it on the stage, because his voice had conjured up these wonderful pictures'.[5] That magic was undimmed when the BBC re-broadcast it half a century later.)

Guthrie was less enthusiastic about Burrell, fearing that the younger man, less experienced, less famous, and lamed by polio, would be unable to stand up to two such powerful personalities. He was open to the jibe of being the Lepidus figure overshadowed by Antony and Octavius, an unfortunate analogy for the other two men as well, but there was more than a grain of truth in the charge, as became apparent later. To begin with, however, Burrell skilfully held the ring between the two competitive stars.

The Sea Lords agreed to release the two actors with a speed and lack of any show of reluctance which Olivier said they both found 'positively hurtful'. He and his two partners met at Denham Studios, where Olivier was just finishing his film of *Henry V*, and Ralph outlined his plans to maintain a repertoire of plays in simultaneous production, a common practice in Europe, but not then in Britain. He also revealed that one play had already been chosen, *Peer Gynt*, as he wished to build on all the work he had recently put into the radio production. Before Olivier had quite absorbed this fait accompli, he found he was saddled with the part of Sergius Saranoff in *Arms and the Man*, while Ralph was scheduled to repeat another earlier triumph as Bluntschli, which he had played to Gielgud's Saranoff at the Old Vic in 1931. Since they had agreed to alternate the leading roles, and Olivier was only going to play the tiny part of the Button-Moulder in the Ibsen, it was finally decided that his starring vehicle should be *Richard III*, with Ralph in the small part of Richmond. Donald Wolfit had recently played Richard Crookback, with great success, so even this part was seen by the actor as a possible cause of invidious comparisons. Olivier feared he might have been astutely and subtly out-manoeuvred by Richardson before they had even started.

They recruited a company whose nucleus had a wealth of experience – Sybil Thorndike, Nicholas Hannen, other Old Vic stalwarts Harcourt Williams and George Relph – and of promise, especially in the leading lady department. Joyce Redman was quickly chosen as one, and in the search for a second, contrasting leading lady, they called on the advice of their old Birmingham mentor, Sir Barry Jackson. With characteristic generosity he invited the two graduates from his pre-war Repertory Theatre to come up and see the juvenile lead in his present company, the strikingly beautiful and talented Margaret Leighton. She had gone to Birmingham when she was only sixteen, and spent most of the next six years there, an invaluable training as Richardson and Olivier well knew from their own experience. They took John Burrell with them, and after seeing her play the stepdaughter in Pirandello's *Six Characters in Search of an Author*, they offered her the parts of the Green Woman in *Peer Gynt* and Raina in *Arms and the Man*.

When the auditions were held in London for the rest of the company, Peter Howell was rather thrown at the end of his prepared audition piece to hear Richardson request, with what would now be called a Pinteresque pause in the middle, 'Have you time ... to show us something else?' But he managed something, and was offered several small parts, as well as understudy to Bluntschli, where he was torn between disappointment and relief that Ralph was never 'off'.

Bronson Albery had previously leased his New Theatre in St Martin's Lane to the Old Vic for a few weeks at a time, when the touring companies came into London, but he was much less happy at the prospect of giving it a long-term home until the Waterloo Road theatre could be rebuilt. Eventually Ralph talked him round. Rehearsal space was offered much more willingly. The National Gallery in Trafalgar Square was still empty of its pictures, which had been sent to safety outside London for the duration of the war, and its Director, Kenneth Clark, was quick to offer its large empty spaces for rehearsals. Diana Boddington had joined as stage manager, and remembers that the first flying bombs had just started their random but deadly attacks on the capital. It soon became customary, when their droning engines suddenly cut out, to dive for cover before the explosion. 'When the V-bombs went over, Beau Hannen and the other actors were getting under the tables, but Ralph and Larry just kept on working.'[6]

The London season at the New Theatre was to open with *Peer Gynt*, but prior to that they decided to have a week's try-out of *Arms and the Man* at the Opera House in Manchester. John Burrell's skilful direction had still failed to overcome Olivier's distaste for Saranoff, and Bluntschli stole all the notices in the northern papers, especially in the *Manchester Guardian*. Tyrone Guthrie came up to see the second performance, and when he told him on their walk back to the hotel that he liked his Sergius, Olivier could not restrain a grunt of such disagreement that Guthrie stopped and said, 'Well, of course, if you can't love Sergius you'll never be any good in him, will you?' This shaft of insight transformed Olivier's performance into a comic absurdity that became the perfect foil to Richardson's Bluntschli when the play opened in London, and made the whole production a great favourite, not just with the civilian audiences but with all the troops before whom it later toured across newly liberated Europe.

Ralph was never really happy in a part until he felt comfortable with all his entrances and exits, and he festered for a while over one of the former. At the end of the scene when Sergius flirts with Louka around the clothes-line, Joyce Redman used to rush off-stage and open a door, and there stood Ralph — revealed for his entrance. When they had been running for about three or four months he sent for Joyce to come to his dressing-room.

'I want to say something to you, you're always very late on your exit.'

'No, Ralph, I'm afraid you're early on your entrance.'

His real objection was that the control of his entrance was in the hands of someone else, but clearly Joyce Redman was in no mood to change the moves at this stage of the run.

He paused for a moment, and then murmured, 'Mmmmm, you're right,' and she was never sent for again.

She also played opposite him as his young love, Solveig, in *Peer Gynt*, which opened the Old Vic regime at the New Theatre on 31 August 1944. Even fifty years later she had a tear in her eye as she recalled how 'on the first night, after the scene in which Solveig sees Peer for the first time, Ralph waited for me after I came off and said, "That moment when we met, we made magic tonight." I've never forgotten that.'[7]

Richardson was always keener to give praise than receive it, and to talk of others' performances rather than his own, once deflecting Daniel Massey's questions about his Falstaff by saying, 'Let me tell you about Sybil in *Peer Gynt*. When she died my heart was in my mouth every time. I felt this little body go, I thought she was dead.'

Harcourt Williams watched the death of Aase, Peer's mother, night after night and thought it a perfect duet, while Ralph

> stretched the wide octave of Peer's life with great skill . . . His old Peer was strange, unearthly and a little terrifying. At first I used to long for something more on those last lines:
>
> > '*My mother! My wife! You holy woman!*
> > *Oh, hide me, hide me within your love!*'
>
> I had a notion that he was holding back the emotion because

he was fearful of becoming sentimental, but after he had
played the part some time the real feeling came.[8]

In recognition of his performance as Peer Gynt, Ralph was
very touched to be presented with the Medal of St Olav by
King Haakon of Norway. Another very knowledgeable eye
cast over the production was that of Michael Meyer, the
biographer and translator of Ibsen, and he felt Ralph was not
sexy enough in the first three acts, 'but he was marvellous in
the last two acts. He had that open-eyed, slightly goofy,
dreamy quality that was very right for Peer.'[9]

Agate, however, made no such distinction.

In plain English, I thought that the production was superb,
that Mr Ralph Richardson was excellent in all three phases,
and that everybody else died or got married or went mad more
than competently. But it was one man's evening as in the case
of this play it always must be. Here is the actor's dream
fulfilled; to be always on the stage and never to stop talking.
But great occasions require heroic response; certainly on
Thursday the response was forthcoming. I left the theatre
humming, 'When Richardson begins to Peer / With heigh!
the doxy over the dale . . .'

In this opening production, as already mentioned, Olivier
played the tiny part of the Button-Moulder who summons
Peer Gynt to his end. In *Richard III* their roles were reversed,
when Ralph as Richmond kills the King in the climactic
battle. He was unhappy in the part, and looks it in the
pictures, wearing a rather unbecoming red wig.

Peter Howell goes further.

Not only did he not like the part, he couldn't learn it. In the
long speech at the end, he spoke absolute nonsense, with

Michael Warre on one side and me on the other, both trying
to keep a straight face, while this magnificent figure talked
with enormous flair and aplomb. I don't know what he said
and I'm sure the audience was completely fooled.[10]

Peter Copley joined the Company to arrange the fight at
the end, as he was an expert fencer, but he had some difficulty
teaching a rather ill-matched pair.

Olivier was so physically mobile, and Ralph was the opposite,
he was the most dreadful fencer, so it was an awfully difficult
thing getting this going. He was always saying, 'Look,
Laurence old chap, there's no need to go so fast.' So it was
never entirely successful. I was backstage once, having gone to
watch the fight from the wings, and Ralph was standing at
the side in armour waiting to go on, there seemed to be a lot
going on, and finally he demonstrated that under his gauntlets
he had made these little metal clips, one fitted over reach
knuckle, it took quite a long time to fit them on all the fingers
of both hands. Because Laurence was sometimes a bit wild, or
alternatively Ralph had got his hand in the wrong place.[11]

When J. C. Trewin wrote in the *Observer*, 'Mr Ralph Richardson lets his Richmond glow like plated Mars', he was quite
unaware that this Richmond was wearing some extra finger-
plates for protection.

In addition to alternating the leading roles and playing
supporting roles to each other, Richardson and Olivier developed an unusual and engaging habit at the final curtain-call
that much appealed to that good company man Harcourt
Williams. After the whole cast had taken a number of calls,
whoever was playing the leading part would take a solo curtain
call. When it was Richardson, Olivier would hold back the
curtain for him, and vice versa, a courtesy usually afforded by

the stage manager. Williams thought it 'a matter of no great importance, perhaps, but significant'.

The fourth and final play of that first season was *Uncle Vanya*, with Richardson in the title-role, and Olivier as Dr Astrov. Neither man was very happy, and many people thought they should have exchanged parts. Ralph's unhappiness was increased by the early rehearsal process. Because the three plays already running were playing to capacity business the opening of *Vanya* was delayed, and the director John Burrell chose to have the cast sit around Sybil Thorndike's dressing-room just reading the play for several days, a practice cordially disliked by Ralph, and ever afterwards actively discouraged by him. As he often said, 'How do I know how I'm going to say the line until I know where I am going to stand?'

He was also fundamentally out of sympathy with his character. Vanya is doomed always to be a failure, but Ralph believed that he would have been a Schopenhauer or a Dostoevsky if he had had the chance. Joyce Redman, who played Sonya, knew that Ralph never liked his part, but still believes there will never be another Vanya to touch him.

> On the first night when he tried to shoot the Professor there was an enormous laugh, and he was so overcome he wanted to leave the theatre and go and hide, because he thought he'd killed the play, until Billee Williams (who was playing Professor Serebryakov) came and told him it was perfect.[12]

There were criticisms of the production, but few of the cast, and Ivor Brown summed up the particular qualities of the leading actor.

> Mr Richardson is a masterly conveyor of what the Elizabethans called silliness and we call simplicity or innocence. There is never any doubt about his acting; his entry always proclaims

RALPH RICHARDSON

the original virtue of mankind (hence his rogues, when he plays them, are irresistible), and the lubberly, earth-bound Vanya, dreaming of the heavens he has never stormed, offers the kind of pathos that he plays to perfection and would disdain to overplay.

This Vanya may have concealed his doubts from this critic, but it was the one play left behind when the Company embarked for war-scarred Europe, at the end of its London season and two brief visits to Glasgow and Manchester.

CHAPTER SEVEN

1945–1946

ON THE first day of 1945 Ralph became a father, and he and Mu christened the baby Charles, although for many years he went by their pet nickname 'Smallie'. On 8 May VE Day found the Old Vic in Manchester, and there was dancing in the streets as the whole nation celebrated the end of a long war. A week later the Company, sixty-six strong, set sail for Europe free at last of Nazi occupation. Their tour was arranged by ENSA, so everyone had to wear uniform, with the honorary rank of lieutenant. The two ex-naval pilots took this seriously, and told Diana Boddington to order Nicholas Hannen to wear the regulation khaki shirt in place of the white one he was wearing.

The first stop was Antwerp, then Brussels as a base for Bruges and Ghent. The Belgian theatres had survived the battles, and were packed with wildly enthusiastic troops and civilians. The scene was very different when they travelled into Germany. They were all instructed not to speak to the Germans, who were also barred from all their performances. Hamburg was almost flattened, but its lovely theatre, the great Staatliche Schauspielhaus, in the centre of the city, was still standing. They played at Lübeck, and ended at Belsen with one matinee of *Arms and the Man*, for the military staff grappling with the terrible and too often hopeless task of saving what lives they could. Sybil Thorndike wrote to her son, 'Driving back in the bus to Hamburg, I couldn't stop crying it was all so fearful and horrible . . . I'll never forget this all my life.'

To round off the tour the company flew from Hamburg to Paris in an Army plane, sitting very uncomfortably on the floor, and were put up in a small hotel in the Place de l'Opéra Comique. They were the first foreign company ever to be given the honour of playing at the Comédie Française, and they were entranced by its luxurious fittings, with dressing-rooms more like drawing-rooms than the tiny cubicles to which many of them were accustomed at home.

Because *Peer Gynt* had been both the opening and the closing performance of the London season, Olivier was determined to go first in Paris with *Richard III*, and frankly admitted in his 1986 memoir *On Acting* that whichever play opened he knew would be 'the big one' as far as the French critics were concerned. It proved to be the big one for the audience too. Olivier had worked out a dramatic end to the fight-scene, full of writhing death-pangs before he expired, and Richmond put his foot on the body to say:

> *God, and your arms be prais'd, victorious friends:*
> *The day is ours; the bloody dog is dead.*

Peter Copley observed that he was about to do this on the opening night in Paris, 'when the applause for the fight and Larry's death was deafening, and it was that sort of applause, staying at a level which says "Do it again please," so Ralph only got as far as "God and your . . . oh, fuck, fuck." He was furious.'[1]

But his fury was greatly compounded the following night by the French audience's excessively cool response to *Peer Gynt*. They seemed bored by the play and its central character, and

Ralph was so hurt that he wandered about the Paris streets on his own for most of the night. The general manager of the Company, Laurence Evans, waited up until quite late for him, but eventually gave up and went to bed. When Ralph did finally return, the hotel was in darkness and all locked up. He shouted, but the only person who heard him was Olivier, who had the best room in the hotel, over the front door. When he opened his window and looked out, Ralph was climbing up the drainpipe. He told him to get down before he killed himself, and went down to unlock the front door. Ralph brushed him aside, muttering, 'Get out of my way,' and walked up the stairs.

What happened next gave Olivier the fright of his life. 'He stood still for a moment, then suddenly lunged towards me and picked me up in his arms like a baby. Within strides, he had crossed the room and was on to the balcony. I thought, "It'll stop now, the joke's over." But it wasn't. He moved with me in his arms across the balcony and held me over the edge . . . When you know there is nothing between you and the hard cobbles sixty feet below, except a pair of strong arms, time really does stand still.

'Look, why don't you pull me back like a good boy? I'm beginning to feel really nervous.'

Finally he was lifted back on to the balcony, put down, and his angry friend went off to bed. Olivier was even more astonished by their conversation over breakfast the next morning.

'Ralph, that was rather a near one, wasn't it?'

'Yes, we were both very foolish. It was a double fault.'

Olivier was too flabbergasted to respond.[2]

The only discrepancy in this story appears to be over the date. Writing thirty years later, Olivier sets it after the first night of *Richard III*, but both Laurence Evans and Peter Copley firmly place Ralph's nocturnal wanderings on the following night, after *Peer Gynt*. Laurence Evans puts the reason for the explosion of rage down to Olivier's failure to go round to the Richardson dressing-room to congratulate him after his performance, a slight he felt even more after his perceived failure with the French audience.

The competitiveness between the two friends never rose to such deadly heights again, and the matter was soon forgiven, if never forgotten. But there was a certain edge to their scenes together in the opening double-bill of the second season at the New Theatre – Shakespeare's *Henry IV, Parts I and II*. In the first play Olivier played the fiery Hotspur with a stutter, and in the second the near-senile Justice Shallow with a falsetto voice, fighting off an imaginary swarm of bees. His scene-stealing antics as Shallow did not, however, prevent Richardson's Falstaff from carrying off the honours in both Parts of *Henry IV*.

Despite his initial reluctance, when he came to play the part Richardson revelled in the realization that, unlike Shakespeare's four great tragic heroes, 'he is not projected at breathless speed to his doom. Falstaff proceeds through the plays at his own chosen pace, like a gorgeous ceremonial Indian elephant.'[3] For all those who saw it, his Falstaff was the greatest of his string of memorable creations in those extraordinary seasons at the New Theatre. Half a century later it still stands tallest in the memory of Sir Peter Hall.

> Of the performances I've seen in my life I'm gladdest I saw that. It's just terribly sad that he didn't do it again, because he was a relatively young man when he did it then, and a whole generation of people didn't have that life-enhancing experience. Because he caught that, Falstaff is melancholy, and Falstaff is finally about being a death's head, and Falstaff is a cheat and a liar and a trickster, but most of all he is a life-force and that is what Ralph was, and I just loved that.[4]

It was this histrionic ability to create the contradictions in the character without clashing that determined an eleven-year-old Daniel Massey to seek a career in the theatre when he grew up, after seeing both Parts in the same day — a direct echo of his hero's own revelation on seeing Benson's Hamlet twenty-five years earlier.

Another young scion of a theatrical dynasty, Edward Hardwicke, was taken backstage by Sir Cedric to meet his father's old friend, and was even more impressed by the Falstaff costume and make-up close to than he had been from the front. Hardwicke senior thought it 'the only Falstaff played as Shakespeare wrote him', in both his wit and his make-up.

Alix Stone constructed a convincing outsize anatomy in silk quilting and towelling, that gave him not just the great belly but fat, gnarled and varicosed legs, unhampered by the great boots in which many Falstaffs have to hide their own normal legs. This allowed him a lightness on his feet and a dignity that captivated an undergraduate and would-be critic named Kenneth Tynan.

> Here was a Falstaff whose principal attribute was not his fatness but his knighthood. He was Sir John first, and Falstaff second, and let every cock-a-hoop young dog beware ... Richardson never rollicked or slobbered or staggered: it was not a sweaty fat man, but a dry and dignified one. As the great belly moved, step following step with great finesse lest it overtopple, the arms flapped fussily at the sides as if to paddle the body's bulk along. It was deliciously and subtly funny, not riotously so: from his height of pomp Falstaff was chuckling at himself: it was not we alone, laughing at him.[5]

There were two particular 'moments', worthy of his earlier stage-wife Madge Titheradge, that impressed several critics.

J. C. Trewin captured them most vividly. The first was in the tavern scene of *Part II*.

> Richardson silenced a momentarily restless house when he turned aside with the low 'Peace, good Doll! do not speak like a Death's head; / do not bid me remember mine end', he and we caught sight of the abyss. The second moment came during Falstaff's half-puzzled appreciation at the start of the royal rebuke. Surely it was the Boar's Head humour again – Hal at his tricks? As the King spoke, 'Know the grave doth gape for thee thrice wider than for other men,' we had the last hint of the true Falstaff, a kindling of the eye and a swing of the body as he prepared to launch an answering quip. We could see the line coming when, cruelly, it was quenched with, 'Reply not to me with a fool-born jest,' and the spark died and Falstaff faded into a man old and tired; the King had killed his heart, and what was left to do?[6]

Falstaff had his back to the audience while the King rejected his old drinking partner, and the way in which he tried to control his tears as he turned to face the audience wrenched the hearts of his audiences; and not only them – Michael Warre, who played Hal, was so moved by the actor's reaction to his speech that at nearly every performance after he delivered it and exited, he burst into tears himself off-stage.

Agate was unstinting in his praise: 'he had everything the part wants – the exuberance, the mischief, the gusto'. Brown thought it the best thing Richardson had done and the best Falstaff he had seen. That was a verdict that still stands today for many people, like the playwright Christopher Fry.

It is not often that a moment in a performance stays as clearly and poignantly in the memory as when it was first said – Gielgud and Richard II's speech in Pomfret Castle, 'I have been studying how I may compare', is one of them – but most movingly of all was Richardson's Falstaff, in the little scene with Doll Tearsheet, 'Sit on my knee, Doll', with his 'Do not bid me remember mine end', and the playing of 'I am old, I am old'. There was all human mortality in it, moving out into the audience like a slow sea-wave.[7]

It was perhaps because it came closest to satisfying that most self-critical of actors that Richardson always refused to repeat the role, though he was often begged to, first by John Gielgud, and then much later by Peter Hall, 'but he wouldn't do it again, I tried and tried, God how I tried'.

When the play went to America at the end of the season Ralph told Otis L. Guernsey Jnr of the *New York Herald Tribune*, with typical self-deprecation, 'Not until you play one of the classic roles like Falstaff do you realize how small the mere actor is in comparison to these magnificent personalities. It's like trying to play a huge organ' – he spread out his arms in illustration – 'with too vast a keyboard to reach the stops up at the top and down at the bottom.'

His American audiences seemed to share the British view that this Falstaff did manage to reach all those stops. They had a little more difficulty with the diction, but he explained that this was not the result of poor projection,

We aren't speaking as we would speak normally, that would be too clipped. We are trying to give an impression of old-style English speech, just as one of your actors would alter his inflection if he were playing an American of the early days. I, for instance, say 'Ye' for 'You' and 'La'' for 'Law', and I don't wonder that some of it is not understood.

He yielded centre-stage to Olivier in the next double-bill – of *Oedipus* and *The Critic* – playing Tiresias in the former, like 'one of Blake's ancient, sorrowful spirits', as Desmond MacCarthy put it in the *New Statesman & Nation*. Michel St Denis took over the production of *Oedipus* when Tyrone Guthrie gave it up, horrified at the intention of pairing it with Sheridan's *The Critic*. There were those in the audience, too, who found this frothy confection hard to take after the shattering effect of Oedipus blinding himself at the end of the first half of the evening, with Olivier's blood-curdling prime-val scream of pain off-stage before he entered with blood streaming from his eyes.

Ralph had the tiny and mute part of Lord Burleigh in the second piece, directed by Miles Malleson. *Punch* ended its rave review with 'a last word for Mr Ralph Richardson, speechless yet in spate. Has Burleigh's shaking of the head ever been more portentous? It implies all that Puff wants it to suggest – and a great deal more besides.'

Olivier's nightly feat of athleticism as Mr Puff, when he swept up into the flies on a painted cloud, nearly ended in disaster one night, when the rope for his descent down the curtain came adrift, and he only saved himself by grabbing a wire in the other hand until the stage staff could rescue him. In New York he was once flung painfully on to the stage, tearing his Achilles tendon.

The two co-stars' respective acting styles were well-demonstrated by their very different triumphs in this season. Richardson worked from the inside out, intuiting the main-spring of his performance before adding the make-up and costume and external effects; Olivier from the outside in, worrying first about the look of the part, the most appropriate of his endless succession of false noses, and what spectacular leaps or falls he could achieve, before developing an interpre-tation to go inside all those effects.

Usually critics can only observe the actor's approach to his work from the front, but it was during a performance of what

became known as *Oedipuff* that Harold Hobson was granted a
rare insight backstage. Because Ralph's two appearances were
so brief he had allowed the critic to interview him in his
dressing-room after he had exited as Tiresias. Not expecting
to find a visitor present, Olivier suddenly arrived, made-up for
his climactic entrance.

> Richardson sat in a corner, puffing away at his pipe and
> talking quietly and calmly. Olivier burst in, a wild look on
> his face, peered at himself in the looking-glass, shrieked in a
> distraught voice, 'It's a rotten shame,' and then, red paint
> pouring from his eyes, groped his way along the wall to the
> door. A moment later there rang through the New Theatre
> Olivier's tremendous cry of horror and distress as the self-
> blinded Oedipus. These proceedings somewhat distracted me,
> but on Richardson they had no effect whatever. He just went
> on talking quietly, the apparent essence of an ordinary man.
> But, of course, only an extraordinary man could have contrived
> to behave ordinarily in such circumstances.[8]

It was obvious that both Oedipuff and Falstaff had to be
taken to Broadway, and rather reluctantly *Uncle Vanya* was
added to the repertoire for the six-week season at the Century
Theater, but for markedly fewer performances than the others,
and it was received much more coolly too by the critics
and audiences. Ralph's Vanya suffered critically more than
it had in London, precisely because the Chekhov was presented
in tandem with the Shakespeare. Robert Garland in the
Journal-American took against play, production and players,
beginning with the title-part: 'As the evening's foremost
woe-is-me-er, he is John Falstaff with his stomach held
in and his smirk removed. His speech is Falstaffian, his
leg-slapping is Falstaffian, his thumb-pointing is the same.'
For good measure he added, 'and as the family physi-

cian known as Astrov, Laurence Olivier is his familiar actorial self'.

Fortunately the two double-bills were smash-hits, and Garland's dismissiveness was outweighed by Louis Kronenberg's 'Ralph Richardson's Tiresias is large and implacable, with something about it that suggests the Barrymores.'

But Ralph was lonely in New York; he had had to leave his wife behind with Smallie, a deprivation rubbed in by Vivien Leigh's presence alongside Olivier. After the performances he often supped alone at a quiet eating-place near his hotel, with a little leather-bound copy of one of his nineteenth-century favourites – Conrad, Dickens or Henry James.

Once there was a rehearsal in his large suite, and Peter Copley noticed how very impersonal it was. 'The only thing he had out was all his painting equipment, his easel and a canvas on it which was covered, and all his painting things; and they were all facing the window, and we all came to the conclusion that Ralph was filling his time by painting the opposite hotel out of the window, but we never knew.'[9]

Had they had the temerity to peep under the cover they would in fact have seen a rather more interesting representation on the canvas than of the wall of the opposite building. Soon after his arrival Ralph rang his New York agent for someone to come round and hear his lines, with the request that she would also pose in the nude while doing so. Since this was New York she probably asked for a double fee for the double duty.

Before leaving the USA he announced that from now on he planned to alternate three years of the Old Vic with two years of film work. This was more for financial than creative reasons, since he admitted that film 'is a wonderful medium, and I love it, but I find that I cannot increase my talent by working in pictures, any more than a painter can do so by increasing the size of his brush'. But although this alternation made perfect sense for the actor, it had other repercussions for a co-director of the Old Vic, and lit the long fuse to the explosion that finally erupted the following year.

Richardson had just signed a new contract with Alexander Korda, who soon guided him into half a dozen of his most outstanding screen roles in as many years, but his first post-war film was for the ex-private soldier and youthful genius, Peter Ustinov. During the war the latter had worked with the Army Kinematograph Service, and while still in uniform had researched and written a dramatized documentary for the Air Ministry about the discovery of radar. This subject immediately appealed to the scientifically minded Richardson. Before the war his investigations had led to him being mentioned in two Royal Society pamphlets, on such abstruse subjects as 'The Quantitative Evaluation of Light' and 'The Application of Neon Lighting'. Radar was even more exciting to the ex-naval airman; and he began the film with Ustinov in late 1945, while he was still playing Falstaff at the New Theatre.

The first-time director was delighted to gain the services of one of his actor-heroes, but thrown into a quandary on the third day of shooting, when the actor arrived full of beans, 'bellowing his delight at being alive, but whistling like a kettle on certain sibilants, a sound which he evidently attributed to someone other than himself, since he kept looking around him to find its origin'. Ustinov guessed that he had left home without his rather complicated bridgework, which repaired the crash-damage to his mouth from motor-bike spill or aircraft prang. Sending his assistant, Michael Anderson, off to telephone the Richardson home, his attempts to delay the shooting merely infuriated his star.

'Why can't we shoot?'

'The camera is broken.'

This was not the cleverest response. Ralph immediately advanced on the cameraman, Jack Hildyard, to help mend it.

'I hear the camera is broken.'

'No.'

Hildyard had not heard the earlier exchange, but the sound-recordist was all too aware of the problem. When Ustinov hastily said it was his mistake, the problem was in fact with the sound-recordist, Ralph turned a beady eye on that operator. The latter invented a technical problem that sounded gobbledegook to the non-technical director, but seemed to satisfy the more knowledgeable actor. At that point the assistant director returned with the news that there was an urgent telephone message from the actor's home, and he rather grumpily went off to take it.

When he reappeared a couple of minutes later he looked unwell, holding his hand to his brow. Ustinov went to him anxiously.

'It's nothing, just a migraine. I have some powders on prescription for them, and like a fool I left them at home. They're bringing them out straight away. I'll go and lie down until they arrive.'

He disappeared into his dressing-room, and twenty minutes later a Bentley arrived at the studio gates, to deliver a small packet for Mr Ralph Richardson. A short while afterwards a rejuvenated actor reappeared. 'I feel much better now. *Mens sana in corpore sano.*'

The sibilance had disappeared. That day's shooting, and all subsequent ones, went well, and the film was eventually a great success on its release in 1946.[10]

The summer of that year saw a couple of strains in the Olivier–Richardson relationship which have gone down into legend, and become much embroidered in the process. The first was on the social front, and revealed the hazards of playing host to Ralph in party mood.

He and his wife drove down to Buckinghamshire to spend the weekend with the Oliviers at their recently purchased old country house, Notley Abbey. As it came into view Ralph stopped the car and said to Mu, 'I hope to God I don't put my foot in it this time.' His last social visit to the Olivier home had been a couple of years before the war, on Guy Fawkes night, when they were living at Durham Cottage in Chelsea. November the 5th was also Vivien Leigh's birthday, so Ralph arrived with a huge box of fireworks, and took the largest rocket out into the garden. It was the size used to attract attention if a ship was sinking. When he lit the touchpaper it zoomed straight into the dining-room, burned up the new curtains, set the pelmet on fire, and broke lots of Vivien's priceless antique porcelain.

Aghast at what had happened, Ralph fled, saying to Mu, 'Let's get out of here, these people don't understand us.' Much later he said, with more than a touch of irony, 'I have to admit that I was very hurt, next day, when nobody rang me up to say, "How kind of you, Ralph, to have thought of bringing those fireworks."'

He took no fireworks to Notley Abbey, and behaved with great care under the watchful eye of his hostess. Over dinner they discussed their plans for the future of the Old Vic. Laurence Olivier talked enthusiastically about the early history of the Abbey, and invited his guests to come and view the frescoes painted by the monks on the beams in the attic. The wives declined, and the two men clambered up into the loft. They were gone some time, and then Vivien Leigh's worst fears were realized, with the sound of a splintering crash from above.

Dashing upstairs, she saw a gaping hole in the ceiling of the main guest-room. Despite his best intentions Ralph had quite literally put his foot in it this time. The attic was not floored over, and it had to be traversed by walking on the rafters; Ralph moved back to admire a fresco and stepped straight through the plaster. In the interests of a good story this mishap was expanded later into him crashing bodily through the ceiling on to the bed, but much later still Ralph insisted, when telling the tale, that it was only his leg that went through. In any case, that was quite sufficient to ruin both the evening and Ralph's reputation as a guest, as he recognized: 'There was a rational basis to Vivien's fury, which we must salute. If you prod a tigress twice in her lair, you must not expect her to purr.'

Back in London, Richardson was rather surer of his footing when the three co-directors met to discuss the plays and parts for the coming season, and Olivier was left ruefully recognizing that he had been outsmarted once again. Since he had made the last choice – of Oedipus and Mr Puff – for himself, it was now Ralph's turn to choose first. He said he would like to play Cyrano de Bergerac, and John Burrell agreed. But that was also a role that Olivier coveted, so, believing that Richardson really wanted to play Lear, he nominated himself for the King. The other two agreed, and Burrell declared the meeting closed. When the two actors went to lunch the next day in their usual pub, the Salisbury next to the New Theatre, Olivier confidently offered to swap parts.

'What's that?'

'I'll give you Lear, if you give me Cyrano. Much better way round, don't you think?'

A long look, then 'No', to the surprise and consternation of Olivier. He had no desire to play Lear yet, nor was he ready for it, a view later confirmed by the critics. But he was now stuck with it, and did not help his chances of success by choosing to direct the production himself as well.

Ralph never did play Lear, and resisted many blandishments to do so. The only person he had ever told he wanted to play it was his partner, which was why the latter chose what he thought, wrongly, was a good bargaining counter.

The wariness of that part was still apparent in 1975, when

Sir Peter Hall and Donald Sinden went round to see him after a performance of *John Gabriel Borkman* at the National Theatre. When Ralph heard that Donald was going up to Stratford to play Lear, the younger actor was nonplussed to be told, 'Ah, my dear fellow, that's the terrible thing about our profession, you've been in the business what – thirty years? You think you know what you're doing, then one day you're walking along, and you suddenly say, "Ahhh, I've got my foot in a *Lear*!" '[11]

Sinden says it was not until he started rehearsals that he realized how perceptive a remark that was. Ralph also declined to repeat the role of Kent, in which he had made such a success to the Gielgud Lear in 1931. In fact, though the third Old Vic season at the New Theatre saw the two friends still sharing the same dressing-room, they were not using it on the same nights, as they never appeared together on the stage then or, as it turned out, ever again.

CHAPTER EIGHT
1946–1948

THE GREAT ATTRACTION of Richardson's and Olivier's first two Old Vic seasons was the prospect of seeing two actors at the height of their powers playing opposite each other, with all the dramatic tensions they brought to their stage partnerships. But the third season at the New Theatre failed to offer their fans the same excitement. Olivier only appeared as King Lear, and that for just forty-eight performances between October 1946 and January 1947; thereafter he was much engaged with his film of *Hamlet*. The four other plays in this season all featured the Richardson name, in three classics and one new play, *An Inspector Calls*, written by his old friend J. B. Priestley, in which he opened on 1 October 1946.

This was a morality tale set in the North of England of 1912, where the mysterious title-figure exposes how an entire family is responsible for a young girl's suicide. As W. A. Darlington put it,

> All this the inspector elicits, growing from moment to moment less like a police inspector and more like a recording angel. This, I imagine, is difficult to do in a reach-me-down lounge suit; probably impossible to any actor less good or less impressive than Mr Richardson. He does it effortlessly.

James Agate, too, thought he gave the Inspector 'a stern, unangry poise far more effective than all the thunder he obviously has up his sleeve'; and J. C. Trewin praised his masterly exercise in technique: 'He keeps interest at flood in a part that, treated with a judgement less exact, would trickle into tedium: truth from this actor's lips "prevails with double sway".'

But twice in succession critics were out of step with the Old Vic audiences – *Lear* was much panned but sold out; *An Inspector Calls* failed to fill the theatre despite the critical praise. There was dissension behind the scenes too. Basil Dean skated over this in his memoirs, merely saying, 'I found Ralph Richardson unexpectedly reluctant to take direction, perhaps in unconscious rebellion after the years of wartime restraint.'

He was certainly no longer prepared to be browbeaten by a dictatorial director when he thought him wrong. Dean had grown, if anything, more overbearing during his years running ENSA; Richardson was now much more self-confident, and secure in the total trust of his author. The latter had wanted a much more impressionistic production, as it had been given in its Moscow premiere the previous year, but Dean's compromise solution, of a realistic box-set lit in an overall green light, was so unacceptable to both playwright and actor at the dress rehearsal in Manchester that they fired the director. Ralph re-lit it himself, substituting Colour 52, a warm colour, says Diana Boddington, 'and when Basil said, "All right, I won't come near," Ralph said, "Don't come near until after the first night in London."'[1]

Dean kept his credit for the production, but when the play was chosen for the final performance of the season, he was told by Olivier and Richardson that there would be a box reserved for him, though he would not be expected to take part in any last-night reception. This was the first, but not the last, time Ralph would fire his director at the eleventh hour.

He crossed swords too with the formidable Tyrone Guthrie, who directed the next play, *Cyrano de Bergerac*. Guthrie's genius was for choreographing crowds and battle-scenes, and often his principal actors felt he was less interested in directing them than in motivating the bit-part players and spear-carriers. The characteristic sound of a Guthrie rehearsal was a handclap like a pistol-shot to stop and start the action on-stage, and his tall figure and military bearing dominated the proceedings like a drill-sergeant on the parade-ground. Ralph did not take kindly to being given orders. There was a warning rumble at an early rehearsal, noticed by Peter Copley.

> He was moving around and he said, 'I think this is a good place to be, I'll stand here'; and he was dead centre, about three yards up from the front, and Tyrone Guthrie said, 'Ralph, you're not the principal character in this scene, now please just move to the side.' Ralph shuffled away to the side, saying, 'All right, Tony old chap, you don't have to be cross with me, you know, that's all right, I'll go.' He was quite startled at Tony being rather admonitory.[2]

Guthrie was a very energetic director, constantly prowling up and down between stalls and circle, and tension between the two men reached snapping-point towards the end. The actor had been feeling his way round Tanya Moiseiwitsch's set when the director suddenly yelled at him from up in the circle, 'For God's sake, Ralph, play the scene! – play the scene!'

Guthrie's biographer, James Forsyth, sat up in the stalls as all action stopped on the stage, wondering if this heralded the big row they had all been expecting. Richardson came down to the front and glared up into the darkness of the circle. 'I was brought up to find my lights. And I'm finding them, and for the first time in your production. So don't call me a

bloody fool — old cock.' Everyone held their breath but, just
as he had done when faced with a similar challenge by the
same actor's Othello in 1938, the director recoiled from the
showdown. He clapped his hands, and merely said, 'Raight!
On we go!'[3]

At about this time Priestley wrote about his favourite
actor's 'ripe earthiness lit with magic, for which I would
gladly exchange all the romantic profiles in the world'. It is
easy to see why the part of Cyrano so appealed to an actor who
felt that his lack of such a profile denied him the features for
Hamlet or Romeo. In Rostand's swashbuckling romance he
could play the poetic lover underneath the soldier's rough
swagger and disfiguring great proboscis. He had tried out the
part the previous year on the radio, as he had done with Peer
Gynt, from which Olivier should have divined his friend's real
ambitions; but others too were surprised that such a seemingly
quintessentially English actor should attempt the passionate
rhetoric of the Gascon braggart with the quixotic streak.

Many critics compared it with his Falstaff. He showed
W. A. Darlington 'a real man, who wore his gasconading and
posturing and phrase-making as he wore his clothes, because
they were the fashion of his time, and not because they were
essential to his nature'. To others, like Ivor Brown, he proved
'he is not a natural romantic, but he is a great actor'.

Kenneth Tynan faced the classic critic's dilemma, since he
believed no English actor was capable of merging the extravagant and the bizarre into the heroic: 'But in spite of us all,
Richardson is giving a tremendous performance of *something* at
the New Theatre. Not since Peer Gynt has he conquered a
part so thoroughly.' He grumbled that he was too amiable
and not nearly coarse enough.

But his voice is most delicate; breath light of texture; more
buoyant even than that of Charles Trenet. It has the power to

puff itself up amongst vertiginous clouds of sweet rodomon-
tade. It is a yeasty, agile voice. Where Olivier would pounce
upon a line and rip its heart out, Richardson skips and lilts
and bounces along it, shaving off pathos in great flakes.[4]

Tynan particularly admired the playing of the Kiss scene
between Cyrano and Roxane, and their final scene, saying that
Margaret Leighton came emotionally of age as Roxane, and
that this was 'perhaps the best thing she has yet done in
London'.

Peter Copley was cast as De Valvert, bringing his fencing
skills to help Cyrano appear the skilful duellist he must seem
in their great fight to rhyming verse. This was an uphill task.
Most nights his greatest problem was to make sure Ralph did
not drop his sword too soon; but he never forgot the
performance on the day of the announcement of the actor's
knighthood in the 1947 New Year's Honours List. 'He got a
fantastic reception when he first came on. He gave a performance which the whole cast was watching the whole time, it
rose high above anything he'd ever done before, it was
unbelievable.'[5]

Richardson received a great ovation at the end, and in a
brief curtain speech he spoke of his pleasure in receiving 'an
honour I don't really deserve'. Backstage he was affectionately
addressed by the staff as 'Sir-Rano', and a brass name-plate
was hastily attached to the door of his dressing-room, bearing
his new title. But the question on many lips was how his
partner would take being left out. The answer was – badly.
His first words to Tarquin Olivier on New Year's Day were,
'Your father's not a knight.'[6] To others he put it more
pungently, as he was about to enter as the King in *Lear*: 'I
should have been the fucking knight!'

To those seeking reasons why one had been thus singled
out over the other it was said that Richardson was the older

man, that he had been the first member of the triumvirate and had then recruited the other two; Harcourt Williams even tried to still the gossip and backbiting by inventing the story that only one theatrical knighthood could be offered in one Honours List, so the two men had tossed for it. But nobody believed that, and more credence was given to the theory that Olivier's divorce from Jill Esmond in order to marry Vivien Leigh in 1940 was still considered too recent to allow such an honour, at a time when such things were still regarded as rather dishonourable in royal circles. Olivier growled, 'The King doesn't like me,' whilst it was known that Queen Elizabeth had loved the Richardson performance in *Q-Planes*.

The bitterness and resentment lasted less than six months. In May 1947 the King's Birthday Honours List similarly created Sir Laurence Olivier. Now both new knights were equally embarrassed at their preferment over the man in whose Shakespearean shadow they had once stood, and who had so generously helped them both in their earlier struggles for theatrical recognition – John Gielgud. They lobbied hard on his behalf, but it was another six years before his knighthood was announced in the Coronation Honours List of 1953.

The applause for 'Sir-Rano' had barely subsided when he appeared in a very different guise, as Face in *The Alchemist*, directed by John Burrell, who had done some judicious cutting of Ben Jonson's text. The play was a bit of a rarity at this time, although it had been a favourite in the eighteenth century, and Coleridge had thought it one of the three best parts in existence. But *The Alchemist* stands or falls on the performances, and for W. A. Darlington, 'taken all round, this is the best-acted play that this Old Vic Company has given us. Ralph Richardson's performance is magnificent.' He then hastened to add that 'he is not in a class by himself, however', and thought that George Relph's Subtle, Alec Guinness's Drugger, Nicholas Hannen's Sir Epicure Mammon, and Peter

Copley's Ananias were just as good. He loved Joyce Redman's 'funny little spitfire clown' rather than a trollop, as Dol Common, and was surprised and amused by Margaret Leighton as the buxom and willing widow, Dame Pliant.

The *Manchester Guardian* reviewer was impressed by the ensemble acting in depth and by how the leading actor played as part of the team:

> Mr Richardson as Face, an agreeable rascal and pimp, is the keystone of the whole structure; had he been the least bit more angular, more 'period', all would have been lost beneath that superb thrust of verbal extravagance which must have poured so naturally into the ears of its first listeners. As it was, real significance was gained and maintained. One laughed helplessly.

This acclaim is tribute to how gifted players, most of whom had now played together over a good period of time, could triumph against all the odds. Rehearsals had been particularly difficult. It was the time of the great winter freeze-up of 1947, and Ralph was unhappy that to begin with they had to rehearse in the circle bar, as the only space warm enough to work in. The company as a whole found those early rehearsals very unrewarding, and relations between director and actors became rather strained. At one point John Burrell told Peter Copley that Ananias should jump up on a stool to deliver a particularly long speech. Ralph was standing next to him on-stage and said, 'I wouldn't do that, old chap, if I were you, I wouldn't do that.' So he did not know whom to obey, but eventually thought he had better get up on the stool.[7]

In another scene when Face was working the furnace upstage, as each of his victims came on he would say, 'I think you ought to look round, old chap, and see what I'm doing, examine what I'm doing.' George Relph as Subtle was not having any of that, saying, 'Oh, I think we've got to get on with the scene, I think we'll just keep going.' Finally John Burrell called the whole company together and said, 'Will you please tell me what's the matter, why is everybody so resentful and grudging and unwilling?' This seemed to clear the air, and everyone was agreeably surprised that a production with such a difficult gestation turned into such a resounding success.

The cast were still so shaky on their lines that when Burrell called them on the morning of the opening just to run through their words, George Relph said, 'That's the one thing we can't do. We don't know them!' This appeared to be all too true that night, when Ralph dried stone-dead on his first line. No one could remember another occasion when the first voice anyone heard was that of the prompter. In less accomplished and experienced hands such an unfortunate start could have destroyed the whole of the performance.

One of the greatest successes was Alec Guinness, who played Abel Drugger, a part that Garrick and Kean had chosen to make their own, and Alan Dent echoed Hazlitt's description of Kean, saying that 'the mixture of simplicity and cunning in the character could not be given with a more whimsical effect'.

Guinness found he needed more than cunning to cope with Richardson, even though he had had considerable experience with that generation of leading actors. He had been discovered by Gielgud, and played Osric to his Hamlet and to Olivier's, before playing the Dane himself under Guthrie's direction at the Old Vic.

After war service in the Navy he rejoined the Old Vic Company in 1946 to play Eric Birling in *An Inspector Calls*. The family are dining in full evening dress when Inspector Goole arrives, and one night Richardson came to Guinness's dressing-room to tell him that his patent leather shoes squeaked terribly, and to do something about it. When told that neither oil nor Vaseline seemed to work, Ralph said, 'Try water.' The following evening, when Guinness looked for his shoes during a quick change of clothes he found them standing in a bucket of water. He squelched even more noisily through the last act, and then missed the next two performances through near-pneumonia. When he went to apologize for his absence he was greeted with, 'Oh, have you been off, cocky? I didn't notice.' The shoes were never mentioned again.[8]

But it was the third collaboration that proved the most difficult for both of them. This was *Richard II*, with the King played by Alec Guinness, who found it impossible to escape from his memory of John Gielgud's performance in 1937, when he had played Aumerle; this was also Ralph Richardson's first attempt at sole direction, and he seemed incapable of inspiring confidence in his actors. His only advice to his leading man was to pick up a pencil and say, 'Play it like this pencil, old cock,' which Guinness found no help at all. He lacked the directing skills shown so often by Gielgud and Olivier, and he seemed incapable of communicating to his cast what he wanted, or how they might achieve it. When he rehearsed the first part of the play, with the challenges before the King between Bolingbroke and Mowbray, played by Harry Andrews and Peter Copley, Ralph let it run for half an hour or so, then stopped them, saying, 'Ah yes, the movement's all right, but the speaking is absolutely terrible.' To the actors' frustration, he did not find it easy to elaborate on that. One young man in the cast stepped forward and said, 'Sir Ralph, where do you wish me to be at this point?' 'Oh now, just merge into the scenery, old chap, merge into the scenery', a dismissal which rather upset the actor.[9]

Richardson had not intended to act in his own production until Bronson Albery, a governor of the Old Vic as well as the owner of the New Theatre, pointed out rather sharply that if he did not act, he and Olivier would be in breach of their contract, which bound one or other of them to be in the cast of every Old Vic production. So rather reluctantly he agreed to play John of Gaunt.

He asked Michael Warre to design historically accurate costumes, but then refused to wear his collar up, like everyone else in the cast, as was correct for the period, but flattened his down so that, as Alec Guinness put it, 'It differentiated him from the rest of us, of course, but made him look like a large, bearded Peter Pan.' This Richard was also unhappy with his actor-director's injunction, 'Don't come within six feet of me,' while he stood centre-stage; as he says, 'not easy for the actor playing the King'.[10] Kenneth Tynan thought the potentially fine Richard promised by Guinness's acting in the opening scene 'was ruined by the dowdy unsuggestiveness of Ralph Richardson's production. Sir Ralph, I begin to think, has a common-place mind behind all that marketable technique; a mind mole-like in its earthiness. He tried to make Mr Guinness bellow, which is like casting a clipped and sensitive tenor for Boris Godounov.'

He thought the rest of the cast made heavy going of the play, and that 'the producer himself, a sedentary lion, roared John of Gaunt tediously to his grave'.

Gaunt has one of the most famous speeches in the whole of Shakespeare, which generations of schoolchildren have had to learn by heart. Philip Hope-Wallace accused Ralph of delivering it 'as if it were an inner monologue by T. S. Eliot with a kind of pattering, musing, ruminative "I've-just-thought-of-it" air, which would do splendidly for Old Peer Gynt but does not, I swear, for old Uncle Gaunt.' Whether it was one of those ruminative pauses, or a genuine 'dry', at one schools matinee he only got as far as: 'This royal throne of kings, this scepter'd isle / This earth of majesty, this . . .'

when he hesitated, and 800 treble voices prompted, '. . . seat of Mars'.

He was rarely fazed by this. He had exactly the same experience at a Stratford matineee of *The Tempest* in 1952, when the schoolchildren shouted out Prospero's lines to him. All he said when he came off then was, 'They know it better than I do.'

Despite their ups and downs on-stage, Richardson and Guinness became fast friends, and although they only worked together thereafter on screen, they saw each other quite often socially. One day Alec Guinness arrived at the Athenaeum for lunch, to discover Ralph holding forth about politics to a group of Treasury mandarins. 'After a bit he got up, patted me on the shoulder and disappeared. After some time one of these eggheads leaned towards me and said, "Tell me, you seem to know who that fellow was." I told him I certainly did, he was a most important actor.'[11] More recently he confided that he found him

a rare bird – observant, reticent and rather cunning. There was theatrical trickery of a selfish kind in some of his acting. On the other hand he had imagination and pondered, probably at home, about what he was about to do. He was also, like all the best actors, a little dangerous.[12]

When the Old Vic season ended in May 1947, Richardson embarked on his first major film for Alexander Korda since *The Four Feathers*. This time he was playing Karenin, husband to Vivien Leigh in the title-role of *Anna Karenina*. She was going through a difficult patch in her marriage to Laurence Olivier, and fell out with the French director, Julien Duvivier, and was understandably unresponsive to the wooden performance of Kieron Moore as Vronsky, the man for whom Anna leaves her husband.

The physical conditions were the very reverse of the first months of the year at the Old Vic. Then Ralph and the cast had shivered backstage at the New Theatre, and endured frozen wash-basins; now at Shepperton the cast were bundled up in furs during a heat-wave, tramping through artificial snow. But he enjoyed the part, and in his usual fashion went to great lengths to be true to Tolstoy's descriptions of his character. Vivien's friendship for Ralph had survived his two damaging visits to her home, and she warmed to the truthfulness and emotional power of his performance.

Judy Campbell, one of his later leading ladies, remembers being bewitched by them both at the time the film came out, but when it was reshown on television,

> I was so disappointed in everything except Ralph's Karenin, which was extraordinary. When he was on the screen he filled it, Vivien seemed to have shrunk. I always remember him sitting at the dinner-table twisting that wineglass, and then quite suddenly stabbing a finger at her, without looking at her; and then looking at her later, and it was just utterly unexpected. It took your breath away, like the shark appearing in *Jaws* when you weren't expecting it.[13]

But the strength of their scenes together only underlined the fatal miscasting of Vronsky who, Dilys Powell observed, 'might be playing a professional dancing partner instead of a headstrong Tsarist officer'.

The film was unfavourably compared with the Garbo 1935 Hollywood version, and lost Korda a lot of money. The only reputation enhanced by this costly failure was Richardson's. He was keen to repay his employer's wartime support, and post-war generosity in releasing him to work in the theatre, so it was a happier outcome for both men that their next film was such an outstanding success, winning first prize at the

Venice Film Festival, the British Film of the Year Award, and the New York Film Critics Award.

This was *The Fallen Idol*, based on a short story by Graham Greene, and directed by Carol Reed. For once, Korda recognized that this gifted duo did not need his customary interventionist style of support, and the two of them refashioned the shape and the thrust of Greene's original story. As Greene explained, 'The subject no longer concerned a small boy who unwittingly betrayed his best friend to the police, but dealt instead with a small boy who believed that his friend was a murderer and nearly procured his arrest by telling lies in his defence.'[14]

Carol Reed's sensitive direction drew faultless performances not just from Ralph as Baines (the butler and mistakenly suspected murderer), but also from Michele Morgan as his mistress, Sonia Dresdel as his cold-hearted wife, and especially from Bobby Henrey as the distraught boy, Felipe. The film is quite frequently reshown on television, and still grips the viewer's attention. It remained one of the actor's favourites, and he often talked nostalgically about it to the director Hugh Hudson, when they were shooting his last film, *Greystoke*. The younger man shared his admiration: '*Fallen Idol!* What a wonderful, economic film – ninety minutes, so tight, a perfect little film, our films today are all so long.'[15]

Ralph's next film was also an adaptation of a novel, this time by one of his very favourite authors, Henry James. *Washington Square* was first adapted for the stage by Augustus Goetz, and then turned into a screenplay by Goetz and his wife Ruth. Both play and film were given the title of *The Heiress*. Paramount Films negotiated with Korda for Ralph's services as the father, and cast Olivia de Havilland as his daughter, with Montgomery Clift as the fortune-hunting suitor.

Before flying to Hollywood, Richardson made a brief sortie

into management for the first time, taking Wyndham's Theatre for *Royal Circle* by Romilly Cavan, directing it himself and playing a Ruritanian king called Marcus Ivanirex. Although supported by a strong cast, including his wife Meriel Forbes, Jessica Spencer, David Hutcheson, and Dame Lilian Braithwaite as the Queen Mother, his production was dismissed by the *Daily Mail* reviewer as 'little more than a musical comedy from which someone has carelessly omitted the music'. On the first night the applause from the expensive seats was topped by some boos from the gallery. According to John Gielgud, Ralph thought they were calling 'Mu Mu', but even friendly critics like Brown, Darlington and Hobson thought the evening a waste of time for actors and audiences alike. The play opened on 27 April 1948, and was never intended for a long run, since Ralph had to sail for the USA before the end of May, but as it turned out he still found himself with time on his hands before he left London with Mu and 'Smallie'.

His first experience of the movie capital of the world was not much happier than his first visit to Broadway thirteen years earlier. He wrote to Diana Boddington:

> Dearest Diana,
> How are you my pet?
> I am constantly thinking of you.
> I think that I am about
> 6000 miles from you
> but that makes no difference
> at all – isn't nature wonderful.
> It is not very beautiful
> here, but for the climate,
> which is extraordinary, day
> after day of perfection from
> dawn to sunset.

I ventured to admire some
of the trees, 'They are NOT
INDIGINIOUS' I was
sharply informed: crushed
for a while I ventured
again on the beauty of the
birds 'THEY are migratory'
—. I dont know at all, &
I certainly will not express
an opinion again, but
between you and me the birds are
most beautiful — there some
humming birds in our little
garden that are a
constant joy — I look at
them and I think of you,
it is really quite nice here!
Ever with love   Ralph

His English reserve made it difficult for him to strike up a close rapport with the American cast, who had their own tensions anyway. None of them really got on, and they were so studiously polite to each other that Montgomery Clift said it was 'like we were made of glass'. Clift was both scared of William Wyler and convinced that the director was favouring Olivia de Havilland. He wrote to a friend: 'She memorizes her lines at night and comes to work waiting for the director to tell her what to do. You can't get by with that in the theater and you don't have to in the movies. Her performance is being totally shaped by Wyler.'[16] She was in safe hands there, and her performance won her a second Academy Award.

Ralph indicated his own unhappiness in a postcard home to his dresser.

Dear Betty,
Hope you are well. We are working very hard. Miss
deHavilland is a wonderful actress. I am not doing so well.
Love, Ralph

Publicly he was always gracious about his co-star, but much later, when pressed by Michael Meyer, he confessed he would not choose to work with her again, because she had a clause in her contract to say she would not be required to act after 5 p.m., and so he ended up playing many of his close-ups to her understudy, which Meyer thought 'an intolerable way to treat an actor of Ralph's distinction'.[17]

But it made no difference to his performance, which overshadows all the others. His technique certainly intimidated Clift, who moaned after the thirtieth take of one of their scenes, with Ralph producing the same immaculate performance each time, 'Can't that man make any mistakes?' A young British actor, Anthony Hopkins, who was to work with Ralph himself in films twenty years later, saw *The Heiress* at the time and found 'the way he expressed his absolute disappointment in his daughter was both terrifying and moving'.[18]

The film turned out to be a great critical success but, in spite of the leading lady's Oscar, it was a box-office failure. Ralph was so taken with the story and with his own part, however, that he repeated the role on the London stage the following year.

But he had to navigate some very stormy waters before he reached the safe haven of the Haymarket Theatre again, for it was while he was away in Hollywood that he suddenly received the bombshell news of his dismissal from his directorship of the Old Vic. The triumphs of his previous four years at the head of the Company were about to end in bitterness behind the scenes, and incredulity outside, when the news finally became public.

CHAPTER NINE

1948–1949

THE MANNER AND the timing of their dismissals were unexpected and offensive to both actor-knights, but the possibility had been aired between them towards the end of 1947. The growing campaign to set up a National Theatre, with a state subsidy administered through the infant Arts Council, had resulted in the setting-up of a National Theatre Board under Oliver Lyttelton to consider the options. Richardson and Olivier attended a meeting of this Board to discuss how they and the Old Vic might be involved in the campaign. This resulted in a twelve-year mandate to the two of them to bring together a repertory of actors strong enough to form the nucleus of a National Company. As they left the meeting they discussed how they would subsidize their own financial sacrifice over such a long period by each taking time out to make lucrative films. (That sacrifice had been considerable already – the top Old Vic salary from 1944 to 1946 was only £40 a week.)

But then Ralph chilled the euphoria with a sudden premonitory warning.

> Of course you know, don't you, that all very splendid as it is, it'll be the end of us. It won't be our own dear, friendly, semi-amateurish Old Vic any more. It'll be of government interest

now, with some appointed intendant swell at the top, not our sweet old friendly governors eating out of our hands and doing what we tell them. They're not going to stand for a couple of actors bossing the place around any more . . . We shall be out, old cocky.

The sweetest of these friendly old governors was already lost to them. Lord Lytton had been Chairman of the Board at the Old Vic in Lilian Baylis's day, and it was he who had invited Ralph to become a director in 1944, and negotiated his release from the RNVR. When Lytton died in 1947 he was succeeded briefly by Lord Hambledon, until his death in March 1948. The new Chairman then appointed was the far from friendly Lord Esher, who wasted little time in terminating the contracts of the directors. He chose his moment with some care – one director was 6000 miles away in Hollywood, another was leading an Old Vic tour twice that distance away in Australasia, and neither could fly home at short notice for a showdown. Only John Burrell was left in London holding the fort, and Esher almost succeeded in opening a rift between him and the others.

The fateful document was a four-page Private and Confidential Memorandum on Future Administration, in which the Board of Governors argued that to create the 'corporate entity' required to develop the Old Vic into a National Theatre, it was necessary to replace the current set-up with a full-time administrator forbidden to act or direct, and under him an artistic director appointed for only one year at a time. The justification for this triumph of bureaucratic over artistic considerations was that the future developments could not be administered 'by men, however able, who have other calls upon their time and talent'.

Esher neglected to tell Burrell that he had sent copies out

to Richardson and Olivier, so that Ralph at first thought that Burrell must have been privy to the plot. But he was instantly reassured by the latter's cable protesting that the memorandum had been prepared 'in camera without my knowledge'. He ended the cable to both his colleagues abroad: 'Important that we react in a united way, and avoid attempts to drive wedges between us while separated'.

From California he received a reply saying, 'Dear John did not realize memorandum could have been prepared without your knowledge so replied to Esher copy to you and Laurence same post STOP Will of course take no further action STOP United we stand STOP Love Ralph'.

In Australia Olivier received Burrell's cable before Esher's air-mailed missives, and after reading them in astonishment cabled Burrell, 'Ah me, I see the downfall of our House – Larry'. He had been incensed as much by the tone of Esher's covering letter as by the memorandum: 'Time, in its tiresome way, has marched on since you have been away . . . I am sorry to bother you with these things', with a personal dig even in the perfunctory note of thanks at the end: 'We fully realize the sacrifice you have made and the unceasing work that the great position you have made for yourself entails.'

When Burrell submitted a formal request that nothing further should be done until both his two colleagues had returned from abroad, which in Olivier's case could not be until November, a full four months hence, Esher disingenuously said, 'It was indeed unfortunate that two out of the three directors of the Old Vic Theatre Co. should have been out of the country at the time when these important matters came up for consideration.' Not only had he chosen the time, he had asked them to keep the news confidential for the time being, so they were able neither to lobby together behind the scenes, nor to make the matter public without laying themselves open to charges of breaching confidences. So Esher could agree to delay until November, confident that he had brought off a fait accompli.

He was not the only villain of the piece, however. Tyrone Guthrie, who had been instrumental originally in bringing on board first Richardson, and then Olivier, had begun to have reservations about the consequences early on. He complained that no money was saved despite the box-office success, and said that within two years it became apparent that 'the two stars must decide either to be actors, making films and radio appearances, going to America, Australia and so on, or else to be managers of the Old Vic. They tried, and failed, to have the cake and eat it.'[1]

There was more than a touch of injured pride in his criticisms. Guthrie had carried the burden of Old Vic administration after the death of Lilian Baylis, and right through the difficult war years; he had retained the title of Administrator of the Old Vic and Sadler's Wells during the first couple of years of the triumvirate, and directed the highly successful *Peer Gynt* and *Cyrano de Bergerac*. But his outrage at the *Oedipuff* proposal was compounded when Olivier carried off the double-bill brilliantly without him, under the direction of Michel St Denis and Miles Malleson respectively. His biographer James Forsyth suggests that by the end of 1947 Guthrie may have resented the fact that their greater public acclaim had brought the two actors the knighthoods he felt he deserved just as much.[2]

John Burrell's wife, Margaret, understandably aggrieved by his machinations, called him 'the rogue elephant who kicked the whole thing down'. While all this had been hatching behind closed doors, Burrell had been happily making plans for the next few seasons. The Oliviers were to revive *Richard III* and *The School for Scandal* after their Antipodean tour, followed by Olivier's *Othello*; James Bridie's

Lancelot was to feature Olivier in the title-role and Richardson as Merlin.

Ralph had already put in motion with the BBC the idea that he should do Ibsen's *Brand*, using the radio production as a try-out for the stage, a sequence that had served everyone so well with *Peer Gynt* and *Cyrano de Bergerac*. After the rupture with the Old Vic Board, he kept to his arrangement with the BBC, who broadcast *Brand* in the Third Programme on 11 December 1949, but sadly he never did repeat it on-stage.

It was true that there had been some critical rumblings about standards falling after those first three heady seasons, and J. C. Trewin said that the Old Vic had become pretty boring in the absence of the two stars, but most people thought that that would soon be rectified on their return. Still only the principals involved knew what was afoot. Before the news broke, Esher tried another ploy on Olivier, which the actor only revealed publicly in his memoirs thirty years later; he was outraged when it was obliquely suggested to him, in the privacy of the peer's house in London, that the real aim of the exercise was to make him the sole director, instead of having to share power with his two colleagues. But Olivier was not about to betray his partners in such a nakedly self-serving way, and by now the three of them had recognized that they had lost the battle, and decided to leave gracefully, without public recrimination.

There was one final bitter confrontation in private. Early in December the special meeting was at last held to discuss the Esher memorandum, and even now the three directors were not allowed to argue their case together. They were summoned in before the Board one at a time, and each came out looking white-faced and furious. Whatever agreement of silence was made, it was kept; now all the protagonists are dead, and the Old Vic files have been destroyed.

The public fall-out was considerable when the news of

their 'resignation' was announced the following day. A hot debate ensued in the press as to who was to blame for the rupture, and some teeth were set on edge by the sound of axes being ground. Basil Dean, still smarting from his treatment over *An Inspector Calls*, and now a possible candidate for the newly invented post of Artistic Director, wrote in the *New Statesman* that the very success of the two actors had 'only helped to confuse the picture and delay the day of reckoning for those who sought to give the Old Vic the authority and status of a national theatre as it were overnight'.

Llewellyn Rees, Drama Director of the Arts Council, and the governor of the Old Vic largely responsible for proposing an administrator with no creative responsibilities, was appointed as the first holder of that position. He was soon writing to Lord Esher: 'The Administrator's position must be equivalent to that of Miss Baylis at the Old Vic or Mr Hugh Beaumont in H. M. Tennent Ltd.' His major achievement seems to have been to provoke the later resignations of Michel St Denis, Glen Byam Shaw and George Devine from their directorships of the Vic Centre, which housed the Old Vic School, the Young Vic and the Experimental Theatre.

In his chronicle of the early years at the Arts Council, *Offstage*, Charles Landstone acquitted his friend Rees of acting to his own advantage, asserting that it was Lord Esher who told Rees that he was the only man equipped to become the new administrator.[3] But whoever's initiative it was, the results were singularly unhappy ones.

Esher did not take kindly to the public questioning of his action. The impresario Stephen Mitchell accused the Board in the *Daily Telegraph* of being incompetent to run the country's most important theatre. 'It is disturbing that people so little qualified should be so responsible for our highest artistic endeavours and be given so much money to play around with in an industry in which they have neither trained nor laboured.'

Right: Arthur Richardson, Ralph's father (seated centre), in school staff group. (Cheltenham Ladies' College)

Below: Richard Coaker in *The Farmer's Wife*, with Primrose Morgan, directed by H. K. Ayliff, Birmingham Repertory Company tour, 1925. (Theatre Museum, V&A)

Petruchio in *The Taming of the Shrew*, with Phyllis Thomas as Kate, directed by Harcourt Williams, Old Vic, 1931. (J. W. Debenham/Theatre Museum, V&A)

Above left: Iago in *Othello*, with Edith Evans as Emilia, directed by Harcourt Williams, Old Vic, 1932. 'We have seldom seen a man smile and smile and be a villain so adequately.' (J. W. Debenham/Theatre Museum, V&A)

Above right: Henry V, directed by Harcourt Williams, Old Vic, 1931. 'If he had walked over Waterloo Bridge and down the Strand as he appeared on the stage, the whole of London would have followed him.' (J. W. Debenham/Theatre Museum, V&A)

Below: 'I have put on so many make-ups that sometimes I have feared that when I go to wipe it off there will be nobody left underneath.' (Hulton Deutsch)

Sergeant Fielding in *Too True to be Good*, with Ellen Pollock, directed by H. K. Ayliff, New Theatre, 1932. (Theatre Museum, V&A)

Right: Dr Clitterhouse in *The Amazing Doctor Clitterhouse*, with Joan Marion, directed by Claud Gurney, Haymarket, 1936. (Theatre Museum/V&A)

Left: Charles Appleby in *Eden End*, directed by Irene Hentschel, Duchess, 1934. (Janet Jevons/Theatre Museum, V&A)

Below: The Ghost in *Hamlet*, with Robert Harris as Hamlet, directed by Harcourt Williams, Old Vic, 1932. (J. W. Debenham/Theatre Museum, V&A)

Sam Gridley in *Bees on the Boatdeck*, with Rene Ray, directed by Laurence Olivier and Ralph Richardson, Lyric, 1936. (Theatre Museum, V&A)

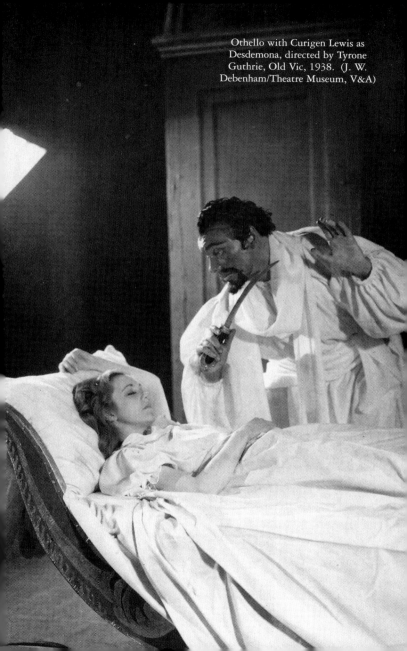

Othello with Curigen Lewis as Desdemona, directed by Tyrone Guthrie, Old Vic, 1938. (J. W. Debenham/Theatre Museum, V&A)

Above: The Boss in *Things to Come*, with Raymond Massey and Margaretta Scott, directed by William Cameron Menzies, London Films, 1936. (Korda Collection, Central Television)

Below: The keen amateur pilot in 1938; two years later the Navy was less enthusiastic about his flying prowess. (Hulton Deutsch)

Peer Gynt, with Sybil
Thorndike as his
mother, Aase, directed
by Tyrone Guthrie,
Old Vic Company at
the New Theatre,
1944. 'He had that
open-eyed, slightly
goofy, dreamy quality
that was very right for
Peer.' (John Vickers)

Above: John Burrell, Ralph Richardson, Tyrone Guthrie and Laurence Olivier in 1944 discussing the opening Old Vic season at the New Theatre.
(Hulton Deutsch)

Below: Bluntschli in *Arms and the Man*, with Margaret Leighton as Raina and Laurence Olivier as Saranoff, directed by John Burrell, Old Vic at the New, 1944.
(John Vickers)

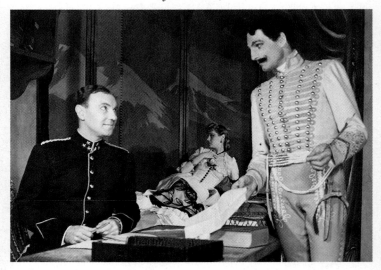

Above: Richmond in *Richard III*, with Laurence Olivier as the King, in the fight scene at the end, directed by John Burrell, Old Vic at the New, 1944. 'Look, Laurence old chap, there's no need to go so fast.' (John Vickers)

Below: When Laurence Olivier re-created his Richard III in his 1955 film, Ralph Richardson played the Duke of Buckingham. 'Say, have I thy consent that they shall die?' (Korda Collection, Central TV)

Programme of the second Old Vic Company season at the New Theatre, 1945–46.

Ralph Richardson and Laurence Olivier in ENSA uniform on the steps of the theatre at Belsen, before the performance of *Arms and the Man*, 1945. (Diana Boddington)

Falstaff in *Henry IV Part II*, with Joyce Redman as Doll Tearsheet, directed by John Burrell, Old Vic at the New, 1945.
'Peace, good Doll! do not speak like a Death's head;
do not bid me remember mine end.'
(John Vickers)

Uncle Vanya, with Laurence Olivier as Dr Astrov, directed by John Burrell, Old Vic at the New, 1945. 'Many people thought they should have exchanged parts.'
(John Vickers)

Inspector Goole in *An Inspector Calls*, with
Marian Spencer and Margaret Leighton,
directed by Basil Dean, Old Vic at the
New, 1946. 'A stern, unangry poise far more
effective than all the thunder he obviously
has up his sleeve.' (John Vickers)

Cyrano de Bergerac, with Margaret
Leighton as Roxane, directed by Tyrone
Guthrie, Old Vic at the New, 1946. 'He
is not a natural romantic, but he is a
great actor.' (John Vickers)

Above: John of Gaunt in *Richard II*, with Alec Guinness as the King, and Margaret Leighton as the Queen, directed by Ralph Richardson, Old Vic at the New, 1947. (John Vickers)

Left: Reading telegrams of congratulation on the announcement of his knighthood in the New Year's Honours List, 1947, watched by Margaret Leighton (left) and Diana Boddington in his dressing room at the New Theatre. (Photograph courtesy of Diana Boddington)

Esher refused publicly to give his full reasons, standing on the justification of a system where 'independent and intelligent minds, free from both profit and prejudice, should control public enterprise'; and sneered that Mitchell's inability to grasp these traditional virtues betrayed 'a lamentable ignorance of how things are run in this country'.

The net effect of all this upheaval and jockeying for power was that the Old Vic suffered several difficult years, the establishment of the National Theatre was delayed for more than a decade, and the theatrical paths of the two actor-knights now diverged for ever. They would meet in a handful of films, but never again stride the boards together. There was no rupture between them, but their different natures and ambitions led them to choose different routes in pursuit of their stage careers; the ways in which these subsequently developed made it at first difficult for them to play opposite each other on an equal basis, and eventually impossible.

Olivier continued as an actor-manager, firstly under his own banner, 'Laurence Olivier Productions', at the St James's Theatre, and later at Chichester and the National Theatre. But Richardson turned to the management of Tennent's, where Hugh 'Binkie' Beaumont repaid his trust over the years by starring him in a number of critical and box-office successes, many of them at the Haymarket. His one great period of actor-management had ended in a rebuff that hurt him deeply. Henceforward he would stick to the actor's last. For those who regretted that decision it is worth balancing the subsequent laments of others that Olivier's burdens of administration and direction kept him away far too often from the thing he did best – acting. Richardson wanted to act, even more than his audiences wanted to see him act, and any gap between engagements, however brief, made him decidedly restless and unhappy.

He never spoke publicly about why his and the others'

contracts were not renewed, nor how he felt the whole affair had been handled, except for the laconic remark that ' a fired butler doesn't complain of its master', which reveals how he felt his erstwhile employers had treated him. This analogy appealed to Olivier, who repeated it himself later.

The travails the three partners had endured together were not quite over for two of them. Richardson invited John Burrell to direct the stage version of *The Heiress* at the Haymarket but, perhaps because he was so exhausted by the whole painful saga of their dismissal, Burrell proved unequal to the task. During the early chaotic rehearsals Gillian Howell, who was playing his niece, was puzzled by the sight of Ralph searching about as if looking for something, as they walked through the pass door to go on-stage for notes. Asked what it was, he said, 'I've lost my talent. It wasn't very big, but it was shiny.'[4] (He used variants of this line to other actors on other occasions when he was unhappy with his performance – sometimes it was 'a shiny little box with R.R. on it, with my talent in it, I seem to have lost it'.)

Despite the lack of clear, firm direction, Gillian Howell was impressed by how hard Ralph and his co-star worked during rehearsal.

> It was an eye-opener to me as a young actress to watch how Ralph and Peggy Ashcroft came back each day with more thoughts, more ideas, more work done – ordinary actors tend to go on from where they were the day before! He said that he included every thought, move, motivation and reaction during rehearsal – and then just let them all go. I think that was his genius.[5]

His genius could not flower in a directorial vacuum, however. With a week to go before the pre-London opening in Brighton, John Burrell limped on to the stage on the

Friday, to announce: 'Ladies and Gentlemen, I am sorry to tell you that I am leaving the production, and on Monday morning John Gielgud will be taking over.' Binkie Beaumont was the one who grasped the nettle, but the initiative seems to have come at the request of the play's American authors, Ruth and Augustus Goetz. It is unclear whether Ralph lent his weight to their move to oust his old friend and partner, but both he and Peggy Ashcroft certainly acquiesced in the decision, as an unhappy necessity.

It was a particularly sad conclusion for John Burrell. On top of the Old Vic Board terminating his contract, he had now lost the confidence of his remaining partner, and his theatrical career in his home country was effectively ended. He went into self-imposed exile in America, where he taught drama, with just the occasional directing engagement in the American theatre or television, and he died there in 1972.

The Heiress cast were naturally apprehensive at the thought of a new director coming in and changing everything at such a late stage, and Gielgud himself was quite worried about what he might have let himself in for. Fortunately he had seen the play in New York six months before, with Basil Rathbone and Wendy Hiller. He went down to the carpenter's shop at Waterloo to examine the set before he met the company on the Monday. When he arrived he found James Donald, who was playing the young fortune-hunter Morris Townsend, sitting gloomily on the steps of the empty stage, saying, 'I've offended Sir Ralph.'

When the cast assembled, their new director told them he did not want to change anything, just see what he could do to help, and could they run through the play for him? He then told them that everyone was standing about when they should have been sitting. 'You look as if you're going to catch a train, you're all on the platform waiting to take off, and one can't attend to the dialogue.'[6]

All the details had been neglected, which were so important to a period play – they needed props, fans and muffs,
noises off-stage of carriages driving up; the set was totally
repainted in olive-green instead of cream; and before the cast
quite knew where they were, everything had been changed.
Peggy Ashcroft was lost in admiration. 'We were hamstrung
and couldn't get unknotted . . . He was wonderful. It was like
somebody unlocking a puzzle.'[7]

Unlocking Ralph's puzzles took a little longer. His problem was translating his film performance of Dr Sloper into a
stage one. It is most unusual for an actor to make the film
first, then re-create the part on-stage before an audience; the
process is usually the reverse, as with Olivier's two assumptions of Richard III, Gielgud's Cassius for Stratford repeated
in the Hollywood *Julius Caesar*, or Kenneth Branagh's more
recent *Henry V* for the Royal Shakespeare Company and then
for Renaissance Films.

Ralph put his finger on the difference between the two
performing media when he said, 'I've never been one of those
stage chaps who scoff at films. I think they're a marvellous
medium, and are to the stage what engravings are to painting.
The theatre may give you big chances, but the cinema teaches
you the details of craftsmanship.'[8]

Gielgud quickly realized that Richardson was still engrav-
ing his performance for the screen close-ups, instead of
painting it for the theatre's long-shot.

When Ralph poured out the sherry or the port he took hours
over doing it, and he kept going to the door and looking into
another room. I said, 'Ralph, when you've decided who's done
the murder in the other room, perhaps we can go on with the
scene.' I had to convince him that these things wouldn't work
in the stage version, and he immediately understood.[9]

When the revamped production opened the following Monday in Brighton it was a great success, and after a glittering first night in London on 1 February 1949, it ran at the Haymarket for 644 performances, although Ralph surrendered the part to Godfrey Tearle after a year. His respect for Gielgud's direction was revealed to Gillian Howell one night at the curtain-call when she remarked to him, 'It seems to have gone very quickly tonight.'

'Oh, yes. Johnny's in front, and I've taken out some of the goldfish.'[10]

One or two of the critics praised Gielgud's direction, though unaware of the scale of his salvage operation at the time. Many of them waxed enthusiastically about Richardson and Ashcroft as father and daughter, though here too, for different reasons, some of the more reflective observers struggled to pinpoint just why they were so impressed.

Harold Hobson wrote in the *Sunday Times*: 'Of Miss Peggy Ashcroft's Catherine one hesitates to speak simply because everything one says must be inadequate. For her performance all superlatives are pale and feeble things.' W. A. Darlington said in the *Daily Telegraph*: 'Ralph Richardson plays her father, with that unobtrusive certainty of touch which makes him an actor at once easy to appreciate and difficult to anatomize.'

Hobson chose to end his 1958 monograph on the actor with his memory of this performance, recalling that the reason why Dr Sloper is so hard on his plain, gauche daughter is because her mother died giving birth to her. His sister pleads with him to show a little mercy towards her niece, reminding him that his wife had died a long time ago. The critic said a decade later he could still see him,

a cruel, relentless figure whose cruelty and relentlessness were due to a great grief within; and I can hear his voice ring out,

'That is no consolation', every word spoken as if it were a note in music, resonant, reverberating, echoing down the corridors of interminable years of sorrow. The emphasis on the word 'that' was terrible; at one stroke it destroyed all the healing properties of time, and the 'consolation' lingered on the air like the distant and dying tolling of a bell.[11]

The experienced theatre and radio producer R. D. Smith admired the way he avoided all the traps that snare the less aware actor playing a despotic father, and especially the ensemble playing of stars and supporting cast:

In sickness and death he maintained a consistency of character that ought to be common enough but is, alas, rare even in actors of the front rank. Peggy Ashcroft was, quite simply, faultless and the purity and force of her thinking and feeling left one shaken and elated, as one can only be when someone of genius is playing with a first-rate team in material of high seriousness.

One junior member of this team was reprimanded for not being quite serious enough. Donald Sinden was making his West End debut as Morris Townsend's young cousin, a tiny part with only six lines and one piece of business. Then, as now, he was hungry for laughs, and was encouraged by his director, a touch rashly, to seek them. He got them with every line but one – 'How do you do, Miss Sloper' – and he thought it would be nice to get a laugh on every single one of his few lines. He worked out a way of getting a laugh on 'How do you do, Miss Sloper', by tripping over the hearthrug and saving himself by grabbing at Peggy Ashcroft's hand, and that did get a laugh one night, which thrilled him no end. In the interval the call-boy came and asked him to go to the No. 1 dressing-room on the third floor to see Sir Ralph. 'So I went along and he said, "Well done, cocky, I've seen you working for that, congratulations, well done, you've done it [pause], but I don't think we really need it do we?" I said, "No we don't," and it was out.'

Donald Sinden today describes Ralph's performance in the play as 'mesmeric', and he often made a point of watching from the wings.

> He gave instructions to the stage-management that on no account was he ever to be prompted. He would always get out of it, but he would sometimes say the most astonishing things. In one scene Ralph had to say, 'And what's he done with the money? He enlarged his capacities in Europe!'
>
> One night he said, 'And what's he done with the money? He enlarged his experiences in Africa.'
>
> His sister's response was, 'Yes he admits he's been wild, Austin, but he's paid for it.'
>
> 'Ah, so that accounts for his impoverishment.'
>
> One night he said, 'Ah, so that accounts for his impotence', which did complicate the plot considerably.[12]

Ralph's occasional transpositions and inspired paraphrases, when he was momentarily at a loss for the right word, line, or very occasionally, entire speech, became legendary; not least for the aplomb and total authority with which he carried them off, right through his career. This aspect of his stagecraft astonished his fellow-actors, and usually deceived his audiences.

He showed the trick once, towards the end of his life, to David Storey, during rehearsals for the play Storey wrote for him, *Early Days*. Ralph had been asked to do a Shakespearean speech on television, to reopen the arena at Alexandra Palace, and he asked for suggestions as to what piece he should choose. After Storey and the cast had made various suggestions, he suddenly said, 'I think I shall do my speech from *Richard IV* or *Henry X*, I know it by heart.' And he did this speech of supposedly Shakespeare, which was complete and utter rubbish, but sounded absolutely authentic. It was a great Shakespearean speech, it went on and on, and he declaimed several minutes of this wonderful rhetoric, and said, 'Shall I stop, or continue? That's the speech I used to do whenever I dried in Shakespeare, no critic ever noticed it, no audience has ever made any comment on it whatsoever.' David Storey was very impressed, and said it sounded just like many Shakespeare speeches when one did not quite get all of it, but it sounded like what should be there.[13]

The long and happy run of *The Heiress* meant that the 'first-rate team' Reggie Smith described above forged lasting friendships which in Ralph's case spanned three generations. Gillian Howell's married name was Cadell, and her husband John was the son of Jean Cadell, who had been with Ralph at Birmingham Rep. Gillian's eldest child, Simon, was born shortly after the Haymarket run, and twenty-two years later he joined the cast of *Lloyd George Knew My Father*. His sister Selina played Ralph's daughter in *The Fruits of Enlightenment* at the National Theatre in 1979, but she had an even greater stroke of good fortune much earlier than that, because he became her godfather at Gillian's request.

Selina's earliest memory of this 'wonderful, mysterious and charming man' was when she was only about four or five, long before she realized he was famous. Her mother took her to the Richardson house in Hampstead,

and shambling down the stairs came this enormous man, and I was nervous at first, but within minutes I had been charmed, because this enormous man bent down to me, and told me that he had an animal that he would like me to meet. He said I had to be very, very quiet, and go upstairs to the attic with him. I know I just did what I never did with people, which was to leave my mother's hand and go with this man. He was mesmerizing, and I went up the stairs with him, and I can feel now my little hand in his big paw. He didn't speak, and we went up for what seemed to me forever, to the top of that house, which was converted into an attic, and he opened the door and it smelt of hamsters' cages, and then we went through another little door, and there was sawdust all around, and suddenly in the corner there was a ferret. I didn't know it was a ferret, until Ralph told me that this was a ferret he'd found on Hampstead Heath with a broken leg, that he'd mended it, and he'd been looking after it ever since, and it was almost ready to go back to Hampstead Heath. And he stood, waiting for it to calm down, because I suppose I'd rattled around a bit. In some way I had handed myself completely over to this atmosphere, and waited for this little creature to come up to Ralph, which it did, and it got on to his hand, and he just held it there and let me stroke it, and it was enchanting.

On the same visit, when I left, Ralph gave me an envelope, and it was the most beautiful envelope, not the usual shape, more square; on the outside was my name, which he misspelt – CELINA – and inside was this wonderful scroll of flowers and my name again, and this enormous piece of white paper, which was a £5 note, which I'd never seen before. I remember being terribly impressed by that, and the fact that I was the only member of my family to have been shown the ferret.[14]

The Cadell family were not alone in enjoying and building on this connection with Ralph in *The Heiress*. Peggy Ashcroft had worked briefly with Ralph at Birmingham Rep and then in the 1930 Robeson *Othello*, but it was in this long run that the two of them forged a partnership that would be repeated again in the work of playwrights as different as Henrik Ibsen and William Douglas-Home, and a lifelong close friendship. John Gielgud was directing Ralph again, for the first time since the 1933 *Sheppey*, and their renewed partnership grew over the next thirty years into one of the glories of the English stage.

More importantly, the personal trough of 1948, with the blow to Ralph's pride and self-esteem inflicted by the abrupt end of the Old Vic triumvirate, was succeeded by another peak of critical and box-office success. He now consolidated his considerable reputation with some very confident performances on stage and screen, and found himself much in demand as a performer, speaker, and business adviser.

CHAPTER TEN

1950–1951

As he grew older Ralph encouraged the image of himself as delightfully vague and engagingly eccentric, but he was profoundly practical about all matters affecting his work, and he was very conscious of his own worth. His BBC file reveals this last quality, with a courteous but determined argument over fees.

The standard BBC fee in 1945 for top-rank actors in major radio plays was 50 guineas, which Ralph was paid for his Cyrano de Bergerac in March 1945, and the following month for Falstaff in each Part of *Henry IV*. When he was asked to play a major part in the BBC Victory Programme, he pointed out that he was still being offered exactly the same fee as before the war, and requested an increase to 75 guineas. Val Gielgud, Head of Drama, was concerned about setting a precedent, which would immediately open the doors to a flood of similar requests; but after some protracted and high-level internal BBC consultations it was accepted that Ralph would decline to appear on the air unless his reasonable request was met, and thereafter his standard fee became 75 guineas, at which it remained fixed for some years.[1]

He enjoyed the medium of radio, and appeared on a fairly regular basis over the years, but chose the occasions with some care, severely rationing the talks and interviews he gave.

Woman's Hour was entranced with his talk on 'Romance', but failed to persuade him into further such appearances. He declined a request to contribute to another feature in the BBC's North American Service, excusing himself by pointing out that he spent every Tuesday and Thursday at the Board of Trade, trying to help solve the problems of film distribution – a task that many actors would have found neither appealing nor very comprehensible.

The beginning of the 1950s was in general a fertile and creative time for Richardson. The long run of *The Heiress* was followed by another, in *Home at Seven* at Wyndham's Theatre, which left him the time and inclination to explore the potential of other media and their relation to the theatre. At the end of 1949 he gave an illustrated lecture on 'Theatre and Screen' at Grosvenor House in London for the *Sunday Times*, in connection with the National Book Exhibition.

Just after the war he was instrumental in saving and restoring the bombed remains of Pollock's Toy Theatre, together with Alan Keen, the antiquarian bookseller, and he later became President of the Pollock's Club. His interest in this venture extended to getting J. B. Priestley to write an hour-long play for the Toy Theatre about highwaymen, *The High Toby*; and in 1949 the cardboard cast was given voice with a 'first night' cast that included Sir Ralph and his wife Meriel Forbes, Phyllis Calvert, Peter Cushing, Esmond Knight, and J. B. Priestley himself.

Ralph's love of books also received practical expression, when this avid reader was translated into a publisher as the result of two wartime friendships. The first invitation came from Max Reinhardt, whom he had met looking for a partner on the squash court. Their military status was rather different – Ralph was now a Lieutenant Commander, and Max was an Aircraftman II, the lowest rank possible; but they were equally matched on the squash court, so they played together regularly. After the war, when Max Reinhardt was publishing accountancy textbooks with some success, a squash-court conversation that included another keen athlete, Anthony Quayle, ended with a decision to publish books on subjects which interested all three of them, such as theatre, and Richardson and Quayle joined the publishing board. Their first venture was to republish the Bernard Shaw/Ellen Terry letters.

Soon afterwards another of Ralph's wartime friends reappeared in his life. Their previous collaboration had been over the lead-covered 'secret books' at Eastleigh. Now 'Boy' Hart was running the merchant bankers Ansbachers, who were keen to buy a publishing company. He asked Ralph's advice, who felt unqualified to give it, saying, 'Don't be silly, talk to Max Reinhardt.'

The upshot was the purchase of The Bodley Head, a long-established and distinguished company, which had published *The Yellow Book* and many other notable literary works. Quayle and Richardson now joined the Board of Bodley Head, which soon also welcomed J. B. Priestley, and later Graham Greene. These two authors did not always see eye to eye, but Ralph always felt he was surrounded by congenial friends, and he remained a director to the end of his life. Apart from the regular Board meetings, he and Max lunched together regularly in the upstairs room at Rules restaurant. Ralph enjoyed tête-à-tête lunches much more than the big publishing parties which were commoner in the 1950s than they have become in the present days of conglomerate publishers, but Max Reinhardt thought they were necessary then, even if his squash partner did not. 'He hated parties. I threw a big party in Lower Sloane Street, and Mu loved it, but Ralph sat on the steps downstairs and talked to our driver.'[2]

Ralph always arrived at Board meetings and lunches full of ideas for titles they might publish. He took particular pleasure in their decision to revive the Nonesuch Press and reprint the Folio Edition of Shakespeare, with the Quarto readings in the margins, to mark the Coronation in 1953. As a former student of book-binding he always took a professional interest in the finished product too. He liked to demonstrate how to crack open a well-bound book without breaking its spine.

The enigma of Ralph was that all these eminently practical qualities were combined with an ability to dream that lifted him way out of the normal run of actors. It was this ability that marked out his acting style, as he once revealed to Patrick Garland in a television interview.

> I don't say it's a trick. but what I think it is — it's partly dreaming. You see acting, isn't it, is make-believe, and to make people believe you've got partly to believe it yourself. Not all the time, but some of the time in each play you really believe that it is really happening; I mean you're acting enough to know that's true. So in a way it is forced dreaming to order. The curtain goes up at eight, and at eight precisely you must partly dream.[3]

This ability was particularly useful in *Home at Seven*, in which the central character is entrapped in a waking nightmare. R. C. Sherriff's play showed a bank clerk, David Preston, arriving home from the City at his usual hour of seven o'clock on a Tuesday, but believing it is still Monday. In the missing twenty-four hours, a total blank in his memory, the safe has been robbed at the local club where he is treasurer, and a man has been murdered — the only man he has ever really hated. The suspense lies not so much in the suspicion of others as in his own growing fear that he may have been the perpetrator of both crimes, and that the shock may have provoked his amnesia.

The intrusion of such events into respectable, middle-class suburbia gripped the attention by the truthfulness of the playing. For the *Observer* critic,

> Sir Ralph's David, with 'the dark space in his memory', goes straight to the heart. Some actors turn a room into a stage whenever they enter; but as David Preston moves about his house with that typical walk, stiff yet springy, you feel that he has indeed known the place for years. So complete an illusion is less usual in the theatre than one might imagine. Both Sir Ralph and Marian Spencer (well cast as the devoted wife) create it at once.

This paper's critic thought the other characters were a credit to the BMA, the Law Society and the police, 'and if there is an Incorporated Association of Barmaids, then Meriel Forbes should take its diploma'.

The *Sunday Times* reviewer, too, was moved to lyrical vein.

> The chief value of the piece, of course, in spite of its other clevernesses, is David Preston's character, and Sir Ralph Richardson's performance. Sir Ralph is the Wordsworth of our actors in that he sees poetry in the commonplace. Dickens, admirable fellow, made ordinary people exciting by discovering all kinds of strange wonders in them: that is, he showed that ordinary people are extraordinary. Such is not Wordsworth's way, and it is not Sir Ralph's. Both move the spirit by a single and straightforward statement of fact . . . I hope it is clear that I consider this to be a remarkable performance.

Most of the other notices were equally laudatory, and even the dissenting *Evening Standard* fastened its severest criticism to the fact that the plot device 'reduced Ralph Richardson to a comparative spectator, which is equivalent to putting a muzzle on Hamlet'.

The actor clearly never felt the muzzle the critic saw, since he repeated the part on BBC Radio the following year, and then re-created it in his one and only venture into film direction. The moving spirit here was again Sir Alexander Korda, who chose *Home at Seven* as his first experiment in transferring recent stage successes economically on to film. There were a number of changes – the film-script was adapted by Anatole de Grunwald, and two of Korda's contract artistes, Margaret Leighton and Jack Hawkins, were brought into the cast – but the biggest innovation was in the way the film was made. It was rehearsed on the actual set at Shepperton for three weeks, just like a stage play, then shot in thirteen and a half days, rather than the eight weeks which would have been customary under the usual method of production. (Korda was so taken with the results, both artistic and budgetary, that he rapidly shot three other films in the same way, including one with Ralph, this time acting only, in *The Holly and the Ivy*.)

But despite his success, Ralph was never persuaded to repeat the experience of being a film director, unlike Olivier, whose appetite fed on success in this medium. He modestly gave much of the credit to his collaborators: 'I am extremely fortunate in having a great artist beside me [Korda] and to be able to turn to the author [Sherriff] on the set. I believe that in making a film of a play it is important not to deviate from the author's original intention.'[4] That expressed belief shows how far removed his approach was from that of many other film directors, then and since. (There is one other reason why Sherriff's play was always fondly remembered by the actor. He had the acumen to buy a 25 per cent interest in the stage rights, which brought him in a steady and substantial income over the nine-month run of *Home at Seven* at Wyndham's; it also restored his faith somewhat in his own theatrical judgement after the mere five-week run of his previous venture into management with *Royal Circle*.)

It was Richardson who suggested to Korda that Joseph Conrad's *Outcast of the Islands* would make an interesting film. The omens were favourable – Carol Reed was brought in again to direct, and a strong cast included Robert Morley and Wendy Hiller as Mr and Mrs Almayer, Trevor Howard as Willems, the title-figure gone to the bad, and Ralph Richardson as the white-bearded Captain Lingard. The exterior scenes were shot on location in Ceylon, and the whole sweep of the film was much more ambitious than the earlier Korda/Reed/Richardson collaboration on *The Fallen Idol*, but it failed to repeat the success of the earlier film. Captain Lingard remains a rather remote figure, and only catches fire in his magisterial denunciation of Willems at the end, when he declines to shoot him after his betrayal: 'To me you are not Willems, the man I thought much of and helped, the man who was my friend. You are not a human being to be forgiven or destroyed. You're a bitter thought, something without bodily shape. You are my shame.'

Carol Reed was impressed by his star's discipline and attention to detail. On one particularly hot and steamy day on location, he said he would only be shooting medium close-ups, so it was not necessary to change into full costume as the merchant sea captain. But Richardson still appeared correctly dressed right down to the boots, explaining that 'if I had on my own shoes it might show in the shot from the way I stood'. (Similarly, when his publisher friend from the City, Max Reinhardt, advised him after the Brighton preview of *Home at Seven* that he was much too well dressed for a bank clerk, he asked the theatre's wardrobe to dig him out an ill-fitting suit.)

Outcast of the Islands was Wendy Hiller's first experience of working with Ralph, and she came to the conclusion that he

JOHN MILLER

was a very simple, reserved, shy man who felt he had to make himself interesting, and that a great deal of that was 'a good old acting job'. Whenever they met afterwards, and did plays together, she always used to think he was still making his mind up as to what character he was playing off-stage.

> When we were doing *Outcast of the Islands* the Make-up room was upstairs at Pinewood, and if Ralph was coming downstairs and I was going up I could see Ralph making up his mind who he was, for that greeting – whether he was going to be hail-fellow-well-met, or whether he was going to be very distant, or whether he was going to put an arm around me, or was he going to speak at all? I wasn't only unsure, he was unsure too, and I think that was because he was so shy, he couldn't be himself, which was a very special and original self.[5]

His fourth film in little more than a year made, appropriately, the biggest bang. This was *The Sound Barrier*, directed by David Lean. Originally Lean did not think that Richardson was capable of playing the lead, until Korda persuaded him; afterwards the director said he thought he gave one of his very best performances. As a keen amateur flyer before the war and a professional pilot during it, Ralph was particularly keen to tackle this part, and as the industrialist hell-bent on developing the first jet-plane to break the sound barrier, he dominates the film, as his character does his family and colleagues. For an actor always so concerned about his first entrance, Lean devised one that was satisfactorily suspense-building. Nigel Patrick, as Ann Todd's fiancé, about to meet his prospective father-in-law for the first time, waits in a drawing-room with her and her nervous brother, Denholm Elliott, all with obvious trepidation as they hear the tycoon approaching. The camera shows his hand on the outside door-knob through the door that is slightly ajar, and we hear him finishing a conversation outside. The drawn-out tension of this delayed entrance before he bursts through the door is as dramatic as any of the test-pilot sequences. The bitterness between father and daughter, after both her brother and her husband are killed in pursuit of his supersonic dream, recalls the depths of similar feelings in *The Heiress*, although the later film has a moving reconciliation at the end. The British Film Academy gave the Best Male Acting Award of 1952 to Ralph Richardson for his perform-ance in *The Sound Barrier*; it also won him the New York Film Critics Award for Best Actor.

This flurry of filming was fitted in around his first stage appearance in one of the classics since leaving the Old Vic, as Vershinin in Chekhov's *Three Sisters*. Again he was surrounded by a strong cast – Renée Asherson, Margaret Leighton and Celia Johnson as Irina, Masha and Olga, Eric Porter as Solyoni, Harcourt Williams as the doctor, Walter Hudd as the schoolmaster, and Diana Churchill as Natasha. This was a special Festival of Britain production mounted by Tennent's in association with the Arts Council. Individual performances were much admired, but Peter Ashmore's production as a whole was felt to be somewhat less than the sum of the parts. Ralph's positive personality did not quite fit the useless colonel, and Ian Hamilton thought he was overshadowed by his stage partner: 'The part of Masha demands considerble virtuosity, and Miss Margaret Leighton displays it. This is the finest performance, and it would not be unfair to suggest that it outshines Sir Ralph's in the last scene.'

T. C. Worsley went further in the *New Statesman*, and was largely dismissive of both production and cast.

And Sir Ralph Richardson? Even he, it seemed, was oddly at sea – all over the place. Partly it is, I think, that he has developed almost to a point of schizophrenia his tricks of voice which, by now, bear simply no relation to the words he is saying. Whenever he is not speaking, when interjecting a smile or a grunt, or just acting, he is as masterly as he used to be.

But he thought Vershinin played the parting from Masha at the end excellently, which again proves how subjective two critics' reactions can be to the identical performance.

As Ralph approached his next great watershed year of 1952 he could look back on a happy run of major film successes, from Baines in *The Fallen Idol* to J.R. in *The Sound Barrier*, and on two of his last three plays enjoying long and happy runs. The working atmosphere always mattered a lot to him. This was one reason why he never contemplated abandoning the stage to become a full-time film actor, as some of his own contemporaries did, and as many more were to do in later generations of actors.

His different reactions at the end of the working day are indicative of his sensitivity to atmosphere.

It may be something to do with the hours that one spends in the film studio. You get there very early, but when the day's over and the director says, 'Right, it's a wrap-up' I'm out like a rabbit. I'm half-undressed by the time I get to my dressing-room, I've taken the things to the dresser, and I'm away, because I've got to get out of it. This moment, 'Boys, it's a wrap-up', what a joy it is – more joyful really than when the bell comes at school when I was a boy, which I hated. [Everyone else in the film world calls it a 'wrap', only Ralph called it a 'wrap-up'.]

A curious thing, though, in the theatre, when the curtain comes down, you go to your room, you sit there; and you eventually say to your dresser, 'Well, I'm going to make a great effort of will, I'm going to get out of this theatre.' And on the way down to the stage door very often you find yourself just wandering on to the stage. I often do. Quiet now the audience has gone. Just walk about on the stage and think perhaps of the mistakes you made, and the movements. You don't want to leave it. In the theatre there's a sense, rather like after a meal, of fulfilment after playing a part in a theatre, even though it hasn't been a good show you've done. It's rather the difference between eating a meal when afterwards there's a sense of fulfilment, you just want to sit by the table for a while, you don't want to get up; or eating a ham sandwich in a railway station when you want to bite it and go off. I can't express it, but that's the difference.[6]

That reluctance to leave the theatre was more than the usual actor's need to unwind after a performance, and was noticed by all the actors who played with him over the years, and inspired many stories, told with awe and affection, which will emerge later.

But the 1952 season saw him much less keen than usual to linger on the stage of the Shakespeare Memorial Theatre at Stratford-upon-Avon, where he had at last been lured by his young friend and admirer from the pre-war Old Vic and that wartime Gibraltar beach, Anthony Quayle.

CHAPTER ELEVEN

1952

ANTHONY QUAYLE had taken over from Sir Barry Jackson as Director of the Shakespeare Memorial Theatre in 1949, and he instituted a policy of attracting the 'Great Big Names', as he put it, to lead the Company. A good, if not great actor himself, he proved to be outstandingly successful as the man at the helm, and his ability to attract the leaders of the profession made Stratford for the first time a truly national rather than a provincial institution.

John Gielgud led the way in 1950, with his Angelo, Cassius, Benedick and Lear, with Peggy Ashcroft as his Beatrice and Cordelia; the following year the young Richard Burton made his name in the cycle of Histories, with Michael Redgrave at the head of the Company. For the 1952 season Quayle turned to Richardson, inviting him to play three leading parts opposite Margaret Leighton.

The first production was not new, but a revival of Michael Benthall's *Tempest*, with Loudon Sainthill's sumptuous costumes. Michael Redgrave, Richard Burton and Alan Badel were succeeded as Prospero, Caliban and Ariel, by Ralph Richardson, Michael Hordern and Margaret Leighton. Many actors whose testimony appears in this book used the same word, when asked to describe the Richardson acting genius –

'magical'; but he seemed quite unable to conjure up this quality as Prospero, and appeared rather bemused and strangely detached from the proceedings on-stage.

He was detached enough at one matinee to observe a party of schoolboys in red blazers sitting in the stalls. He told his dresser, Gladys Varney, 'Go and get some of that boy's mousy hair for my moustache.'

'Which boy?'

'The one with the same colour hair as yours – mousy!'[1]

Macbeth's hair colour eventually appeared nearer the shade of the boy's blazer than of his scalp.

When Ralph accepted the part of Prospero it was without too many apprehensions, but he later drew a vivid distinction between his and Gielgud's assumptions of this role and less grand ones.

> I think I could come on and say, 'I'm from the Gas Works, I've come to read the meter,' and I believe that people would believe me. But it's strange that John Gielgud, whose acting I admire extravagantly – I think he's one of the greatest actors living – could not come on and say, 'I'm from the Gas Works, I've come to read the meter.' People would not believe that he came from the Gas Works. Then, the other curious thing is that at the end of *The Tempest* he comes on and says, 'I am the Duke of Milan,' and you believe it. He *is* the Duke of Milan, and it's absolutely splendid. Now I have played in *The Tempest* and I have said, 'I am the Duke of Milan,' and no one has believed me for one moment.[2]

This uncertain opening to the season was followed by an almost unmitigated disaster. Most actors are so superstitious about the bad luck traditionally associated with *Macbeth* that they will only refer to it as 'the Scottish play', and Ralph had

had his qualms too. The previous year, at a Foyle's Luncheon celebrating the publication of the new *Companion to the English Theatre*, he ended his speech with a prophetic shiver,

> Shakespeare said of the actor that he was an abstract and brief chronicle of the time. 'Out, out, brief candle!' cries Macbeth,
>
>> 'Life's but a walking shadow; a poor player,
>> That struts and frets his hour upon the stage,
>> And then is heard no more.'
>
> I do not like being called a candle, even for Shakespeare, and to remind me that I am particularly abstract and brief depresses me![3]

He rarely spoke at length about any part before he had revealed it to the audience, but in his lecture on 'The Actor' to the Royal Society of Arts on 3 March 1952, for once he laid bare the demands placed on him by the playwright.

> Sometimes an actor may be meagre in his measure, sometimes rich. I am at the present moment engaged in studying one or two of the great parts of Shakespeare which I am going to attempt to perform at Stratford-upon-Avon this year. When one takes one of these parts to pieces and studies each word, one finds oneself surrounded by an immense store of verbal jewellery. The first task in such a case is to avoid the embarrassment of so many riches and to endeavour to construct a clear, straight path from one point to another, and, while hoping to preserve in its place every detail, ever to keep moving, resisting all temptations to pause to pick up a delaying jewel.
>
> Shakespeare offers such wealth that the difficulties of dealing with his material are very great and many. The conception of the poet is so lofty that it is hard for the ordinary mind to move at such heights: as it is hard for the

explorer to walk on Everest; and then, up at these heights, Shakespeare demands a rapid pace. He is always in a hurry to tell his tale, and trying to keep up with him is a tremendous effort. I am, for instance, studying Macbeth. The beginning of this part is an example of the speed at which Shakespeare works. Macbeth enters, makes one short observation on the weather and is immediately plunged into the drama of murder. Only one second is allowed for the establishment of the character, before events sweep upon him.

'We have not time for this,' Shakespeare seems to say – 'I am in a hurry, friend; come, let's get on with it.'

The director was also keen to 'get on with it'. John Gielgud had played the murderous King twice himself, and was determined to have an uncluttered set to keep the action moving, so his design was mostly black velvet drapes as a background to the silvery costumes and flaming torches, with very little furniture except in the banquet scene. He explained why in a programme note:

I am producing *Macbeth* in this new manner because I've come more and more to the conclusion that Shakespeare never intended it to be done as a strictly historical play set firmly in the eleventh century, encumbered with melodramatic horned helmets, cloaks falsely baronial, bagpipes, tartans and the rest of it. The less 'realistic' we can make it the better.

Richardson went along with this approach, hoping that, 'freed from place and special costumes, we can at last extend the imaginative scope and pour everything on to the target'. He was happy to be in the hands of an old friend whose judgement had always proved sound before, and who was uniquely responsive to his needs. 'Gielgud's method could be dangerous if adopted by some other producers. He brings no detailed notes, he has no obsession about unalterable positions. He fits in with the mood of the players, his mind superbly flexible.'

But flexibility was what was lacking in Richardson's Macbeth. It was not from lack of knowledge of the text; as he said, 'I've played every other part in it, but not the cocoanut!' He had, in fact, played the 'cocoanut' himself on BBC Radio, as long ago as 1933, when his 'deep and resonant' voice had made his Scottish King 'singularly impressive'. But Richard Findlater found that his voice two decades later was 'feathery, anxious and springy', and Ivor Brown deplored the metronomic inflection and curious mildness with which he seemed 'to parse the lines as he went on'. W. A. Darlington too was disappointed:

> Better than any other actor on our stage he can use an ordinary character to suggest the universal, the supernatural, the transcendent. He has not his superior when comedy in the grand manner is required. But high and solemn tragedy seems to take him out of his stride.

For J. C. Trewin, 'Richardson haunted the tragedy like a sleepwalker (an odd transference here) with a look of fixed astonishment.'

Kenneth Tynan appeared to be seeking to inherit James Agate's crown as the master of invective, blasting director and star in his opening paragraph:

> Last Tuesday night at the Stratford Memorial Theatre *Macbeth* walked the plank, leaving me, I am afraid, unmoved to the point of paralysis. It was John Gielgud, never let us forget, who did this cryptic thing; Gielgud, as director, who seems to have imagined that Ralph Richardson, with his comic, Robey-esque cheese-face, was equipped to play Macbeth; Gielgud

who surrounded the play's fuliginous cruelties with settings of total black, which is about as subtle as setting *Saint Joan* in total white.

But he reserved his deepest thrusts for the actor, with two cruelly memorable images, as 'a sad facsimile of the Cowardly Lion in *The Wizard of Oz*'; and 'Sir Ralph, who seems to me to have become the glass eye in the forehead of English acting, has now bumped into something quite immovable.'

The *Times* reviewer was more measured in his analysis of why the production failed, and put his finger on the central weakness: 'The plain truth is that Sir Ralph Richardson's playing of Macbeth suggests a fatal disparity between his temperament and the part.'

Ralph conceded that for once the imaginative leap into the heart and mind of the character might be too great for him. He saw Macbeth 'as a taut violin string calling for a gigantic poetic effort. Men and women can know unhappiness, but few of us have to go through the tremendous ordeal of that doomed creature. It's rather like tackling a piece of music by Beethoven.'

He certainly shrank from conveying the unrelieved villainy of the character, but another reason for the 'fatal disparity' was shrewdly diagnosed by Gielgud. 'The great difficulty with both Othello and Macbeth is that they are great heroes with no sense of humour.'[4] Ralph always sought to bring out the humour in a part, even in Ibsen, as a means of making his portrayal deeper and more rounded. But over and above Macbeth's lack of humour was Ralph's failure, for once, to believe in the character himself. As he confessed to his director, '"Well, if I can't see the dagger, cocky, can you wonder the audience can't either?" Which was very endearing, but didn't help the production; he was very unhappy, so it wasn't much good'.[5]

There was a sub-text to his unhappiness, which was only apparent to some members of the Company, and this was caused by a change in his relationship with his leading lady. Ever since Margaret Leighton had joined the Old Vic Company in 1944, Ralph had taken her under his wing, and she had become rather a protégée of his. He helped to get her a long-term contract with Alexander Korda, and the two of them had many successful partnerships on stage and screen; he introduced her to her husband Max Reinhardt, and the two couples frequently dined together on a Sunday evening after the men had played a strenuous game of squash.

Their close personal and professional relationship was sundered by the arrival of a young actor in the Stratford Company, Laurence Harvey, who swept her off her feet into a passionate affair and eventually into a rather short-lived marriage. Some members of the Company, like Michael Hordern, felt that Ralph's hurt disapproval of their affair affected his concentration. 'He couldn't take his eyes off Margaret Leighton, on stage or off. He was absolutely adrift all season.'[6]

The critical savaging of his Macbeth prompted Ralph into one of those self-deprecating 'Richardsonisms' that has been passed on from actor to actor. The morning after the first night he and Raymond Westwell both arrived at the theatre at about the same time to collect their mail from the stage door. Either Westwell failed to see his colleague, or was too embarrassed to refer to the previous night's débâcle, but neither man spoke to the other. When they met that evening for the second performance Ralph said, 'You cut me this morning. If you do it again, I shall bruit it abroad that you were seen playing Banquo to my Macbeth.'[7]

The humour of this remark could not conceal the deep sense of failure that he carried with him for long afterwards. Twenty years later he was filming *A Doll's House* with Anthony

Hopkins, whose own self-confidence was rather undermined over lunch one day, when the older man suddenly said,

'You're playing the Scottish King, aren't you?'

'Yes, I am.'

'My God, I don't envy you that. When I played it, I'd have blacked the boots for the entire cast rather than go on-stage. It takes fifteen men to play that part.'[8]

His reluctance to go on-stage in the part at one matinee led to a startled stage manager having to say to him, as he was waiting in the wings to go on: 'But Sir Ralph it's *Macbeth*, not *The Tempest*.' He had come down in the wrong costume and make-up – every actor's recurring nightmare.

After such a wounding failure, it is a mark of the actor's resilience that his third role was seen by most people as a success. It was his idea to do *Volpone*, and he so transformed his make-up and his performance that critics and audiences could scarcely credit that it was the same actor who had so disappointed them earlier in the season. Harold Hobson thought he put more effort into the make-up than the performance, with such a pasty complexion that 'he looks like a corpse dressed up for a party'. His enormous, sometimes excessive, attention to how he looked in a part gave even the actor the occasional pause for reflection: 'Indeed I have put on so many make-ups that sometimes I have feared that when I go to wipe it off there will be nobody left underneath!'[9]

For his readers in the *Daily Mail* Cecil Wilson tried to imagine the actor's state of mind: 'As he approached his third and last new role of the season, Sir Ralph Richardson must have felt rather like a boxer with one round left in which to save his title after being hammered all around the ring.'

In this production even the ring did not stand still. George Devine and his designer, Malcolm Pride, managed to get the old pre-war stage machinery to work, with its sliding stages, revolves and massive lifts. Volpone's huge four-poster bed slid out of view as the Senate rose from beneath the stage, and houses revolved in the corners. The *Evening Standard* reviewer said admiringly, 'The stage ascended, dived, capered sideways – did everything, in fact, except sit up and beg.'

Devine was anxious that all this activity should not be slowed down by his leading actor, and kept urging him to keep up the pace. Anthony Quayle was playing Mosca and observed how Ralph always agreed with his director, 'Absolutely, of course, I do see.' But when they came to do the scene again he reverted to his old tempo. With a foot in both camps, Quayle was rather torn. 'In the end, Richardson did it his way. In performance the actor always wins.'[10]

Christopher Morahan was Devine's assistant on this production, and at one rehearsal suddenly found Ralph grabbing hold of his forelock, saying, 'What I would like is to have a wig like this laddie's – lank'; a personal embarrassment that did not diminish his admiration for this Volpone, nor his eagerness to direct him at the National Theatre many years afterwards. Most critics thought Volpone Richardson's best performance of the season; the exception was Harold Hobson in the *Sunday Times*, who found it entirely lacking in élan and attack, and compared it unfavourably with Donald Wolfit's recent approach to the part.

Altogether the 1952 season was the lowest trough in Ralph's career, and he never returned to Stratford afterwards. Eight years later he wrote of every actor's ambition to scale 'the four glorious peaks of dramatic literature' – Hamlet, Lear, Othello and Macbeth – and sadly indicated he thought they were beyond him.

> Actors who attempt these great parts may be placed into three
> divisions – those who succeed the first time they play them;
> those who are doomed never to succeed, however many times
> they try; and those who could succeed with practice. Clearly I

don't belong to the first division. It could be that my place is in doomed second ... Is it, on the other hand, quite so proved? Is there not still a chance of coming in with the third division – those who could 'succeed with practice'? ... But truly I imagine that if one were to attain proficiency in these great exercises, the result would be to render to all one's other work an ease, a facility, and a strength. It is for this reason that I envy those who have succeeded.[11]

To others, actors and audiences alike, his other work did seem to possess that ease, facility and strength; but he never wholly escaped those stabs of self-doubt, although they never again cut quite so deeply as in that unhappy Stratford season. The depth was the greater because of the height of his admiration for the master of all playwrights:

I do not think Shakespeare would have chosen to write for actors if he had not considered acting a worthy instrument for his genius. Acting has much in common with other arts. It consists in observing, selecting and composing; in creating order, pattern and harmony; in inventing and imagining, and in bestowing vitality. It is the anatomy of emotion.[12]

His greatest successes in the anatomizing of emotion for the rest of that decade were to be in modern parts, with just one excursion into Shakespeare.

CHAPTER TWELVE

1953–1958

THE RELATIONSHIP between actors and authors can sometimes be as fraught as that between actors and directors, but
Ralph always seemed to retain the respect and admiration of
the playwrights he served, from Shaw and Priestley to Pinter
and Storey. Often they went on to create parts especially for
him, like John Greenwood in *The White Carnation*, which
R. C. Sherriff wrote for Ralph after their huge success with
Home at Seven. In the latter, Ralph had convincingly played a
man who lost his memory; now he played a man who had lost
his life seven years earlier, when a flying bomb killed him, his
wife and guests at a Christmas Eve party. To begin with he
cannot believe he is a ghost, until a friendly policeman
persuades him. While the Home Office and the Church try to
exorcize him, the ghost settles down to improve his mind
with good books and the BBC Third Programme.

If the critics were not quite sure about the play, they
certainly were about the central player, *The Times* finding him
'an authentic Richardson ghost – bewildered and a little
helpless, but intensely human'. For the *Sunday Times* his
performance was 'magnificent'; Harold Hobson went on to
assert that 'there is no other player who can touch the ordinary
qualities of ordinary people with such radiance, nor so marry
the commonplace with the sublime'. Kenneth Tynan in the

Evening Standard saw him as 'a 4-D character in a 3-D world', and tried to make amends for savaging his Macbeth by commending the way 'he guides the play through its shallows with a touch of a master-helmsman. It is a magnificent performance, and I mean no irony when I nominate Sir Ralph as the best supernatural actor of his generation.'

Among the supporting roles Meriel Forbes was picked out for her charming performance, together with old friends such as Harcourt Williams as the vicar, and Campbell Singer as the policeman. But the appeal of these players only sustained a run of a couple of months, followed by a seven-week tour. Ralph's own faith in the play led him to revive it later in the year for a BBC Radio production in the Light Programme series, 'The Stars in their Choices'.

In November 1953 he joined other old friends in a star-studded production of N. C. Hunter's *A Day by the Sea*, otherwise sometimes flippantly referred to as 'Three Knights and a Dame'. The newly-dubbed Sir John Gielgud played a disillusioned diplomat, Dame Sybil Thorndike his mother, and Sir Lewis Casson her ancient brother-in-law, looked after by the drunken doctor played by Sir Ralph. Cecil Wilson added, in the *Daily Mail*, 'And to prove that not all talent is necessarily titled, Irene Worth and Megs Jenkins add tender, eloquent notes to this sigh in a minor key, with its gentle way of breaking into a chuckle.'

Irene Worth's first astonishment at Ralph came on the pre-London tour, in Liverpool, when his hamster escaped in the hotel. 'Three nights later, in the middle of the night, about 3 a.m., Ralph suddenly sat up in bed and said to Mu, "I think Mousey's come home." How you can hear on the thickest of pile carpets that a hamster has returned is beyond me, but Ralph heard it!'[1]

But what happened on-stage took her breath away even more, in the way he continued to explore and develop his role during the run. One night she came down to the wings early before her entrance, when Gielgud and Richardson had a two-handed scene together.

> They began to spar with each other, they were trying to keep each other on his toes, and under all this was the marvellous respect and love those two men had for each other. So there was no rivalry or bitterness, but a sharpness with their ripostes, I thought I've never seen anything like this in my life, and it was really only for themselves, but of course it must have been electric for the audience.[2]

Gielgud was also the director, and he orchestrated some ensemble playing from his distinguished cast that packed the audiences in for a long run, despite the critics' reservations about Hunter's neo-Chekhovian text. W. A. Darlington complained that 'London playgoers are notoriously more interested in acting than in plays, and here is a positive feast of acting provided by a cast which glitters with titles and high talent.'

In the *Manchester Guardian* Philip Hope-Wallace questioned whether the play gained by having such a starry cast: 'With so many big guns on the stage there is some wonder that the explosions are not louder.' Kenneth Tynan thought they were all wasting their time on 'an evening of unexampled triviality . . . It was like watching a flock of eagles and macaws of magnificent plumage jammed for two hours in a suburban birdcage.'

During the run Donald Albery sent Richardson a very different play to consider – *Waiting for Godot* by Samuel Beckett. Peter Glenville wanted to direct it, with Ralph as Estragon and Alec Guinness as Vladimir. Ralph was mystified by it, and sought advice. Irene Worth urged him to do it: 'It's the most wonderful play I've ever read, it's divine, you must do it.' John Gielgud told him he thought it was rubbish, and he should not touch it.

So he turned to the author himself, who came to see him backstage at the Haymarket. But Beckett was as enigmatic in person as he was on the page, and when he was confronted with a list of questions, beginning with 'Who is Pozzo?', he said he could not explain things in that way. Fearing that if he could not understand the play himself he could not possibly hope to make it clear to the audience, Ralph turned it down, a decision he later much regretted.

There were more knights in his next film, *Richard III*. Sir Laurence Olivier re-created his 1944 Old Vic success, with Sir John Gielgud as the Duke of Clarence, Sir Cedric Hardwicke as King Edward IV, and Sir Ralph Richardson as the Duke of Buckingham. He enjoyed playing Richard's accomplice in crime in the film, much more than he had the heroic and rather colourless Richmond on the stage. But his director was not overly happy with his friend's performance, as he confided to his son Tarquin:

> The old bugger won't accept direction. I take him with extreme delicacy out of earshot, when nobody suspects, and try to coax him. 'I'll think about it,' he says, and bloody well goes on playing for sympathy. Buckingham should be detestable, how else can people expect to fall in love with a villain like Richard, if they like his sycophant?[3]

But Buckingham's silky deviousness is well conveyed by Richardson, and one of the most chilling confrontations in the film is when the newly crowned King rejects him with 'I am not in the giving vein today.' All of Buckingham's bitterness and apprehension wells up into Richardson's face and voice on:

And is it thus? Repays he my deep service
With such contempt? Made I him King for this?
O let me think on Hastings, and be gone
To Brecknock while my fearful head is on.

There was very nearly a too dramatic moment on camera for Cedric Hardwicke. Riding a richly caparisoned warhorse, robed and crowned, Hardwicke had to sit majestically as he entered a courtyard in his coronation procession.

I was alarmed to discover that Edward IV's saddle was slipping, and I was proceeding at a full gallop at a 45-degree angle between heaven and earth. I should undoubtedly have been trampled beneath the hoofs of the following procession if Ralph had not rushed forward to retrieve me.[4]

The three old friends from the Birmingham Rep days saw quite a lot of each other off the set too, and on one occasion Ralph's Rolls was stopped for speeding in Regent's Park. The policeman failed to recognize the driver and demanded identification.

'I am Sir Ralph Richardson. Seated next to me is Sir Cedric Hardwicke and behind me is Sir Laurence Olivier.'

This cut very little ice with the officer of the law. 'I don't care if it's the whole of King Arthur's ruddy Round Table – you're getting a summons.'[5]

A Day by the Sea finally came off in 1955 after an eighteen-month run, and Ralph and Mu set off for a tour of Australia and New Zealand, with Terence Rattigan's plays *The Sleeping Prince* and *Separate Tables*. They were joined by Lewis Casson and Sybil Thorndike. The two couples enjoyed acting together, although outside the theatre Dame Sybil put her finger on why the Richardsons are rather different from us, not such madly keen explorers of places and people. Actually, I think Ralph is rather shy. He considers an actor should display his feelings in his art, and off the stage be as private as he wishes. Mu understood this and backed him up in his unwillingness to meet people.[6]

Before leaving Australia he appeared as the Reverend Lambeth in his last film for Sir Alexander Korda, *Smiley*, directed by Anthony Kimmins. He was back in England when Korda died in January 1956, and he and Olivier both paid tribute to him at his memorial service. Korda had guided the Richardson film career for so long that the actor now felt rather at a loss, and his choice of screen roles from now on was much more hit-or-miss.

In September of that year he returned to the Old Vic in Waterloo Road for the first time since his 1938 Othello. He was welcomed back by what Cecil Wilson in the *Daily Mail* called 'the sort of cheering, stamping ovation normally reserved for post-war idols like Richard Burton and John Neville. But it was reserved last night for that sturdy pre-war product, Sir Ralph Richardson.' Michael Benthall's ambitious and comprehensive five-year plan to present the entire Shakespearean canon meant that someone had to tackle the difficult and rarely performed *Timon of Athens*, and Ralph shouldered the burden.

This role of a man who gives away too much to his supposed friends, and then when they abandon him in his hour of need resorts to misanthropic ranting at their ungratefulness, makes forbidding demands on the actor. W. A. Darlington for one thought he rose to them: 'That he dominated the play goes without saying; any Timon must do this. But Sir Ralph did more than dominate the play – quite simply he was the play. Without effort or intention, he reduced the other players to shadows.'

Harold Hobson too was enchanted by the way in which 'all Shakespearean viciousness of phrase is transferred into a threnody, a lamentation . . . It is, quite simply, creative acting of the highest kind in which the actor as artist presents to the world his own vision and thereby enriches it.'

Others were less convinced. J. C. Trewin complained of his rather clipped speech, 'ne'er letting Timon's silver thread upon his lip'. Kenneth Tynan objected to

> a mode of speech that democratically regards all syllables as equal. I select, for instance, Sir Ralph's thanks to the Amazons for enlivening his feast. 'You have added,' he said distinctly, 'worth and toot, and lustre.' It took a trip to the text to reveal that 'and toot' meant 'unto't'. Yet there was in his performance, for all its vagueness, a certain energy, and it was a relief to hear Timon's later tirades spoken with irony instead of fury.

Many more were regrettably denied the chance to hear his speaking of those tirades. Ralph approached BBC Radio Drama with a proposal to record the play with the Old Vic cast, as he had done several times during those Old Vic seasons at the New Theatre. But ten years on, the BBC found it much more difficult to make available the recording facilities Ralph wanted over the period he suggested, and so there is no permanent record of Ralph's performance as Timon.

No one noticed a trick that Ralph played with his make-up, until he confessed it to the *Tatler* when the play had been running for some weeks.

> In *Timon* I wear two quite different false noses, a little one for the first Act, and a larger one for the second. The first got them used to the idea and stopped them from saying I was

depending upon tricks of make-up, and after that they ceased to look with inquiring eyes.

He was not, however, about to give much else away. Pressed in the same interview he replied: 'What sort of man am I? Well, do you know, I've often wondered that myself!'

It was poetic irony that the theme of the play which brought him back to the Old Vic, from which he had been so summarily dismissed eight years before, should be one of ingratitude. The galleryites who cheered his return to the Waterloo Road would have to wait another two decades for the next opportunity.

The beginning of 1957 found him in New York, playing General St Pé in *The Waltz of the Toreadors* by Jean Anouilh. Harold Clurman's production at the Coronet Theater was named Best Foreign Play by the New York Drama Critics, who were overwhelmed by the depth Richardson brought to the old roué, with sudden changes of pace they found 'fabulous', and an astonishing gift of being 'almost simultaneously funny, pathetic and contemptible'.

But Ralph's great success was cut short when he was suddenly afflicted with an incapacitating throat infection, which forced him uncharacteristically to be 'off' for a number of performances, and eventually drove him home to seek an operation. Happily this proved unnecessary, and with the enforced resting of his voice the infection cleared up.

He had already decided on his next play, and was soon fretting to get to work on it. The literary agent Peggy Ramsay had sent Frith Banbury a script by a virtually unknown author called Robert Bolt. The director thought first of Celia Johnson for the part of the wife, and the two of them made a list of seven or eight men who might play her husband, with Ralph's name at the top of the list. As soon as he read the script in New York he said he wanted to play it. Binkie Beaumont immediately put up half the money and Frith Banbury found the balance from his own production company. With two such bankable stars the director said it was his easiest play ever to get off the ground.

The unusual speed with which everything fell into place in setting up *Flowering Cherry* actually caused one early problem with the leading man. Rehearsals were quickly fixed for a certain date, but because Celia Johnson had already promised to take her children for a month's holiday in Cornwall, she asked for a postponement.

During those four weeks the now fully recovered Richardson was champing at the bit, or rather at the text. Frith Banbury suddenly got a telephone call.

'I say, old fellow, Act II, Scene II – "Little rat!" – I can't say that line, old fellow.'

'Oh, Ralph, why?'

'I can't possibly say it, it's all wrong there.'

'Oh, I see. Well, to be quite honest, I'm really working on the set, it's got to be with the designer, and it's got to be at the workshops on Monday, and I haven't really got into the text with that degree of thoroughness yet.'

'Well, I know I can't say it, old fellow.'

'Well, look, I'm phoning Robert Bolt tonight in the country, and I'll tell him what you've said – that you don't want to say "Little rat".'

When the director broke the news to the author he exploded with dismay. 'What? It's the most important line in the play!'

Banbury then asked Bolt to write a long letter to Sir Ralph, copying it to him, explaining why the line was so important, to try to persuade him to keep it in. At the first reading of the play three weeks later Ralph skipped the line, and Celia did not notice the cut. When they blocked the scene at the end of the week they reached the disputed line; she waited and nothing happened.

'Oh, aren't you going to say "Little rat"?'

'Why? Do you think it's good?'

'Oh, yes, I do rather. Doesn't matter, does it, press on, shall we?'

Frith Banbury held his breath, and prayed: 'Now, nobody say anything.' The next day they rehearsed the scene again. 'I could feel the tension in Bolt, it was enormous. Ralph said "Little rat", and nobody said anything. So that taught me about Celia's influence over Ralph.'

It was a lesson well learned. If he wanted Ralph to change something in rehearsal thereafter he always discussed it with Celia beforehand and reached a conclusion with her, before saying, 'Ralph, I don't think this is quite on the rails at the present, I think perhaps this, what do you think, Celia?' The moment she said, 'Yes, I don't think this is quite right,' Ralph would say, 'Oh, don't you, old girl, what do you think?'

'You see, the director is a threat, standing out front, but your colleague is an ally, standing beside you on the stage, and suffers the same way you do, and so you can more easily take it from her, I think.'

This respect for his leading lady's judgement paid dividends on the opening night. Binkie Beaumont was aware that Ralph could sometimes give too much, and was noticeably better on matinee days, so he advised Frith Banbury to have a run-through at 3.30 on the afternoon of the first night. The director asked Celia to request a run-through, and then told Ralph she had requested it.

'Oh really, I wonder why the old girl wants a run-through? Oh well, if she wants it, she'll have to have it.'

'And because we'd had that run-through he was absolutely superb on the first night.'[7]

Most of the critics concurred. The plot, stated baldly, is hardly appealing. A failed insurance manager talks of giving up his boring office job to move back to the country life of his youth and plant his own orchard. His secret drinking and petty pilfering from his wife's purse are gradually revealed, and his wife finally summons up the strength to leave him when she realizes that the country idyll is no more than a fantasy he is incapable of realizing.

Richard Findlater in the *Sunday Dispatch* thought that with this play Richardson had put himself back at the head of his profession: 'Sir Ralph haloes this tedious shammer with a luminous authority, demonstrating the individual talents for comedy, pathos, and even – at moments – tragedy which have been, for too long, buried beneath his mannerisms.'

Cecil Wilson echoed this in the *Daily Mail*: 'Sir Ralph, always a master hand at homely, well-meaning chumps, plays his most triumphant failure.'

Derek Monsey in the *Sunday Express* recalled a familiar description of the actor, wearing 'the look of the wretched Cherry with fine theatrical panache'.

Kenneth Tynan thought the play was flawed, but carried by the strength of an actor of genius, repeating a favourite phrase:

> No doubt about it, Sir Ralph Richardson gave an amazing performance of *something* at the Haymarket last Thursday. No actor in England is more interesting to watch. He is interesting all the time, without respite; even when he plays a dull man, that dull man is never permitted a dull moment ... Those critics who hold that he excels in portraying the Average Man cannot, I feel, have met many Average Men.

The play ran for fifteen months, and made Robert Bolt's reputation as a dramatist. He now realized how the creative process begun by the author is finished by the actor, and after it had opened he told the director,

> It's amazing, you sit upstairs and you phrase a speech until you're blue in the face, and you get the rhythm exactly as you want it, and then Ralph Richardson comes along and makes absolute hay of the rhythm. He chops it about and he makes his own rhythm, and in the end you just have to accept it, because he does something which is pretty wonderful in its own way, though perhaps it isn't what you originally meant, because it can't be associated with Ralph without it having some permanent effect.[8]

It was not just the individual speech rhythms; Anthony Hopkins was impressed by his use of the oddest counter-gesture.

> After he had stolen the money from his wife's purse to buy drink, and she berated the son for doing it, and hauled him off to the bedroom to chastise him, Ralph said, 'Oh, leave it, leave it,' and put his newspaper over his head as if he could hide behind it. A very odd, but very revealing gesture; he had an odd inner approach, which was often expressed in odd quirky postures.[9]

His acute stage sense made him almost hypersensitive to the overall stage picture, which was why he was always so concerned with the details of costume, props, lighting and design. The end of *Flowering Cherry* suddenly broke out of its realistic setting, and opened up to show an orchard growing and blossoming behind him, as he died of a heart attack trying to bend the poker. Frith Banbury was concerned that he seemed to be throwing this final scene away.

'Ralph, you don't seem to bother much about the ending.'

'Well, what's the point of it, old chap, look at all that's going on at the back of me, why should I try?'

The engine of his performance depended on the smooth meshing of all the other moving parts, and he hated any cast changes more than most actors. Wendy Hiller initially found it very difficult when she took over from Celia Johnson midway through the run.

When we started together in *Flowering Cherry* he used to hiss through his teeth, all through my speeches – 'Sss, Sss, Sss . . .' I said, 'Ralph, I don't know if you know that you are hissing, but I can hear you, could you lower it a little?'

He was quite taken aback that he could be heard, because what he was doing, he told me, was keeping up Celia's rhythms. He didn't adjust his own performance to mine – not one jot or tittle.[10]

To this day, Ralph's performance as Jim Cherry remains the one that most moved and impressed his son Charles. It is some indication of the special dimension he brought to the part that when he refused to go with the production to America, and was replaced by Eric Portman, it closed there after only four performances, having clocked up over 400 at the Haymarket.

This transatlantic pattern was significantly repeated with Ralph's next new play, which opened first in London, then in New York, closing rapidly on Broadway but running for a year in the West End. This time the author was not an unknown, but the well-established and successful novelist and playwright, Graham Greene.

CHAPTER THIRTEEN
1959–1962

THE COMPLAISANT LOVER was the surprise comic hit of the season, and the most surprised were the cast, who in rehearsal had not thought it was a comedy at all, but a tragedy. Ralph played a suburban dentist, Victor Rhodes, with Phyllis Calvert as his wife Mary, who is having an affair with a bookseller, Clive Root, played by Paul Scofield. Rather than lose his wife, the cuckolded husband suggests they all carry on as before, and the desperation that keeps this unhappy trio together proved to be irresistibly and astonishingly funny. Graham Greene wrote it first as a novel, then adapted it as a play.

Phyllis Calvert found the story a heartbreaking one.

When we saw the published script it said 'A Comedy', and we were playing it desperately *not* a comedy. We all said, 'Graham, you can't put "A Comedy" on this.'

'Yes, it's going to be a comedy.'

The moment the play opened, it was laugh after laugh. We didn't know, and that was why it was such a success. When it went to America they knew it was a comedy, they played it for comedy and it lasted one week, with Michael Redgrave, Googie Withers and Richard Johnson. Graham

came into my dressing-room two nights before it was opening
in New York and I said, 'What are you doing here, why aren't
you in New York?'

'I couldn't stand it any more. I couldn't watch them
rehearsing, it was too awful.'

He knew it wasn't going to be a success.[1]

Paul Scofield was taken to the Savile Club by his co-star
on the first day of rehearsal, and was caught by surprise over
lunch.

'In conversation he told me how right he thought I was
for the part of Clive Root, "because of the line which says you
look like a gipsy – and you *do* look like a gipsy!"

'Intrigued, I went back to search for this line – and never
found it.'

These two actors each had a very distinctive vocal style,
and Scofield took a little while to attune to the other's
wavelength.

Ralph was an actor of rhythm – he had a beat, a pulse inside
him which dictated to him; and playing opposite him one had
to learn to respect that rhythm. I am inclined to syncopate a
little, and coming in one night with a line a shade later than
usual, Ralph clapped his hand behind his ear as if to say,
'What was that?' His rhythm had been broken – I had let him
down. It was the discipline of music.[2]

The rehearsal period was originally set for four weeks, with
John Gielgud as director, and when he was delayed in America
they lost the first week. But he was experienced in directing
both the men, and after only two weeks' intensive rehearsal
the play was ready to go on, so he said, slightly to Phyllis
Calvert's surprise, '"I'm going away, I'm not going to do any
more, I'll only ruin it." So for the last week we just ran

through it every day, and that's how it remained for the rest of the run, just like that.'

Gielgud as director believed in keeping a watchful eye on his productions during their run, but he had to go to America for six months after *The Complaisant Lover* opened, so Phyllis Calvert says they were all rather dreading his return.

> We finished the performance, and John came round the corridors. I was going up to my dressing-room and I said, 'Oh, I suppose we'll be rehearsing tomorrow?'
>
> 'No, dear, nothing has changed at all. You're all exactly as when I left, except I'm going down to see Ralph, and ask him to cut out a few of his dancing-steps.'

Ralph acted with his feet, which could be very expressive, and several actors observed how in comedies he often entered trotting. He was physically as well as vocally impressive; and his always intensive pre-rehearsal study of a play usually revealed to him the psychological motivation of the other characters as well as his own.

Phyllis Calvert could not understand why Mary should invite her lover to the house.

> It was playing with fire, and she's not entirely stupid; this worried me a great deal but I went on with it, and then I was sitting in the prompt-corner with Ralph one day and I said, 'Why is she such a fool, why does she invite her lover there?'
>
> He turned round and said one word, which gave me the clue to the whole thing: 'Vanity, my dear.'
>
> She wanted to show off her house to her lover – that aspect of the thing had never occurred to me at all.[3]

There was a difficult piece of business with a trick cushion that played music whenever someone sat on it. The dentist is a compulsive practical joker, and this particular joke recoils on him as he collapses on it at the moment when the mood suddenly switches from comedy to the grief of betrayal.

Scofield found Ralph's playing of this breakdown scene 'poignant and disconcerting' to the audience, and the growing tension between the two men a lesson in controlled power.

> Playing my scenes with him, I found the gradual hostility, which grew in him throughout the play, almost frightening. Something very hard – an iron in his soul – something dangerously combative, very masculine; and very consistent throughout the run, no change of voltage, just sometimes more alarming.[4]

One night the tape of the jingle music from the cushion went awry, and the cushion played 'God Save the Queen'. Ralph continued as if nothing out of the ordinary had happened, and made no complaint afterwards.

Peter Copley caught the final week of the pre-London tour, in Brighton, and wrote to congratulate his old friend. Ralph replied, in his flowing handwriting:

Theatre Royal
Brighton
12 Jun 59

My Dear Peter,
Thank you very
much for your kind letter.
It is your own good
nature to find sermons

in stones – but we are
lucky, I think, to have
found a good play,
and this luck I
most heartily and
speedily wish you.

EVER.   Ralph.

The layout of his letters was as characteristic as the stylish calligraphy with which they were penned, with such broad margins that the words formed a column down the middle of the page. This may not have been just his painter's eye for pleasing composition; when the radio producer Piers Plow-right directed him in some readings in the late 1970s, he found that Ralph appeared to have developed tunnel vision, and could only read down the middle of the page.[5]

In *The Complaisant Lover*, while the actor was giving all due credit to the author, the *Times* reviewer stressed that

the success of the turn from light, almost farcical comedy into serious comedy is not all due to the skill of Mr Greene's writing. Much of the credit must be given to Sir Ralph Richardson. He makes a masterly transition from the suburban zany by way of bitter tears to the simple man who in his desperate trouble has nothing but his natural goodness to help him.

That goodness was natural to the man as well as to the actor, though his trust was not always repaid. Phyllis Calvert was horrified by his reluctance to suspect villainy in anyone.

We were parking our cars round the back of the Globe one night, and I noticed he didn't lock his car. So I ran after him. 'Ralph, you haven't locked your car!'

'I don't lock my car, never locked my car, never locked it here.'

'Well, I always do.'

Of course his car was pinched that night.

The play ran for a year. Paul Scofield originally planned to leave after six months to play Shylock and Petruchio at the Stratford Memorial Theatre; but he said he could not educate his children on Stratford's top salary of £60 a week, and when they refused his request for £80 a week he decided to complete the year at the Globe instead. He did, however, take a two-week break, when his substitute was Alan Dobie.

The latter was initially rehearsed with the understudies. He asked the director, 'Where do I sit, Sir John?'

'Oh, sit wherever you feel comfortable.'

When he rehearsed with the principals Ralph entered and addressed an entire, quite long speech to an empty chair (where Paul usually sat), then swung round, saw Dobie and said, 'Ah, perhaps it might be better if you sat here.'[6]

As the play approached the end of its year's run Phyllis Calvert asked Ralph anxiously, 'Do you think that they'll want us to go on tour?' As a widow with young children she hated being away from home for any length of time. Ralph cured her of this aversion with his forthright reply: 'If you don't go on tour the theatre will die!'

During the run of *The Complaisant Lover* Ralph found himself in the slightly unusual position of speaking Graham Greene's lines by day on a film set, as well as by night in the theatre. The author had adapted his novel of *Our Man in Havana* into the screenplay of the film directed by Carol Reed, with whom Ralph was delighted to be working again, playing a cameo part of the Intelligence Chief, 'C'. The film as a whole, despite a starry cast, was not a success with the public,

however. The central figure, Wormold, was played by Alec
Guinness, one of whose sharpest memories of that film is the
object-lesson in upstaging in the last scene, between Richardson and Noël Coward, 'and the director wickedly and funnily
left the camera running'.[7]

It was the last time Carol Reed directed Ralph, and the
respect and affection he inspired in the actor was expressed in
moving terms when Reed died. Edward Fox was among the
mourners at the church. 'Carol Reed adored Ralph, and one of
the most lasting memories I have of Ralph was his magnificent
reading at Carol's funeral service, it was heart-rending.'[8]

In his next film, as Sir Edward Carson, QC, he cross-
examined Robert Morley as Oscar Wilde, summed up by one
critic as 'the only worthwhile part of an otherwise forgettable
film'. He followed this almost immediately with the role of
General Sutherland in Otto Preminger's *Exodus*. After the
death of his film patron, Alexander Korda, it had looked for a
while as if his screen career might be over, so the four films he
made in 1960 were particularly welcome. His were not the
leading roles in any of them, but he was just pleased to be
getting film offers again, saying, 'I don't mind how small the
part is so long as it is interesting.' When he was asked to play
Themistocles in *The 300 Spartans* he commented: 'An interesting old bird. A kind of Winston Churchill of his time. It's
not a large part, but an actor shouldn't be ashamed of playing
a small part any more than a novelist is of writing a short
story.'[9]

He did, however, end up feeling rather ashamed of his
next choice of play – Enid Bagnold's *The Last Joke*, directed
by Glen Byam Shaw. The only reason he asked to be in it was
to act with John Gielgud again. The latter played a Romanian
prince, and Ralph appeared as a Levantine millionaire who in
one scene had to change his trousers on-stage. Both actors
quickly regretted getting involved, and attempted to improve

matters by re-arranging the dialogue, much to the fury of the author. Anna Massey played Ralph's daughter, and remembers him going to great lengths to find a fob-watch that made the right sound when he dropped it, but all these effects were of no avail to save the play.

The critics were dismayed at this latest offering from the author of *The Chalk Garden*. Frank Lewis in the *Sunday Dispatch* called it 'a meaningless jumble of pretentious whimsy, preposterous melodrama, and laboured poetic symbols'; Robert Muller in the *Daily Mail* 'a perfectly dreadful charade, both baffling and boring'; and Milton Shulman in the *Evening Standard* snorted, 'It is a long time since such a caravan of over-blown nonsense has rolled into the West End masquerading as a serious vehicle for some of our best actors.'

Even Harold Hobson in the *Sunday Times* was provoked into heavy irony: 'At its opening night everything came out of the top drawer. The dresses were by Balmain, the acting by Gielgud, Richardson, Flemyng, and Massey, the guns by Bapty, and the apathy and boredom by an audience of rank and beauty.' When Anthony Cookman wrote in the *Tatler*, 'Sir John and Sir Ralph seem happy enough giving bravura performances of parts which possibly strike them as fantastically thin', his guess was more accurate than his observation.

Before this doomed play ended its brief run, Ralph received an unexpected visitor from his youth. He had not seen Charles Doran since their touring days; 'the guv'nor' was now over ninety, he had lost a leg, and was being looked after in a nursing-home. He sent a message that he would like to come to see his old pupil at the Phoenix Theatre. Ralph was touched that Doran still remembered him, and said he would like to see him after the matinee.

But I was just making up and putting on this toupee, and somebody came in and said, 'Look, Charles Doran doesn't think he can wait until the end, because we've got the car for him and could you see him now?'

'Well, of course. But could he come up the stairs?'

'No, but he's at the stage door.'

'Yes, where is he? I'll come down and see him.'

So I ran down the stairs and there was Charles, great big moon face, didn't look any older, and I hadn't seen him for thirty years, and I said, 'Oh, Charles, how nice to see you.'

He looked at me for a moment. He didn't change his expression, and then he said, 'Ralph, what a beautiful wig-join!'[10]

It was perhaps as well that he offered no comment on the performance that went with the wig-join.

The Richardson–Gielgud friendship survived *The Last Joke*, and their partnership was renewed the following year, with much greater success, but before that Ralph crossed the Atlantic again to make a film of one of the great plays of American literature, Eugene O'Neill's *Long Day's Journey into Night*.

The rest of the cast were all-American – Katharine Hepburn as Mary Tyrone, Jason Robards Jnr and Dean Stockwell as the two sons – and so was the director, Sidney Lumet. The latter soon learned to modify his directing style to the needs of his English star, who gave him a baleful look after an eleven-minute answer to a very short question, and said, 'Ah, I think I know what you want – a little more flute and a little less cello.' The clear implication, 'and a lot less words from you', was not lost on the director, who said that 'from then on working together was joyful'.

The family quartet demands four powerful and sensitive actors, and here they were not equally matched. Stockwell was generally seen as inadequate, and the two who attracted most acclaim were Robards as the eldest son, the self-despising alcoholic, and Richardson as the flamboyant Irish actor, James

Tyrone. Katharine Hepburn gave a magnificent performance as the mother succumbing to her drug addiction, but she never quite overcame her casting against type. Francis Wyndham pointed out in *Sight and Sound* that 'Mrs Tyrone should be the stupidest member of her family, but Katharine Hepburn cannot help playing her as if she were quite the most intelligent.' But he had no reservations about her husband: 'Richardson's mannerisms, which can be fatally distracting, are here absorbed by the histrionic character he portrays.'

The film retains great interest for students of acting, and of these actors in particular, although the general cinema-going public regarded it as an art-house movie, and the distributors treated it as such. But the cast enjoyed the experience, and Katharine Hepburn still affectionately remembers her screen husband as 'a remarkable creature'.[11]

In November 1961 Tennent's announced their forthcoming revival of *The School for Scandal*, the first in London since Olivier's for the Old Vic in 1949, with a cast including Ralph as Sir Peter Teazle, Anna Massey as Lady Teazle, Margaret Rutherford as Mrs Candour, Meriel Forbes as Lady Sneerwell, and John Neville and Daniel Massey as the Surface brothers, Joseph and Charles. With designs by Anthony Powell, and direction in the hands of John Gielgud, everyone looked forward to a stylish night out with Sheridan. The critical expectations seemed too high to be met, however, and in the reviews there is a tone of disappointment that the sum of the evening was not greater than the individual parts, although this reaction was not reflected at the box-office, which set a new record for the first week at the Haymarket of £5500.

Ralph made himself at home, as elegantly as usual. Anna Massey regularly took tea with him in his dressing-room in the interval. The eighteenth-century porcelain, fine damask napkins, and a fire in the grate set off the pair in costume 'just like the Teazles at home', as she describes this backstage scene. He told her he had been reading Lamb's *Essays* to find his characterization of Sir Peter.

Sir John Gielgud has told in his Foreword of the problems Ralph had with his entrance, but there was no uncertainty about the textual key to his interpretation of Sir Peter. This came in the screen scene, as Lady Teazle is discovered, when after Charles Surface's astonished 'Lady Teazle, by all that's wonderful!' there came an anguished 'Lady Teazle, by all that's damnable!' from her husband.

Daniel Massey was moved at each performance.

> Every night my heart used to go into my mouth, because although he was a great comedian he was I think pre-eminently the great tragic actor. His whole being simply punctured, like the apple in the advertisement suddenly drained of fluid becomes dry and wrinkled. But of course when you sink everything into that one line, so much of the rest of the part goes for nothing, and all that comedy in the man, that Ralph had at his fingertips, he simply rejected for the wronged husband.[12]

John Neville, too, remembers 'how very touching he was in the screen-scene; I played Sir Peter myself a couple of years ago at the National, and he wasn't as ill-tempered and grumpy as I certainly was with her.'[13]

The critics objected to this lack of testiness. As *The Times* complained: 'Sir Ralph has no difficulty in making his reading consistent with itself, but while we admire his accomplished acting we cannot help ruefully reflecting that it is a reading which takes much of the fun out of the part.' The *Sunday Times* thought he was 'touchingly kind and generous-hearted, but too much like a country squire', and that there were only two convincing people of fashion – Meriel Forbes and Margaret Rutherford.

Kenneth Tynan was entranced by Ralph's response to the disclosure of Lady Teazle behind the screen: 'His eyes melt; his normally frisk demeanour turns suddenly leaden. The pathos hereabouts is not to be found in Sheridan. It may well be said that Sir Ralph belies the text: my reply is that he transcends it.' W. A. Darlington believed that 'Ralph Richardson's Sir Peter was effortlessly right throughout', and although he thought a little more work was needed before the production showed its full quality, he observed significantly that 'the laughter was continuous and hearty, and the pace was brisk'.

Quite a lot more work had to be done anyway, as John Neville was committed to leave the cast after six weeks, to join Laurence Olivier's inaugural company at the new Chichester Festival Theatre. He knew how much Ralph hated cast changes during a run, so he was particularly touched by two gestures just before his departure.

After one matinee Ralph knocked on his door.

'Johnny, are you in?'
    'Yes, Ralph.'
    'I want you to meet a very dear friend of mine.'
    So I opened the door, and in his arms was a ferret.
    'Hello, this is my dear friend Sam, the ferret, and this is Johnny Neville', introducing us as if we were two adults.[14]

At his final performance he was even more moved when Ralph and Daniel Massey composed quite a long poem about him leaving and going to Chichester, and came and recited it in his dressing-room.

Richard Easton took over Joseph Surface for the rest of the

Haymarket run. Gielgud wanted him to take hold of Lady Teazle, just before the servant enters to announce her husband's arrival, as if only the interruption prevents him from seducing her there and then. Daniel Massey heard Sir John say, 'Can't you sort of fiddle about with her?' and then Sir Ralph add, as he got up in the stalls, 'Listen, I think I know what you want, Johnny.'

Massey remembers that his demonstration to Easton was extraordinary. 'He took hold of Anna, like Clint Eastwood or someone, talk about sex-mad, I mean he really held her lustfully.'[15]

The production played to packed houses for six months, and then an American tour necessitated some further cast changes. Gwen Ffrangcon-Davies and Geraldine McEwan took over from Margaret Rutherford and Anna Massey, Richard Easton now replaced Daniel Massey as Charles Surface, and Gielgud himself took over as Joseph. Although he joked about being 'the oldest Joseph Surface in the business', the comic timing of the two knights now made the screen scene the highpoint of the evening.

The cavernous O'Keefe Centre in Toronto seated nearly 3000, compared with just over 800 at the Haymarket, and the producer Derek Glynne, who arranged the North American tour, was impressed by Ralph's response to it. 'A lot of actors used to take one look at that vast auditorium and say, "Will I be heard?" But Ralph had a different approach, he was a real professional. He said, "When you're out front there, give us a shout if you can't hear me."'[16] He needed to reach right to the very back, since the run there was sold out, and so was the seven-week run at the Majestic Theater on Broadway, despite a newspaper strike.

John Neville regretted that his commitments to Chichester, and then his directorship of Nottingham Playhouse, drew him out of Ralph's orbit for six years, until they recorded a *son et lumière* soundtrack together. Ralph invited him home for a cup of tea, but as they got out of the Rolls in Chester Terrace he decided that what they really wanted was 'a little drink'. They went up to the top-floor study, and were brought scotch and vodka. 'There you are, Johnny, that's your bottle, and this is my bottle.' They settled down to a long conversation about a J. B. Priestley season which Ralph wanted to put on with them both taking part.

'Suddenly there was a tap-tap-tap at the door of the study. Ralph went and opened the door, and a parrot walked in.

'"Ah, José, how are you? Come and meet my friend Johnny."

'So we were introduced, again like two adults.'

The parrot climbed on to the desk, went to a jam-jar full of pencils, plucked one out and started crunching it up in its beak, to Ralph's distress. 'Oh, José, José, why are you doing that, you know you have your own pencils, why are you doing that to my pencils? Come on, old chap.'

Sheridan played a hand in forging some happy friendships for Ralph, some of which were renewed in *The Rivals* four years later; but he was keen to move next to a twentieth-century classic he caught in an off-Broadway production during the run of *School for Scandal*. It was Pirandello's *Six Characters in Search of an Author*, and he invited the young American director, William Ball, to come and stage it again in London with a British cast.

CHAPTER FOURTEEN
1963 – 1964

THE REHEARSAL period for *Six Characters in Search of an Author* was rather longer than usual, partly because it was scheduled to open the new theatre that was being built as part of the Mayfair Hotel. It was not complete when rehearsals began, and was still not finished by the planned opening date, which had to be postponed. Initially this long run-up was a help to Ralph, as it gave him more time to study the part. This enigmatic play is full of theatrical trickery – it opens with a group of actors in rehearsal, when suddenly the stage is invaded by six ghostly characters from an unfinished play, by an author now dead, seeking help to rescue their own destinies from limbo. The play was then fifty years old, but had not been performed in London since before the war. Shaw thought it one of the five best plays he had seen, high praise from that knowledgeable and severe ex-critic.

Ralph played the father from the world of the other play, with particularly strong support from the two women in his character's life. His wife was Megs Jenkins, who had played opposite him in *A Day by the Sea*, and his step-daughter was Barbara Jefford. He had seen her play Imogen in *Cymbeline* at the Old Vic, in the same season as his *Timon of Athens*, and had sent her a congratulatory note. Thirty years later she still finds it difficult to pin down the way he worked.

You have to preface everything you say about Ralph by saying he was unlike anybody else. He approached things obliquely, but not like some people do because either they can't think of anything else to do with it, or they want to be different from other people; it seemed to me to be an innate quality that he had, and it wasn't a self-conscious thing to my mind, it was built in to Ralph.[1]

But his own obliqueness did not extend to going along with new-fangled experimental techniques by his directors. The delayed opening because of the building hold-up reduced William Ball to calling the Company together one day and announcing: 'We have to do something to keep this fresh, and I don't want to over-rehearse it, so I suggest it would be interesting if we did an improvisation.'

At the same point in rehearsals of *The Complaisant Lover*, the director John Gielgud had simply absented himself. This time it was the leading actor, sitting there with his hat on his knee, who quietly got up and left the room. The whole idea was dropped, the story got around the theatrical grapevine, and none of Ralph's subsequent directors ever brightly suggested improvisations to him. Actors who tried it on him also got short shrift.

He had his own way of suggesting the inner depths of emotion. One of the most compelling scenes is where the ghostly characters re-enact the events of their family life, when Ralph had to make lascivious advances to his step-daughter, Barbara Jefford. 'His surreal quality affected the way in which he did *not* touch me; in the seduction scene his hand was inches from me, and was so effective, it gave an extra dimension to it, because we weren't real people.'

She was also touched by the expression of his friendship, off-stage:

He was very sweet to me, my father had died a couple of years before, and Ralph became a kind of father-figure to me. He used to write me little notes about our health, 'from your doctor', and he used to draw a little doctor, in the little brown hat he always wore with both sides turned up. We got on very well, and that is why I imagine he later invited me to be his Portia, and to play Helena in the *Dream* as well, in South America.

The critics thought them well-matched, both giving remarkable performances. Pat Wallace in the *Tatler* supposed

that every three or four decades an actor with these proportions of voice and presence turns up in this country and I can't help feeling that such a one provides a healthy, slightly larger-than-life antidote to the Method School. However that may be, Sir Ralph surely interprets Pirandello's meaning and, with Miss Barbara Jefford as the step-daughter, presses out every drop of tragi-comic value.

Philip Hope-Wallace in the *Guardian* admired their and Megs Jenkins' fire-power, 'quite as powerful as one can tolerate in this small enclosure, admiration continually going out to the way they contain and control their performances'. Bernard Levin in the *Daily Mail* thought Sir Ralph 'as mannered as ever, if not more so; but beneath the mannerisms he conveys most movingly the agony of the man who has everything except forgetfulness'.

But J. W. Lambert felt, on the contrary, that he had

discovered a legato line long missing from his speech. Gone are the outrageous caesuras, the mysterious 'sforzandi' which have for long lent a grotesque and often irrelevant extra dimension to his roles. Out flow the long lines, phrased and shaped with a musician's art; and from them echo the regrets, the helpless rages, the incurable dismay of all human weakness.

W. A. Darlington, with his *Daily Telegraph* column headlined 'SIR RALPH'S TOUCH OF MAGIC', proclaimed that this was the key to the quality of the production: 'It is Sir Ralph's special gift that he can imbue an apparently normal human character with a touch of the supernatural, and this faculty never had a better vehicle than here.'

Once again one detects a note of astonishment in the admiration, that reveals how the actor never lost the ability to surprise even his most seasoned observers. This was best summed up by T. C. Worsley in the *Financial Times*:

> Sir Ralph has now developed a style so idiosyncratic and personal that one is sometimes frightened that he is going to exercise it in the blue, as it were, with only a passing reference to the character he happens to be acting. But here the style and the character fit to perfection ... out of all the possible gestures and intonations that could have been used the only absolutely right one has been selected on every single occasion, and that one is always enough because that one is the only absolutely right and exact one. This is what style in acting means.

If Ralph's style and power almost burst out of the confines of the little 300-seater Mayfair Theatre, he could hardly have complained about his next arena not stretching far enough to display his talents. Indeed, it was a particular thrill to him to be invited in 1964 to lead a British Council tour through South America and Europe, to mark the Quatercentenary of Shakespeare's birth. A three-month tour through climatic extremes, with an especially gruelling programme of social events to show the flag and celebrate the Bard, would have deterred many men of sixty-two, but Ralph chose his two parts cannily. Both of them – Bottom (for the third time) and Shylock (for the first) – are relatively short parts, and make maximum impact with less than half-a-dozen scenes each.

The British Council formed a special Shakespeare Festival Company, in association with Tennent's. Wendy Toye directed *A Midsummer Night's Dream* and David William *The Merchant of Venice*. As the leader of the Company, Ralph was invited to advise on casting. He was keen to work with Barbara Jefford again, and also Alan Howard, but after that his ideas disappeared into a time-warp of his own. He would suggest one 'wonderful young actor' after another, who would then turn out to be either very old, or dead.

Brighton's Theatre Royal was usually Ralph's last stop before a West End opening, but this time it was the springboard for Mexico City. Ralph was still experimenting with his make-up for Shylock, as Barbara Jefford discovered at the first dress rehearsal, when she went to wish him good luck before it started. 'He was sitting at the mirror, and I could see his reflection in it when I opened the door; I remember starting back, it was remarkable – I remember a lot of green, like an Abanazar kind of character. He toned it down a bit as we went on.'

But only a bit. His conception of Shylock was still an exotic one when he repeated the role three years later at the Haymarket. During that run the radio producer John Powell went backstage to see him after a performance, to discuss a new broadcast production of *Cyrano*.

'There he was in this extraordinary make-up, and wig, and incredible nose and huge, but huge eyelashes, and him saying, "Do you think this is a bit over the top, old boy?" Of course it wasn't, it was exactly right for the performance.'[2]

Irene Worth, too, was overwhelmed by the look and the

interpretation. 'His Shylock had an antique Jewishness, he was a Semite from antique time, his noble behaviour, his grief over Leah – to sell that ring of Leah's! That was one of the unique qualities of Ralph, his observation and insight.'[3]

The British Council Report proudly boasted that the tour 'included the first visit of a representative British Shakespeare company to Quito in Ecuador'. Barbara Jefford understood why they were the first, when she passed out with altitude sickness after the opening performance there. 'They wouldn't have opera or ballet in Quito; Shakespeare was supposed to be less taxing, but in fact it needs a great deal of breath, you could only do about half a line at a time.'[4] Thereafter they put oxygen cylinders behind the trees, for the fairies to have quick draughts of oxygen before their dancing.

Ralph's wisdom in his choice of parts was now seen to be vindicated. If they had been more physically demanding he would have found it difficult to cope with all the other pressures on him. He was often required to meet the Presidents of the various countries they visited, sometimes even being summoned to the presidential box *during* a performance, which breached Ralph's conception of the proper distance between actor and audience.

He was also unhappy with the Latin tradition of a very much later curtain-up. In Madrid the curtain did not rise until a quarter to eleven in the evening, an interminable delay for a man who was usually enjoying his first or second drink after the show by that time.

But he had the great comfort of his wife's presence on the tour as she was playing Titania in the *Dream*, and she also took off him most of the burden of the constant packing and unpacking. The only occasion on which he exploded was in Athens, when someone failed to notify the Company about an official lunch; Barbara Jefford had departed on a trip to Delphi, and Ralph's absence as well provoked unfavourable comment in the Greek press, which made him very angry that someone else's incompetence had made him appear unmannerly.

In general, however, the tour was a great success, with sold-out performances and mostly favourable notices. Some critics, especially on the east coast of South America and in France, would have preferred a more sophisticated production, but Peru welcomed 'impeccable theatre', and the Director of the Teatro Español in Madrid 'a spectacle of perfect art'. The Portuguese commented on 'the tremendous impact of Sir Ralph Richardson's acting', and the Spanish on the 'beauty and expressiveness of Barbara Jefford's voice and actions'.

Ralph found himself back in Madrid sooner than he would have wished, for the filming of some of his scenes in David Lean's *Dr Zhivago*. He had a two-week break in the middle of filming, and when he and his wife returned to Madrid from England, Alec Guinness telephoned their hotel to invite them to dinner. They were reluctant to go out, but Mu invited Guinness round for an omelette, providing he came early. When a waiter holding a menu opened the door to the suite, Sir Alec saw his old friend advancing on him muttering, 'Who can one hit, if not one's friends?', and then Ralph knocked him down. As the waiter fled, the actor got to his feet, rubbing his jaw, saying, 'What was all that about?' Mu said apologetically, 'He's very tired.' As if to confirm this explanation Ralph was now sunk into a deep armchair, seemingly fast asleep.[5]

The blow was never explained, nor ever mentioned again between the two men. The victim forgave if he never forgot it, and is still rather puzzled about why it happened. 'I certainly didn't hold it against him ever. It in no way interfered with our relationship. I don't think his blow was directed against me as such, but to express his exasperation – probably at being back in Madrid. It was never apologized for or discussed.'[6]

The exasperation was not just with the location, but to some extent with the film's director as well. The Spanish countryside was standing in for Russia at the time of the Revolution, which required the spreading of tons of artificial snow, and the epic sweep of David Lean's vision involved more hanging around for the actors than on most films; so Lean never stood as high in the Richardson list of favourite film-makers as Carol Reed or Alexander Korda. Sitting in the back of a car on location, after one seemingly endless wait for the right sort of sky, Ralph sighed and remarked to Tom Courtenay, 'Sometimes you have to be a businessman', suggesting he could tolerate all these delays only if the pay was good.[7]

The lack of a sympathetic rapport with David Lean, however, did not prevent Ralph from giving a moving portrayal of Alexander Gromeko, who takes in the young orphaned Zhivago and brings him up as though he were his own son. The old man's bewildered stoicism in the face of hardship and rough treatment after the Revolution touches the heart even more than the descriptions of those scenes in Pasternak's masterpiece.

Ralph returned from Madrid with a feathered addition to his succession of pet rodents. Alec Guinness had often talked about his own South African Grey parrot, and Ralph was now determined to have one too. His choice was a Green Brazilian parrot, which he found in the flea-market in Madrid; the owners turned out to be two small boys, who delivered José to the Richardson hotel suite. They had no cage for it, so it perched on the back of a chair, pecking at everything within reach. When the boys produced a camera, Ralph's natural inclination to pose for a picture was soon corrected. 'No, no! Fotografia of José!'

José's sharp beak and sharper temper frightened everybody except his indulgent owner, who kept him on a perch, not in a cage. After he bit the chauffeur, Ralph clipped his wings so that he could not fly; but in compensation for this restriction he then regularly used to take José for a ride on his motor-bike, sitting on his shoulder while he chugged at a slower speed than usual round the Outer Circle of Regent's Park.

While he was finishing the Shakespeare tour, the director of his next play was sitting in the Greek sun, trying to make sense of the script of Tennent's new vehicle for Ralph – Graham Greene's *Carving a Statue*. After he had read the script Peter Wood thought he must have been sent only the first two Acts, but Binkie Beaumont assured him that this was the entire play as far as the author was concerned. When both the actor and prospective director were back in London, Beaumont suggested they had better meet to sort out the problem.

Peter Wood was another for whom Ralph's Falstaff had been a transforming experience, the more so because it was the very first play he saw that was not a pantomime; ever since then he had felt that Ralph could play the rejection of love like nobody else. The two had worked together in the 1950s, on a Caedmon recording of *Measure for Measure*, so they already had quite a good working relationship, and the director had learned that a sentence beginning 'With due respect' prefaced a tricky situation.

When he arrived at the Hampstead house he was taken up to Ralph's top-floor eyrie. Ralph began, 'With due respect, I find this a most extraordinary suggestion. Why would Poet' (his nickname for the author) 'send us a play which was not yet finished?'

'Well, there it is, it isn't finished. That play is a three-Act play and there's an Act missing.'

'You'd better talk to Poet.'

The author invited the director to lunch at Bentley's, gave

him a lavish lunch with a lot of caviar, lobster, vodka and white Burgundy, and over the Poire Wilhelmine and the black coffee finally said, 'Now, what was it you wanted to talk to me about?'

By this stage of the meal Peter Wood was not at his most coherent, and it was only many months later that he realized that that was the intention, 'and fundamentally these brilliant old trouts hadn't any intention of doing anything to this play'.[8]

The problem with it was that although it was a brilliant idea – for fifteen years an eccentric sculptor had been trying to build a gigantic image of God, of which only the huge feet could be seen on the stage – the script itself failed to work dramatically. At one point during rehearsals Ralph was in despair at this, and reached out to his director for help. They took off in the Rolls to Shoreham-by-Sea, and walked on the pebbly beach of Ralph's childhood, while he talked of his early life there, of his loneliness, and of his friendship with Hackenschmidt the wrestler. Peter Wood thought at the time that he was practising for his autobiography, 'but of course he wasn't doing any such thing, he was trying to reach me, and I was too insensitive to know that. It's one of the regrets of my life that I couldn't see past the whole Pollock's Toy Theatre which was his character, to the guy who operated the Theatre.'

They shared a lighter moment one lunchtime at English's Oyster Bar in Brighton. Ralph appeared to be feeling his age, and made rather heavy weather of the walk. When they arrived, a very beautiful girl, whose mini-skirt showed off her long legs to great advantage, was descending the steep staircase as Ralph opened the door; his instant change of mood astonished his companion. 'Ralph lost at least thirty years, as he held open the door, and leaped up the staircase like a gazelle as she stood at the bottom. I've never seen anything like it.'

When the play opened in Brighton it soon became plain that it was not working, and the director said it proved that he had been right all along, that all of it was not there, and he demanded that something should be done about it. But he had not bargained for what happened next. An envelope arrived by special messenger at his Brighton hotel, containing a note to him in longhand from Graham Greene, and a typewritten letter addressed to Ralph, which was highly vituperative in tone, and ended: 'I had hitherto supposed that the vices of the English theatre lay at the door of the office of the Lord Chamberlain in St James's Palace, but I come reluctantly to the conclusion that it lies at the threshold of the vanity of ageing and incompetent actors like yourself.'

Horror-stricken, Peter Wood rang Graham Greene's hotel.

'Graham, under no circumstances must you send this letter!'

'It's gone.'

In the morning Ralph telephoned. 'I've had a very disturbing missive from Greene' (he had ceased to be 'Poet'), 'do you know anything about it?'

'No.'

'Funny, because he said he'd sent you a copy. I suppose you realize that if Greene should show up at the stage door of the Theatre Royal here at Brighton, only one course would be open to me?'

'What is that?'

'I would be forced to knock him down!'

The actor–director relationship took years to recover from this episode, and the latter is still unsure whether it was because he had lied about having seen Greene's abusive letter, because he had become privy to the sharp difference of opinion between actor and author, or because his insistence that a new Act was needed irritated both his distinguished collaborators, 'Ralph because he didn't want to learn it, Graham because he didn't want to write it'.

There was also, as with his Vanya, an unwillingness to see his character as a failure; Ralph saw him as a modern Michelangelo, and wanted to play him as a genius. The combination of his determined misconception, and the author's failure fully to dramatize the predicament of the failed artist and the wider theme of icon worship, meant that the press were bewildered, the audience was confused, and Ralph's tenancy of the Haymarket's No. 1 dressing-room was of short duration this time.

Philip Hope-Wallace in the *Guardian* found the play 'a laboured parable', and the *Times* reviewer decided that 'its theatrical impact is melodramatically threadbare'. W. A. Darlington began his *Daily Telegraph* notice: 'It is not very easy to stick any kind of informative label on Graham Greene's *Carving a Statue* at the Haymarket'; and Felix Barker ended his in the *Evening News*: 'I may be a false prophet but, though Sir Ralph gives his best performance for years, I can visualize few audiences for this muddled parable once the more zealous converts from Farm Street have bowed the knee.' His prophecy was only too accurate, although Graham Greene did not share his views about Sir Ralph's performance, complaining privately and later publicly that the two of them had throughout seen the character quite differently. It was the last time they worked together in the theatre.

Peter Wood feared it would be his last opportunity as well. Fourteen years later, when he was about to direct *The Double Dealer* at the National Theatre, Peter Hall asked him whether he should invite Ralph to play Lord Touchwood. His wry response was, 'Peter, after *Carving a Statue* I'm sure neither he nor I could bear it.'

So I got a note from Ralph, an abject, charming note, which said, 'We didn't hit the mark with *Carving a Statue*, I know, and I feel that I must make some latter-day apology.' It was a

charming, charming letter, naughtily obsequious, because he's
not an obsequious man.[9]

He was indeed anything but obsequious, as he was shortly
to demonstrate to the director of his next film, to the
amusement and admiration of its star, Charlton Heston.

CHAPTER FIFTEEN
1965–1966

KHARTOUM WAS the story of how General 'Chinese' Gordon, sent to evacuate the Sudanese capital before the Mahdi's troops overran it, stayed on and was speared to death there. Charlton Heston learned a Victorian English accent for Gordon, Laurence Olivier reprised his Othello accent for the Mahdi, and Ralph Richardson researched Gladstone more fully than the director, Basil Dearden, either expected or wanted. Ralph insisted on wearing the little black finger-glove Gladstone sported to conceal the loss of his left forefinger in a shooting accident which Dearden thought might be distracting to filmgoers, since it was never explained in the script. But Dearden was not Korda, and Ralph refused to give way.

The first day Heston and Richardson were due at Pinewood together they arrived in the car park almost simultaneously. As the American got out of his new XKE Jaguar, he saw his colleague climbing out of his Bentley.

> Since we hadn't been introduced I thought, 'Well, this is not the time to go over,' because he was putting things in his briefcase; but just as I was turning away to go inside he closed the door of his car, patted the bonnet and said, 'Goodbye, old fellow, back in a while.' He was saying goodbye to his Bentley, I thought it was just marvellous.

When they came to shoot their big scene together, Ralph had some more surprises up his sleeve. He would never have treated Carol Reed, one of the directors who had been wooed by Charlton Heston to make the film, as he did Basil Dearden.

The General and the Prime Minister met at a railway station and held a conversation in a waiting-room, then Gladstone went outside to get on the train, finishing with a little exchange through the window of the train. Ralph had quite a long speech, with several moves and bits of 'business', so the director said, as he was lining-up the master-shot, 'Now, Ralph, let's just run through this once for the camera, right?'

'Oh yes, quite. Well, I do the speech here, and I move around the table I expect here, and I'm putting my coat on as I go, and at the end I turn here, and I pick up my hat, and put on my hat and take the gloves, and out.'

'Yes, that's right, the moves seem about right. Would you like to just rehearse it once for the camera, and sound?'

'Yes, yes, quite. Well, as I say, I do the scene here, I pick up my coat and put it on, and I'm walking around acting all the time, and then I get to this spot at the other end of the table, so we're back in shot, right? And then I put on my hat and the gloves, and I'm off.'

'Well, that's fine, yes, well, we'll light the shot then.'

When the shot was lit, the actors returned and Basil Dearden tried again. 'Now, do you want to run through the scene before we shoot it?'

'Yes, why not?'

And he went through the same performance once more, still without saying a line of the speech. In a surprising departure from his usual stage practice he did not even rehearse putting on the tight-fitting Victorian top-coat, which had to be timed and co-ordinated with the business with the hat, the gloves and the stick.

His co-star watched all this with some surprise, since in all their other scenes everything had been rehearsed in the normal fashion; he wondered if this was a touch of the eccentricity he had heard about, and who would win the battle of wills.

So finally the director said, 'Well, you don't want to run through the full thing, a dress rehearsal as it were?'
'No, no, let's shoot when you're ready.'
The director clearly thought this was not going to work first time. Flawless – all the stuff with the gloves and the stick, perhaps showing off a bit – maybe it was all done on a moment's impulse.[1]

What seems to work on the set does not always work on the screen, as the star of so many historical epics is quick to acknowledge, but here

when you saw it even in rough assembly, with the close-ups and the turns and the looks that were part of the scene, you understood that this was a master at work, and you also knew that this was someone the camera loved. Now, in film there are many people who are not particularly skilled performers at all whom the camera loves, but if on top of that you get a great actor then you have something special.

The two actors quickly established a rapport that continued off the set. The sequence at the railway station ran long into the evening, and during one break Ralph spilled some coffee on his shirt. His colleague had come out in a track-suit, so he offered, 'Ralph, I have an extra shirt here, it's clean, you're welcome to borrow it, if you like.'
'That's a good chap.'
A couple of days later it was delivered to the Dorchester

Hotel, neatly laundered, with an accompanying note, bearing just a quotation: 'And when he had put on the shirt of the prophet / he found he was mightier than he had been.'

They might share a shirt, but there were some tastes they could not share. The Pinewood dining-room had high-backed banquettes for privacy, and one lunchtime when Charlton Heston was waiting for a reporter to arrive to interview him, Michael Hordern and Ralph sat down in the next booth. 'I was not intentionally eavesdropping, and I heard Hordern say, "What is that strange substance that Chuck has with his biscuits at tea?" Richardson said, "Peanut butter – tried it once – dreadful stuff!"'

In his journal, *An Actor's Life*, Charlton Heston noted for 7 September 1965: 'I worked with Ralph Richardson today. He does a lovely job (of course); an easy, delightful man to work with. We didn't finish the scene, but it runs more than four pages. I think we did it well, I was proud to be acting with him.'

Most of the critics and audiences thought they did it well, too, and it was a reasonable success at the box-office. The screenplay took some dramatic liberties with the historical facts, suggesting that Gladstone showed bad faith more than bad judgement in his dealings with General Gordon. But it was one of the few really inglorious episodes in the career of the great Victorian statesman, and Ralph revelled in showing the darker side of a great man, just as he always looked for the lighter side of villains, like Buckingham in *Richard III*.

Meanwhile, he returned to occupy the Haymarket Theatre for his next three plays, opening in Shaw's *You Never Can Tell* in January 1966. The director was Glen Byam Shaw, who had a happier time than he had with *The Last Joke*, partly because this time Ralph was also much happier with his character as the waiter, William. Judy Campbell played Mrs Clandon, with Harry Andrews as her estranged husband, and one of the trickiest scenes was the lunch-party in Act Two, when they find themselves unwittingly and unwillingly reunited. This scene took a disproportionate amount of rehearsal time, partly because Byam Shaw departed from his namesake's precise stage directions about the seating plan and the serving of the meal. Harry Andrews had developed a fear of forgetting his lines, and began to fret at all this concentration on the waiter's business. After one lengthy discussion with the director about how William should remove a plate just before the irascible Mr Crampton hammered the table where it had been, Harry Andrews suddenly exploded: '"I can't do this, this whole scene is about how Ralph is doing this and that." Ralph immediately apologized: "Oh, you're absolutely right, my dear fellow."'[2]

His concern for detail was just as much for how it affected the others in the cast as himself. Eating and drinking on-stage can be a real trial for actors, but the fish and the soup were always quite good in this play, and the tea in Act Three was always hot. Keith Baxter played the impecunious dentist, Valentine, in love with Gloria, the eldest Clandon daughter, and he thought it would be in character to wolf down the fish at the lunch-table, which much amused the audience. After a while the stage management asked him to tone it down a bit, and eventually admitted it was at Ralph's prompting. He felt a little aggrieved for a time, but a couple of weeks later Ralph said to him, 'Were you very disappointed about the fish?'

'Well, yes, but perhaps it was a bit vulgar.'

'Well, it was rather, but I liked your spirit.'[3] Donald Sinden would have recognized the sentiment, as his over-enthusiasm had been similarly curbed in *The Heiress*.

The critic Felix Barker only realized how thoroughly Ralph prepared when he recognized some business of his on the first night. Weeks before he had dined at Bryan Forbes's house with the Richardsons, and Richard Attenborough and his wife; Ralph was suddenly on his feet removing the plates and clearing them away to the hatch with a napkin over his arm. No one remarked on his behaviour, which had become much more professional by the time it was demonstrated again on the Haymarket stage.[4]

Keith Baxter had been initially so overawed that the director had to instruct him to treat William like a waiter, not like Sir Ralph. The younger man was soon put at his ease. 'Ralph didn't come on until the second Act, and he used to stand in the wings and say to me, "Is it safe to go on, cocky?" as though the audience were sitting there with machine-guns.'

This was not entirely fanciful – Ralph believed that audiences had to be tamed and dominated.

> I think they like being frightened by an actor to some extent, in a way rather like a lion-tamer. The audiences are a little bit like wild animals, they've got to be subjected – you've got to keep them under control or they'll growl. They'll chase you right out of the stage door if you're not careful. And also I think the audience like seeing the act of domination as, indeed, if you went to see a lion-tamer and he didn't have a ferocious moustache and a whip and the lion didn't growl, and he just came on and patted them and walked out, which would be perfect lion-taming if you like, perfect, but it would be a very dull show. I think that's the difference between film-acting and acting in the theatre where these lions are alive.[5]

The critics recognized the effortless way in which he achieved this domination, even as the deferential waiter. *Punch* admired how 'he can make his voice audible throughout a theatre without seeming to raise it, so that what he says always sounds like overheard conversation'. Harold Hobson espied 'a gentleness which is stronger than steel'. W. A. Darlington discerned that 'while most actors play it as a waiter whose experience has made him a philosopher, he makes him a philosopher in grain, who has somehow found himself a waiter'. *Queen* magazine was 'too busy looking at him to watch how he does it, shuffling slightly with bent back, flicking his napkin, ever watchful to arrange a place setting here, or solve a social problem there'.

While Ralph often talked of actors he admired, especially from his youth, Judy Campbell believed his own genius had been very little influenced by the work of others.

> What makes him great to me is the way he is entirely an original, he seems not to owe anything he does to any other actor, it all seems to have been thought out in his own mind; and yet the way of speaking doesn't become mannered, nor indeed the way of performing. It's very individual of him, and though everybody can do an imitation of Ralph, they can't actually imitate the way he performed a role.

So convincing was his waiter that Judy Campbell enjoyed every minute on-stage with him 'because you did feel you were really staying in that seaside hotel, and one had the atmosphere of it'; and when they had all danced off-stage at the end she watched the old illusionist 'regale listeners in the wings with accounts of how he had danced with Fred Astaire, completely convincing the younger members of the cast, who only began to doubt him when he extended the claim to Nijinsky'.[6]

Ralph never failed in Shaw, but only ever appeared in four of his plays. The creative satisfaction was not quite enough for him; as he put it: 'They were very difficult to get right, but they were rather like trams – once you were right it was very boring, because it was either right or it was wrong.' So audiences were denied the chance of seeing what he would have made of Undershaft or Shotover, whose weight and complexity would seem to have been admirably suited to his gifts.

The play ran for nine months, at the end of which Ralph kept his No. 1 dressing-room, and exchanged his costume for that of Sir Anthony Absolute in Sheridan's *The Rivals*. Again Glen Byam Shaw directed, Keith Baxter stayed on to play Bob Acres, and Daniel Massey rejoined Ralph, this time playing his son Jack.

Margaret Rutherford should have been perfect casting as Mrs Malaprop, but her memory was now very uncertain, particularly in her opening, and most important, scene, when often she could remember none of her responses to Ralph. He did his best to carry her through, but Keith Baxter exited one night and met Ralph in the wings, waiting to come on for his second scene.

'Hello, Ralph.'

'Oh, it's Nightmare Tunnel tonight, cocky!'

On another of her bad nights Ralph went up to Daniel Massey backstage and asked, 'How's the old girl with you?'

'Well, she's not too bad.'

'Oh, she's scarce with me!'

When he had his own lapses of memory, he sailed through them with great aplomb. The ending of the play was re-arranged to give the final speech to Sir Anthony Absolute: 'So let me invite you to the New Oxford Rooms where we will drink a health to the young couples, and a husband to Mrs Malaprop.' One night the cast heard him say: 'So let me invite you to the Om-pom-pom-pom, where we will drink a health to the young couples and a husband to Mrs Malaprop.' But nobody in the audience seemed to notice, because he said it with such authority that it was not like a dry or a stumble at all. His inner rhythm, that so impressed Paul Scofield and others, always preserved the metre, even when the words made no sense.

He tried to help Daniel Massey find his best performance, and advised him,

> 'Always come slightly under the target, leave them wanting a little more.'
>
> And I said to him, 'But Sir Ralph, it's all very well, you stand up there and you can afford to say that, most of us have to get on with it to get in the race.'
>
> But I did take his point, of course he's absolutely right — give them everything and there's nothing round the corner.[7]

The critical response to *The Rivals* was not wholly favourable. In the *Daily Mail* Peter Lewis attacked the 'ponderously slow production', and the leading actor for playing old Absolute 'with all the stick-wagging, head-nodding and hand-tossing mannerisms at his command. But mannerisms are no substitute for the old dog's rage and devilment.'

However, Eric Shorter in the *Daily Telegraph* found it a 'delightfully frenzied booming performance ... Sir Ralph exerts his parental authority with great rhetorical flourish. Sir Anthony will never be in safer hands.' The *Punch* reviewer thought it 'his best stage performance for some years'. (The regularity with which this last critical assessment recurs on successive productions makes the reader wonder how the actor kept eclipsing the memory of his previous successes.)

In the *Evening News* Felix Barker harked back to one of the greatest theatrical forebears: 'Just to see Sir Ralph, a quivering, irascible Sir Anthony Absolute, is to have a portrait by Zoffany, and when he flicks Miss Rutherford's nose with his kerchief he is the comic spirit of Garrick reborn.'

Keith Baxter was irresistibly reminded of another image when he was invited up for a drink after the performance.

He'd taken off his wig, and sat in his waistcoat and breeches, with his parrot on his shoulder, looking like this wonderful up-market Long John Silver. The parrot was defecating over everything, with Ralph saying, 'Oh, you need to see the doctor, old fellow.'

Ralph brought the parrot into the Haymarket about once a week, sitting on his shoulder in the Rolls. José did not like it when the car stayed in top gear, so every now and again, Ralph would change down and rev-up, to squawks of delight in Spanish. Ralph had now given up trying to learn the parrot's foreign vocabulary, and was attempting without much success to teach the bird English.

His long and happy run at the Haymarket with Shaw and Sheridan was combined with bringing to the screen another wonderful comic creation – Lord Emsworth in P. G. Wodehouse's *Blandings Castle*. The part brought him millions of new fans, since this production was for the small screen. He had until now been very wary of television, and the little he had done had not endeared the medium to him. His very first experience was in its infancy, when he and Olivier had re-created *Bees on the Boatdeck* in a live performance at Alexandra Palace – no recording was then technically possible, and only a handful of viewers could watch it. In 1962 he played Judge Brack to Ingrid Bergman's Hedda Gabler, and in the same year the Minister of Labour, Sir Stanley Johnson, in Terence Rattigan's *Heart to Heart*, both for the BBC. In 1965 he re-created his more famous Johnson in Priestley's *Johnson over Jordan*, again for the BBC.

Frank Muir was Head of Comedy for BBC Television in the early 1960s, and it had long been his ambition to star Ralph in a comedy series. He felt he had the perfect vehicle in the Wodehouse stories about Lord Emsworth, and eventually

succeeded in persuading Ralph to the same view. It was the
scripts that finally convinced him. 'What I liked was that
there were no jokes. I hate jokes. In comedy you don't want
jokes. What you need is humour.'[8]

There were some early hiccups before Ralph caught on to
the Wodehouse style. One story was based on the fact that he
had to shout 'Pig-hooeee' in a very special way to call the
pigs, and he just could not believe it was credible. So Frank
Muir, anxious not to lose him before they had even started,
said they would find another story if it worried him. Ralph
said, 'No, you shouldn't do that, why am I worrying?'

Frank Muir explained to him,

'The trouble is you're being too thoughtful, you're taking the
story apart as if it were a drama; it's not, with people like
Wodehouse you create a fantasy world – you either go into
that world and accept it on his terms, or you don't go near it.
Once you do Lord Emsworth, you've accepted his terms, and
if Wodehouse says the pig only responds to that call, you
accept that without question, or you don't do it.'

Having accepted it, Ralph turned in a brilliant and
convincing comic performance as the dotty Earl obsessed with
his prize-winning pigs. At the conference with the wardrobe
girl about his clothes she suggested, 'Well, it must be tweeds,
mustn't it?'

'Oh yes, but not thick tweeds. Get me thin tweeds,
because thick tweeds are like cardboard, they don't move in
the way they should move even when you're not speaking. I
want clothes that will move with me.'

With the addition of a battered old hat, and pince-nez on
a ribbon, he was the eccentric old peer to the life. Occasionally
it was difficult to separate life from art. Frank Muir liked to

drop into rehearsals of all his series, and *Blandings Castle* rehearsed just across the road from Television Centre in a British Transport training depot for bus-drivers. One day there was no sign of Ralph, so he asked the director, Michael Mills,

> 'Where's Ralph?'
> 'Oh, he's down in the boiler-room.'
> 'What's he doing down there?'
> 'You know Ralph, he's curious about everything, and he suddenly got curious about the boiler-room and the heating.'
> So I went down and he was talking to a bewildered and totally uncomprehending Nigerian boilerman, with questions like: 'Well, if you turned off the stopcock leading to the water-tank above the bleeder-tank, then how on earth can you gauge . . .?'
> It was just like Ralph, he was a walking curiosity-shop, everything fascinated him.

He was never distracted from the work in hand, however, nor the technical skills required of him. Because he was giving two performances at the Haymarket on Saturdays, a stand-in walked all the moves for the camera rehearsal that day; Ralph came in on the Sunday and hit all his marks precisely for the right camera angles after just one walk-through. This precision was even more critical for the multi-camera television technique than the single film camera he was used to. His television colleagues were as impressed as Charlton Heston had been at Pinewood.

Frank Muir also admired his comic timing in its subtlety.

> He had a line about packing the hamper with the chauffeur, 'and put some Cockburn's Port in – I'd rather like his opinion

on it'. So many actors would have leaned on that last line to get the maximum laugh out of it. Ralph almost threw it away, but not quite, which made it even funnier.[9]

Ralph's wife was also in the television series, playing his sister, Lady Constance, and when he got one of his attacks of cold feet she told him firmly, 'Don't be a fool and weak-kneed. Have a go.' He excused his brief loss of nerve by saying,

I'm sixty-four and that's a bit old to be taking on a new medium. Not that age matters in the theatre. One doesn't feel that one has started. Acting is as complicated as a crossword puzzle. It wouldn't be worth doing if it were easy. In fact it gets harder as you get older.[10]

He never did another television series, only a handful of single plays, and three of those were reproductions of his stage successes. In retrospect, Frank Muir was even more amazed and delighted that it was Ralph he had captured to play Wodehouse's great eccentric; there was only one way he could explain his special genius: 'It's the Ralphdom of Ralph that one has to cling to, he wasn't really quite like other people.'

CHAPTER SIXTEEN
1967–1969

LONDON'S THEATREGOERS were denied a sight of the Richardson Shylock that entertained so many abroad in 1964, but they were given the opportunity in 1967, though in a new production with a different supporting cast. Glen Byam Shaw directed, with designs by Motley set in the eighteenth century.

The critics found Angela Thorne's Portia lightweight, Geoffrey Whitehead's Bassanio chilly, Karin Fernald's Jessica muted, Priscilla Morgan's Nerissa matronly and the production and designs lacking in atmosphere. But their main attention was devoted to the portrayal of the Jew, which Irving Wardle in *The Times* thought 'the sole justification for the show'. His shrewd assessment of the Richardson style unknowingly echoes the actor's own private advice to Daniel Massey, during his previous play at the Haymarket: 'At climaxes he always stops short, leaving a sense of volcanic power in reserve; and he gains effect – both in delivery and movement by holding back the rhythm so that it gathers weight; and then making his effect with swift precision.'

J. W. Lambert in the *Sunday Times* considered it 'a superb performance', one of his half-dozen finest, 'the mannerisms put to work, the characterization infinitely more than a matter of make-up and accent; it contains multitudes'. He particularly admired the refusal to play for easy pathos in the final exit, 'as with a last contemptuous glare at the loutish Gratiano, a pause to drop, rather than fling, the betraying knife on to the floor of the court, he drifts away into a dark night of the soul'.

This effect struck a chord in at least one long memory. When Ned Sherrin told Sir Donald Wolfit he had been to see the play, the actor-manager pricked up his ears.

'Did he drop the knife with a clatter as he left the trial scene?'

'Yes, it was a wonderful moment.'

'Ah,' sighed Wolfit, his point proved, 'Doran's business.'[1]

These two theatrical knights had not appeared together since their time with 'the guv'nor' four decades earlier, and one of the few sentiments they shared was an affection for the old man, and a recognition of what they owed him. (Asked by American journalists in 1947 what he thought about Ralph Richardson's knighthood, Wolfit barked, 'No comment!' Years later, asked by David Storey whether he liked Wolfit, Ralph mused, 'Well, let's say if I saw him coming down the street towards me, I'd not be disinclined to cross over to the other side.')

The Merchant of Venice was the last time Ralph played at the Haymarket, which had been such a happy home for him. Nine out of the ten plays he did there between 1926 and 1967 were great successes and had long runs, the solitary failure being *Carving a Statue*. More significantly, his Shylock was his stage farewell to Shakespeare.

He soon wished it had been altogether his last Shakespearean performance. The following year he played Sir Toby Belch again on television, in an unhappy production directed by John Dexter for ATV. Joan Plowright was Viola, and Alec Guinness's own problems with Malvolio did not prevent him from noticing how Ralph was agonizing over Sir Toby.

In 1969 his self-doubt was expressed much more dramatically in the radio studio. John Powell had invited him to play Dogberry in a BBC production of *Much Ado About Nothing*, with a cast that included Paul Daneman, Cecil Parker, Fenella Fielding, Martin Jarvis, and Richard Goolden partnering Richardson as Verges. After a stumbling first read-through, Ralph had got the measure of the part (which he pronounced idiosyncratically as 'Dog-*berry*', accentuating the second half of the name), playing it absolutely seriously, which everyone except himself found wonderfully hilarious. His worries came to a head in Dogberry's farewell scene, which the producer had set by a quayside, with the idea that Dogberry would back away and fall in the water, with a huge stereophonic splash.

They were rehearse-recording and were ready to record this scene, when the producer suddenly heard Richard Goolden say on-mike, 'John, he's gone, he's gone,' just as he was about to cue everyone from the control-room upstairs. John Powell never moved so fast in his life.

> We all rushed down, and Richard and I caught Ralph in the foyer of Broadcasting House, just about to leave, and persuaded him back. I said if he was worried about it, he didn't have to do the shout at the end, and we would record a separate shout and tack it on, if that was OK. But it was a very strange personality thing with him, suddenly taking fright like that.[2]

The end-result was admired by all who heard it, though Ralph was not among their number. He never listened to his own broadcasts, nor did he ever ask to hear a playback during the recording sessions – he knew instinctively when he had got it right, or when he could improve on it, without having to listen to it back.

He exercised the same self-discipline with his film work – he never went to see the rushes, nor to see his own finished films if he could possibly avoid it. In this respect he was the exact opposite of John Gielgud, who always felt he could learn by watching what he had done, through the camera's eye.

Fittingly perhaps for a man who had read all of Shakespeare by the age of fourteen, he chose the least-heard of anything from that pen, to be his last word on the subject – the two long and moving poems, *The Phoenix and the Turtle* and *The Passionate Pilgrim*, which BBC Radio broadcast in 1976.

When *The Merchant of Venice* closed at the Haymarket Ralph spent most of 1968 in the film studios, playing a string of authority figures in uniform and mufti. In *Midas Run* he did get to act, if not to dance, with Fred Astaire, in a spoof of the British Secret Service. *the bed-sitting room* was a much more surrealistic fantasy, written by John Antrobus and Spike Milligan, and directed by Dick Lester; here Ralph gave another of his great eccentrics, Lord Fortnum of Alamein, who mutates into the eponymous bed-sitting room after a nuclear war.

He was the Foreign Secretary, Sir Edward Grey, in *Oh! What a Lovely War*, Richard Attenborough's film version of Joan Littlewood's smash-hit stage musical about the First World War. The film lacked much of the bite of the stage show, and most of the galaxy of stars in it had too little to do to make a real impact individually.

Two other small parts were David Kelly, the British Minister in Switzerland, in Guy Hamilton's *Battle of Britain*, and Mr Micawber in Delbert Mann's version of *David Copperfield*. Ralph brought his own distinctive presence to all these films, although none of the movies succeeded in firing on all cylinders.

Anthony Hopkins noticed how he seemed to rise above any problems or difficulties when they were working on *The Looking Glass War*. John le Carré's spy thriller was directed by Frank R. Pierson, and Hopkins says it was a very troubled and unhappy set. 'Ralph obviously sensed something was up, but just breezed through it. He pretended to be vague, would come in and say, "Hello, cocky, how are you?" but his eyes took in everything in the room, he had very quick eye movements, his eyes were everywhere.'

Ralph was playing the Head of the Secret Service, a profession he represented several times on film, and once disastrously on-stage; he seemed to love the mystery surrounding such characters. He was attracted by le Carré's complexity of characterization and maturity of dialogue. He described his own character as 'an affectionate man, sensitive, fond of subordinates and protégées, but relentless. An agent is sent over and has to be abandoned: "He'll have to look after himself," the Head says. It comes swift as a knife from a man of humanity.'

Hopkins observed how he stamped his own mark on the part. 'He chose his own clothes, and was meticulous about having the right props. I was fascinated by his use of the fob-watch, and the way he was constantly winding it up.'[3] Watches were always one of his favourite props, and when in doubt he often fell back on a bit of business with one, always with great effect for the character, if not always total relevance to the plot.

He was at a loss to know what to fall back on in the play that marked his return to the stage in 1969. His success in portraying zany eccentrics had prompted the offer. After seeing him in *the bed-sitting room* Oscar Lewenstein was convinced he would be the best choice for Dr Rance in Joe Orton's *What the Butler Saw*; the author had been similarly impressed by seeing Richardson in *Blandings Castle* on TV. Later Orton had second thoughts and pushed the merits of Alastair Sim, but before the play went into production the promising young writer of anarchic comedy was murdered by his lover, Kenneth Halliwell.

The action is set in a lunatic asylum, and the elements of this black farce include nymphomania, incest, transvestism, blackmail and mistaken identity. Through it all stalks the figure of Dr Rance, one of Her Majesty's Commissioners in Lunacy, supposedly trying to restore order, in reality quite the most insane person there. It should have worked, with a cast that included such practised farceurs as Coral Browne, Stanley Baxter and Julia Foster.

Before rehearsals began Ralph said cautiously: 'The worst of our deceiving profession is that you never know. I've seen the cast falling about with laughter in rehearsal, and then no one laughs on the night. What comes out of a play always surprises you; if it didn't, there wouldn't be anything in it. Between a dress rehearsal and what comes out a week later, the difference is immense: it is what comes up when a play meets the audience.'

But the director, Robert Chetwyn, failed to infuse in this cast a belief in the author's comic vision. Peggy Ramsay, the literary agent, who had nurtured Orton through his brief career, saw the production in Brighton, and lamented that 'nobody in the cast is enjoying the play, which never flows, and which doesn't seem to have any fun about it.'[4]

Ralph's regular Brighton fans were outraged by the play. Stanley Baxter said 'there were old ladies in the audience not merely tearing up their programmes, but jumping up and down on them out of sheer hatred. Even the house manager had to leave town.'[5] Ralph wrote a reply to every letter of complaint, but whatever mollifying effect that may have had on the recipients, it did very little for his own peace of mind. He made some adjustments of his own to compensate for the clumsy set. The crucial door leading to the hall was practically out of the sight-line on the side, so he did not use it even when the script specified it, coming through an inappropriate revolving door at the back of the set which, Coral Browne remarked, 'confused an audience and made it seem like he'd come from outer space'.

But there was little he could do about the final scene, when grilles were supposed to drop over each window, locking everyone into the asylum. For some unaccountable reason the director lowered iron bars right across the proscenium, forcing the actors to play the last quarter of an hour divided from the audience by an iron grid.

Ralph had not received boos since *Royal Circle*, and even those boos were fairly isolated and not over-vociferous. The audience response to the first night at the Queen's Theatre on 5 March 1969 went far beyond mere boos. At the opening of the second Act a galleryite screamed, 'Give back your knighthood!' As the cast pressed on they were interrupted by shouts of 'Filth!', 'Rubbish!', 'Take it off!', 'Find another play!'

The anger reached a climax at the curtain-calls, and it seemed to Stanley Baxter as if 'the gallery wanted to jump on the stage and kill us all'. (The shade of Joe Orton was surely at the elbow of the Oxford University Public Orator three months later, when he presented Ralph Richardson for the Conferment of the Honorary Degree of Doctor of Letters, and in one oratorical flourish proclaimed, 'He stands not only between Melpomene and Thalia, but also those other rival virgins of Bacchus' train, and you might expect him to be torn to pieces like a second Pentheus. But he remains intact, true to himself amid all changes of role.')

Few recognized the genuine worth of *What the Butler Saw* until Lindsay Anderson's brilliant revival at the Royal Court six years later. For now, many of the shortcomings of the production were blamed on the author and the cast. Benedict Nightingale inveighed against the leading actor in the *New Statesman*.

Richardson is at his most mannered and monotonous, his most trumpetingly solemn. He can't end one sentence on its

keynote, but bays discordantly into the auditorium, filling his
hearers (onstage I suspect, as well as offstage) with awful
glumness. It's as if the Hound of the Baskervilles has wandered
into a Feydeau farce.

The *Sunday Times* critic tried to absolve him from blame,
and to distance him from the play.

> The only pleasure we could enjoy, apart from Miss Browne,
> was in Richardson's performance as an investigating specialist
> who seemed even madder than everybody else, but mad with
> a severe, confident sublimity worthy of a better part in a better
> play. But even in *What the Butler Saw* Richardson shows
> himself a very great actor.

Ralph could cope with the portrayal of madness well
enough, and did so very touchingly on-stage the following
year in a play which engaged his sympathies; but he found the
constant stress on sexual perversion, even for comic effect,
disagreeable, and in the end he felt he was trapped in 'a dirty
play'.

He had to cope with insanity again that year in a radio
production of Ibsen's last play, *When We Dead Awaken*. This
is rarely performed on-stage, partly because of the difficulties
of staging the mountain avalanche at the end, so it was well
suited to a medium where the listener's imagination could
match the author's. The producer John Tydeman was using
Michael Meyer's translation, and Ralph was the first choice of
both of them for Rubek. Others in the cast included Irene
Worth, Barbara Jefford and Gordon Jackson. When one young
actor had not got a pencil on him, Ralph told him in front of
everyone, 'Let me give you a bit of advice, young man, apart
from your talent there are only two things you need as an
actor; one is a pencil to write down the notes when the

director gives them to you, and the other is a good india-rubber to rub them out when he's not looking.'

He did envisage an important role for the director, however, when necessary. Irene Worth decided to show the woman's psychological shock by speaking in a flat monotone, which may have been medically accurate but made it very boring for the listener. So Ralph had a quiet word out of her earshot: 'Old man, I don't know what you're going to do, but you've got to do something with Irene, this woman is supposed to be mad. I don't know how you're going to do it, old boy, but you've got to drive her mad, you know what I mean – mad, mad, mad, mad! I've got nothing to play off.'⁶

The actress took some persuading, but eventually deferred to the director's judgement, to the relief of everyone else, especially her leading man. He encountered his usual difficulty with foreign pronunciations, and never mastered 'Taunitzer See', but apart from that he enjoyed his work on the play. He asked the translator, 'Do you think Ibsen will be pleased?'

'Over the moon.'

'Oh well, so long as old Henry Gibson is pleased, and the listeners.'

Michael Meyer never minded this flippant familiarity with the great writer's name, as he was well used to Ralph's individuality from their long friendship which had grown from many meetings over lunch at the Savile Club. In his entertaining autobiography, *Not Prince Hamlet*, he traces the development of that friendship in charming detail. He noticed Ralph's phonetic spelling of his lunch order at the club – 'spinich', 'luttace', and 'cheesebord'. Ralph once ordered a jam omelette, and when the waitress returned to say they only had ham, cheese or herb omelettes, no jam, he told her to go back and ask if they could make a jam one for him. She returned to say, 'They want to know who it's for.' He gave his name and she came back the third time to announce, 'Sorry, sir, no jam omelette.'

Richardson turned to Meyer with a very pained expression: 'What I want to know is, who would I have had to be to get a jam omelette?'

None of this nonplussed the writer quite so much as the day his friend suggested he join him after lunch to see the film of Truman Capote's *In Cold Blood*. The Curzon Cinema in Mayfair is only a couple of streets away from the Savile Club, but they were driven there in the Rolls by the chauffeur. Having arrived in style the fifty-year-old author was then told, 'You must have some sweets.'

'No, really.'

'You must have something. Have some chocolate peppermint creams.'

Thinking perhaps he wanted some for himself, Meyer gave in. 'Well, thank you, that would be nice.'

Ralph put his arm round his shoulders, took him over to the confectionery counter and cried, 'A box of chocolate peppermint creams for my young boyfriend here', which caused every head in the cinema foyer to turn in surprise.

Michael Meyer believes that Richardson was a natural Ibsenite and regrets, like many others, that although he did play John Gabriel Borkman in his last years at the National Theatre, and then Old Ekdal in *The Wild Duck*, he never played Solness in *The Master Builder*, Dr Wangel in *The Lady from the Sea*, Pastor Manders in *Ghosts*, or Dr Stockmann in *An Enemy of the People*, in all of which he should have been superb.

But now he returned to a theatre where he had enjoyed some of his earliest successes in 1928, and which was currently the proclaimed centre of new writing – the Royal Court. He had regretted turning down Beckett, and accepting Orton; he hoped it would be his third time lucky with a playwright of the avant-garde. In David Storey's *Home* he reshaped his image and entered a decade of extraordinary success and happiness.

CHAPTER SEVENTEEN

Home — 1970

THE THEATRICAL revolution that George Devine had insti-
gated from the mid-1950s onwards at the Royal Court Theatre
had been regarded rather apprehensively by most of Ralph's
generation, although Laurence Olivier had trodden its boards
for the English Stage Company in John Osborne's *The
Entertainer*, and enjoyed a great personal success.

Ralph's absence was not from a lack of invitations. Lindsay
Anderson had gone round to Ralph's dressing-room at the
Haymarket to ask him to play the title-role in his production
of *Julius Caesar* at the Royal Court, and he was already finding
him difficult to persuade when, to Anderson's fury, Robert
Morley came in and said, 'Oh, you don't want to go to the
Court, because they don't pay you any money.'[1]

David Storey had written *Home* without any thought as to
the casting. When he sent the script to the Royal Court,
Lindsay Anderson suggested they start at the top and work
down; he knew it had to be strongly cast to work on the stage,
because on the page it could seem insubstantial or difficult, so
he sent it to John Gielgud, whose reaction was one of wary
interest. He thought that the play was fascinating although
he did not fully understand it, but feared that Anderson was
hostile to his style of acting, and that maybe the Royal Court
was antipathetic too.

Sir John went down to Sloane Square to discuss it, and was reassured on the last two points,

> and Storey had such charm and put it so nicely, that on the strength of his personality I said, 'Well, I will do the play.' Then they said to me, 'Who do you think should play the other part?' I said, 'You ought to get Ralph, he would be wonderful in it.'[2]

The director was rather hesitant after his previous abortive visit to the Haymarket. 'Do you think he'll want to be directed?'

'Oh yes, as long as he can respect his director.' (That was not a condition all of Ralph's directors managed to meet.)

This time Lindsay went to see Ralph at his home in Regent's Park, and was relieved to find that he liked the play. He liked the idea of renewing his stage partnership with Gielgud even more. Having made up his mind, once again he wanted to begin rehearsals soon.

> He didn't want to wait until the Court's next play but one; he said, 'I want to work, so if you wait until then you'll probably lose me, and I won't do it.' So I went back to the Court and said, 'We've got to do this play next', and fortunately we were able to swap the next two plays and bring *Home* forward.[3]

The director was not deceived by Ralph playing the fool, and thought him very shrewd — 'crazy like a fox, rather than crazy'. The author was confronted by other animal analogies when he visited Chester Terrace.

> Behind the door we heard very loud barking, and when the door was opened it was a man who was barking, and there was

Ralph, sounding very like an angry dog. He said, 'Welcome to the home of a very poor actor' (whether he meant a 'poor' actor, or a poor 'actor', I don't know). Then he turned and said, 'Let's go through here,' and led the way down to the sitting-room; and as we went down the passageway from the door he suddenly became a horse. His back was to us and he neighed like a horse, and kicked out his right leg backwards and it was extraordinary, it was just like a horse's leg coming out. So that was my introduction to him, and it was quite striking really.[4]

Ralph did not want to talk about the play at all, and David Storey felt he could still have said 'No' at that point, but what he really wanted was a reassurance that they were going to go ahead and do it. Gielgud was not sure which part Richardson wanted to play, but Ralph had no doubts about that. '"Oh, I want to do the one with the conjuring act."

"Well, I can't do cards at all, so I'm very glad. I can cry, so it's much better if we do it that way round."'[5]

In other respects they were cast against type. Ralph played Jack, who did most of the talking, reducing John as Harry in one interchange to repeated use of the single word 'Well . . .', in answer to a whole flurry of questions. (When they did their double-act interviews together their natural conversational styles were the reverse of this.)

The play opens with a long scene between the men exchanging pleasantries in hesitant, unfinished sentences, sitting in what appears to be the garden of a hotel or country house. It is only with the entry of two bawdy and loud-mouthed working-class women that it becomes apparent that they are all mentally disturbed patients in care.

Bringing the rehearsals forward meant that for the first week the two actresses, Dandy Nichols and Mona Washbourne, were not available, so they worked only on the opening scene, going through it line by line, and cutting about ten pages out of it, literally so by John Gielgud, with a pair of nail-scissors, which caused a few problems when some lines were put back in.

Both actors were like a couple of highly strung thorough-breds, but to Anderson's surprise it was Ralph who behaved more like the director, making some very cogent and percep-tive comments.

> They were both a bit apprehensive about the play when we got into it, and when we started rehearsing Ralph said more than once, 'Oh, I wanted to drop this, to get out of it, because I suddenly realized what it involved', because he'd thought in the middle of the night, 'I can't do this', and it was Mu who said, 'Don't be absurd, Ralph, get on with the play.'

In the beginning, neither of them wanted to sit still on-stage for more than a few minutes, and their nervousness made them race through the dialogue. Ralph did not want to look out front and play it to the back of the stalls. 'Couldn't we do it into the wings and look out that way?'

But his director was adamant.

> 'No, it won't work that way, we have to see you and follow your thoughts and feelings all the way through.' His instinct was to retreat from that, he needed reassurance, nonsense of course, but he was a strange mixture of modesty and self-knowledge, presence and star-quality.

The author sensed that both actors found it difficult to make the adjustment to a theatre where, as they perceived it, the audience were there to be instructed rather than entertained.

They exuded a distinct lack of confidence all the way through rehearsals, but worked extremely hard, and were always looking for things that weren't quite there, to reassure them. John worked empirically, I felt, through feeling and intuition, towards the part; whereas Ralph worked towards it more mechanically in terms of the narrative. At one point where they were rehearsing above us on the stage he kept catching my eye as he was performing, and then in the middle of a line he suddenly got up, walked over and leaned down and stared for a long time, which he was inclined to do as though he was blaming me, and said, 'Isn't this the point where I could find some stolen jewellery?' As a joke, but he was looking for the narrative, and not finding it; so he was struggling to find the emotional dynamic of the play in that particular way. Being the very eccentric fellow he was, he invented inner analogies which no one could possibly follow, but which were clear to him. Once Lindsay perceived that that was the way he was working he gave up contesting it strongly, as he'd done at the beginning.

He wanted to wear his own clothes in the play, and invited the designer, Jocelyn Herbert, up to his home to choose something,

and I had to say that none of them were suitable for his character. I had terrible trouble with both him and John, because they hadn't ever played their own age on-stage, and they wanted to wear toupees, and I managed to persuade them not to. Ralph wore one of his own hats, with a curly brim, I think to make sure the light fell on his face.[6]

Gielgud remembers not just her persuasiveness, but the fact that she was 'the most wonderful designer, took infinite pains with the clothes which were very simple but very important'.

She also gained Ralph's respect, which was to be important in a crisis on a later Storey play.

The two stars were still unsure whether the whole thing was going to work, so the cast of a visiting American theatre group called Café La Mama who were currently playing at the Court, and the cast of another Storey play, *The Contractor*, which had transferred to the West End, were invited in to the dress rehearsal of *Home*. They were put up in the dress circle so as not to distract the actors. Paul Moriarty, a member of *The Contractor* company, remembers that they were all so moved at the end that they stood up and clapped and roared 'Bravo! Bravo!' with great enthusiasm.[7]

It was a significant moment for the author too.

> I remember Ralph looking up with a kind of genial disbelief, and then John stepping forward and looking up at them saying, 'Oh, we don't deserve it!'
>
> And then a great cry came back, 'Oh yes you do!'
>
> He was very moved, because he began to weep, tears came into his eyes and he was speechless. That was the turning point, obviously, though we weren't aware of it; because we then opened in Brighton for one week, and all I remember of Brighton is the sound of seats clicking back as people left.

What made this the more unnerving was that the exodus continued steadily throughout the performance, even though they were not shouting at the cast as they left, as they had during *What the Butler Saw*. Ralph took it upon himself to reassure the shaken author. 'He took me aside and said, "It's a very good sign in Brighton – if they're walking out in Brighton they won't in London", staring intently at me, as if to say, "Do you know anything different, or am I wrong?"'[8]

This time he was not wrong. *Home* opened at the Royal

Court to an ecstatic response, and soon transferred to the Apollo in Shaftesbury Avenue. Frank Marcus wrote in the *Sunday Telegraph*:

> Sir Ralph finds here the perfect accommodation for his genius. Increasingly in recent years he has dissociated words from meaning; they have become the (sometimes) barely visible tips of the icebergs. But here they help him to suggest, extra-verbally, a whole world – a world that has passed. He conveys with each look, with each turn of the head, with his shadow of a swagger, with his handling of his cane, some lost virtue and some ancient pride. His confinement in the asylum adds poignancy to profundity. He is ripe and mellow, and asserts, as he has always done in his greatest performances, the humanity of the ordinary man.

Keith Dewhurst acclaimed both of the central performances in the *Guardian*, finding the way in which Gielgud interrupted a conversation with tears as 'simply an act of genius: a consummation of his lifetime's integrity'; he saw the same quality in his partner:

> Richardson says broken lines in a way that makes you feel you've listened to a speech. The little angles at which he tilts his hat, the terrible tragic jauntiness of his card tricks, and his walk across the stage in front of the two women are master-pieces of comportment, and his voice has a strange elegiac quality, a cadence of winds and weather, and seasons of the year, that enables him to express like no other actor something that is at the heart of English drama, and thus of actually being English: something instinctive and involuntary in the rhythm of both phrase and situation that recurs whatever the style or generation.

Others found it difficult to distinguish the effects on them of one player from that of the other, because their partnership was so perfectly attuned to each other's wavelength. For the *Times* reviewer,

> The production has the crowning advantage of a beautiful pair of performances from Ralph Richardson and John Gielgud, who from their first moments on-stage play together like two master instrumentalists, Richardson's oboe answering Gielgud's viola in a duet that extracts endless variety from the broken sentences, reassuring platitudes, and 'Godot'-like catalogues of their scenes together. I have never seen theatrical tears shed to better effect.

Jeremy Kingston in *Punch* was also moved by the long hold at the final curtain:

> At the end of the play, as the climax to two perfect, delicate performances, Sir Ralph and Sir John are standing, staring out above the heads of the audience, cheeks wet with tears in memory of some unnamed misery, weeping soundlessly as the lights fade on them. It makes a tragic, unforgettable close.

They had been wonderful foils to each other for four decades now, and their friendship and professional faith in each other had become almost tangible on the stage, especially to other players of great sensitivity. Dorothy Tutin went to see *Home* twice, the first time alone.

> John came on, sniffing the air and sitting down, looking elegant, and suddenly Ralph came on very slowly and sat down. I took myself so by surprise, because after they'd been talking for about five minutes I found I was crying. There was nothing moving about what they were doing, it was the sheer

magic of seeing those two actors together on that stage, it was so wonderful. When I went again with a friend she said the thing that Ralph had in that part, which I hadn't at first realized and she was quite right, was this enormous care for John, that his part seemed to be immensely watchful and caring, so that a lot of those 'What!', 'I beg your pardon?', and 'Ah, well!' on that strange dying fall, weren't just out to the audience, they were warmly towards John, which was what moved so much.[9]

The two actors now played the whole of their opening dialogue sitting practically motionless for nearly twenty-five minutes. The lack of movement, which had so worried them at the outset, was spell-binding for the audience, focusing their attention on the inner life of the two men as the author had intended.

Richard Findlater also caught the value of the special depth in their relationship:

It was hard to imagine that either Richardson or Gielgud would have been so fine in *Home* without the other. Both performances gained immeasurably by reciprocal reflection; both actors listened magnificently; and behind the perfect collaboration and masterly skill of their duets one senses a lifetime's friendship and trust as well as a lifetime's experience.

Every nuance was important in their duets, as Ralph revealed.

Once when we were playing in *Home* I thought he looked very sulky. I said, 'Johnny, did I do something wrong? Did I leave out half a line?' I do that occasionally, you know. He said, 'Oh, no.' I persisted. 'Tell me what I did wrong.' He said, 'As a matter of fact you didn't give me your second "Tut" which

was my cue.' It takes spit to do a 'Tut'. I did the first one and
the second one didn't come off. I'd run out of spit.

They left such an indelible mark on their interpretations
of Harry and Jack that, as their creator ruefully noted, no
other actors would risk comparisons in London for nearly a
quarter of a century, until Paul Eddington and Richard Briers
took on those roles in 1994.

Before Sir Ralph and Sir John relinquished their parts they
took them on to Broadway, and there was a twinge of
nervousness all round about how such a delicately balanced
and very English play would go down with the New York
audience in the much bigger Morosco Theater. At the rehearsal
before the Broadway opening Lindsay Anderson asked the cast
if anyone wanted to change anything.

John was a little unhappy with his entrance with Mona, and
asked if he could change it from upstage right to downstage
left, and I saw a sudden look of apprehension cross Ralph's
face, and he gave a little shake of his head, and I said, 'I think
it would unstitch the whole thing to put in a different
entrance,' and we left it alone.

They never knew how narrowly they missed one new
experience in New York. One night Jocelyn Herbert overheard
Sir John say, 'Ralph, have you ever taken any drugs – have
you tried this thing called pot?'
'No.'
So she made some hash cookies for a party, but neither of
the actors ate them.
Home was a great success on Broadway, but Ralph still had
one little niggling doubt about the narrative structure. Patrick
Garland had been moved to tears by the performance and
went round to say,

'Ralph, it's a beautiful play.'

'Yes, it's a wonderful play, I love it, standing there with my dear old friend Johnny Gielgud.'

'Well, the two of you together are just out of this world.'

'Yes, yes, it's such a good play, but you know every so often I get an impatient feeling of frustration in my whole body, that I want to turn to my old friend Johnny Gielgud just two or three feet in front of me and say, "Now, look here, this is all very well, but where have you hidden the diamonds, Mr Stacey?"'[10]

David Storey would have forgiven him if he had ever succumbed to that temptation, and certainly would not have been surprised if he had. Having watched him all the way through rehearsals and many performances, and spent time with him off-stage too, he came to the conclusion that Ralph had invented a public persona for himself, which became a character that somehow transcended all the parts he played; he then transferred this persona into the parts he came to play over the years, rather than the other way around.

This perception so intrigued the writer that for the first, and only, time he wrote a play with the actor in mind, 'seeing that very strange, elusive countenance and character, his public character and his acting character, and the oscillation between the two like no other actor I knew; I suppose because the public character was so strong, and elusive as well, it had a magnetism and a subtlety and eccentricity which defied definition.'

He later realized that to create a play in that way was a mistake. Because he could see Ralph so vividly in his mind's eye doing it, he cut corners in the writing of the script, and unconsciously made elisions in the text which he would not normally have done. The first person to spot this was Ralph himself, who promptly turned the play down, saying he could not do it. His other expressed reason was that he said he did not like acting quite such an old man on-stage, in a kind of terminal decay.

So *Early Days* sat in limbo until the end of the decade, with the author refusing to let anyone else do it, because he just could not see any other actor playing the part. His patience and loyalty were eventually rewarded, but only after an extraordinary gestation period and agonizing birth-pangs for all concerned.

While the author waited, the actor flung himself into a rich variety of other creations, the first of which put the old team of Richardson and Gielgud back into costume again.

CHAPTER EIGHTEEN

1971–1973

EAGLE IN A CAGE was set in St Helena during Napoleon's last exile; a stretch of the Yugoslav coastline near Split stood in for the South Atlantic. Ralph played Sir Hudson Lowe, the Governor of the island, John Gielgud was a visiting senior Foreign Office official, Kenneth Haigh was Napoleon, and Lee Montague his valet. A young and impressionable member of the cast was Michael Williams, who played the doctor, in a rather nondescript blue uniform. He felt especially overawed in his first scene by the sight of the resplendent Governor in his red tunic, white breeches, big black boots and a plumed hat making him look even taller than his six-foot frame, flanked by six huge extras from the Yugoslav Army dressed in British uniforms.

They were all awaiting the arrival on horseback of Napoleon and his valet, through a specially built archway; they were to dismount and walk through a line of yet more imposing Yugoslav extras. Michael Williams felt there was little place for him in this set-up and asked the American director, Fielder Cook,

'Where do you want me to go, Fielder?'
'Oh, I don't know, go and stand by the side of Sir Ralph.'

So I did, and Ralph looked down on me from his great height and said, 'What are you doing here, m'boy?'

'I don't know, Sir Ralph, I just asked Fielder and he said I had to come and stand by the side of you.'

'Well, we must have an artistic reason for why you're here.'

'Yes, well I suppose we must.'

'I know, you called round for a quick cocktail and you were caught.'[1]

As always, Ralph had boned-up on the real Sir Hudson Lowe, who was a great gourmet, one of whose foibles was that he loved to cook in the open air. Michael Williams had to gallop up the mountain and find the Governor standing over an open griddle cooking their meal before they sat down to it. It was a tricky scene to handle, because there were a lot of props and business, together with some complicated dialogue. All of this was causing Ralph some considerable trouble, and he was also unhappy with the unconventional behaviour of the doctor, who was putting his feet on the table, which he thought went too far. So he had a quiet word with the director, who told Michael Williams to tone things down. It was a difficult scene technically for both actors.

At the lunch-break the two of them set off down a goat-track to the restaurant.

Ralphy was dressed in his dressing-gown and straw hat, with his stick. All of a sudden he stopped, held up his stick to stop me, we were standing on the edge of a drop of hundreds of feet overlooking the Adriatic, and he said, 'You know, m'boy, acting's a great mystery. One day it's there, the next day nowhere to be seen.'

That's helped me through my career, and it's very true.

The shooting in Yugoslavia went on for about ten weeks, and the central section involved the visit of the Foreign Office emissary to discuss what was to be done with Napoleon. The Governor and the doctor were awaiting his arrival up on the mountain and chatting.

Suddenly we heard this voice floating up through the clouds, and Ralph got like a little boy, and he said, 'Oh, my God, my God, it's Johnny, it's Johnny.'

As he got nearer, Ralph leaped to his feet, pulled his straw hat off and waved it in the air, calling, 'Johnny, Johnny.'

John was talking fifteen to the dozen to the group walking up with him, and he said, 'It's my bald-headed friend, Johnny, Johnny.'

And John was still talking away. 'Oh, I do love him, but God he does talk!'

There were other arrivals during the course of the shooting, attracted to the filming and its location. At the time Michael Williams was courting Judi Dench, and she took advantage of a week's break in her performances with the Royal Shakespeare Company in Stratford to come out and join her future husband for a few days. Kenneth Haigh had rented a villa and invited them both to dinner with several other leading members of the cast. They were having a drink on the sofa prior to dinner, and when Ralph leaned over and bit her very gently on the ear, Judi exclaimed, 'Oh, oh, Sir Ralph, you bit me!'

'What's a bite between friends?'

Then he had another gin and said pensively, 'You know, it's a strange thing, but Mr Gordon follows me all over the world.'

On the first day of her visit they went down to watch the filming, as Michael was not on call that day. He warned her in advance, 'Now, you must be aware of the way Ralph gulps his drink, because he doesn't just sip, he throws it down, so when you see him do it you mustn't laugh.'

'No, no, of course I won't.'

So when we got to this beautiful harbour there was this ubiquitous peasant lady who always seems to be around on Yugoslav shoots, who was there with a table from seven o'clock in the morning, sitting at the end of this pier with every conceivable drink that you can imagine. At about midday they broke, and Ralph stomped along in his splendid uniform, and he said: 'Ahh, I think I'd like to try a little of that splendid wine you've got there.'

So the lady poured him out about half of the bottle, and he said, 'Oh, it's a lovely little wine . . .' and immediately this great gulf opened up, and the whole of the glass went down. At which point Jude laughed, of course.

Even after weeks, or sometimes months, of working together, Ralph never ceased to astonish his fellow-actors with his unpredictable behaviour. Kenneth Haigh and Michael Williams went to see him and Mu off when they were leaving. She was packing in another part of the suite, and Ralph offered them a drink. It was red wine, and he slipped some cherry brandy into it. The two younger actors glanced at each other, and Michael thought, 'Golly, he can't do this all the time, because otherwise he wouldn't be doing the great work he is doing.' They could not understand how it never seemed to affect him at all.

Everyone enjoyed working on *Eagle in a Cage*, and it is a very entertaining film to watch, but it attracted little attention on its release in 1971. Some months later Ralph found it difficult to place a face he saw in his club, until a chance remark reminded him that it was Fielder Cook, who had directed the film.

Such forgetfulness is a little more understandable when one looks at his workload at that time. Apart from this film, he had worked on the television recording of *Home* after its American tour, and whilst preparing for his next stage play, John Osborne's *West of Suez*, he also fitted in a TV recording of *She Stoops to Conquer* for the BBC.

Michael Elliott directed this Oliver Goldsmith classic, with Ralph and Thora Hird as Mr and Mrs Hardcastle, and Tom Courtenay as Young Marlow, repeating his recent success in that part at the Garrick Theatre. Ralph had hardly had time to learn his lines, and in one scene could remember very few of them. He apologized to Tom Courtenay afterwards. 'Sorry about the cues, old fellow, I just gave you one or two to keep you going, like a carrot in front of a donkey.'[2]

Tom admired his Charaton pipes, so Ralph sent his driver round with one. When Courtenay went to thank him, he found Ralph going over the script of *West of Suez*. His own lines were all underlined in red, the others in blue. The page was open at a long speech, most of it in red, then one line in blue – 'What school did you go to?' Half a page in red, then another line in blue – 'Oh, really?' Then another stretch in red. Ralph looked disconsolately at the page and said, 'If I had the other part I could go on tonight: "What school did you go to?" See, I know that part.'

He was a little bemused by Thora Hird's non-stop stream of stories. Once, when she paused momentarily for breath, she noticed Ralph's saucer full of coffee. She said, 'Oh, give it here, I'll take care of that.'

'No, no, I like it this way.' And he drank it out of the saucer.

There were a lot of candles on the set for the last scene, so there was candle-grease everywhere. Ralph ate a bit of it, and said to Esmond Knight, 'Would you like some of this candle-grease? It's awfully good.'

After the final recording session everyone was at the party at Michael Elliott's, and Tom Courtenay noticed an empty glass.

'Can I fill your glass, Sir Ralph?'

'Yes, please.'

'What is it?'

'Gin.'

'Anything in it?'

'You can spit in it if you like.'

More gin was consumed, undiluted, with Anthony Page, when the director went to the Richardsons' house in Regent's Park to discuss the script of *West of Suez*. Ralph was keen to cut rather a lot of it, particularly in the controversial scene at the end where a hippie comes on and curses everyone, which he did not think was very well written. The two of them had long discussions, and Anthony Page felt 'it was a bit like negotiating for a carpet with a carpet-dealer in Turkey sometimes'.[3]

(Interestingly, the actor used the same imagery in attempting to explain the mysteries of the play to the television producer Tristram Powell after one performance: 'It's like a carpet isn't it, with threads running through the patterns.')

Finally, very little of Ralph's part was cut, and as rehearsals went on the director felt that any reservations the actor may have had tended to disappear. It helped that he had loved the first volume of John Osborne's autobiography as a piece of writing, and shared the author's love of literature. For all his premonitions about learning the part, he took to it like a duck to water, and in the confrontation with an aggressive journalist at the end, when she attacks his values and he attempts to run rings round her, he showed his gift for finding the comedy in the scene.

In the play he is a famous writer, Wyatt Gilman, who has four daughters. They all come together in the Caribbean home of one of them, and discuss the decline of the old country. The action of the play revolves around Gilman, and ends with him being shot by the revolutionaries. It was a meaty part, and Ralph made the most of it.

His youngest daughter was played by the twenty-two-year-old Penelope Wilton.

> One of the greatest things about him, when you were on-stage with him, or when you watched him from the audience, was his stillness. He listened frightfully well, there was an enormously relaxed stillness about him as a performer, and that's quite hard for an actor. I had very few lines and I was very young, and he said to me once when we were rehearsing, 'Often the thing you throw away is as important as the thing you say.'
>
> What he was trying to say was, you don't have to hit every word as if it's of equal importance. Then he thought for a minute, and said, 'Still, I suppose you've got to know where to throw it.'
>
> I think he was thinking, 'I'd better not say that, or we might get nothing, at least now we're getting something.'[4]

His death-scene in rehearsal did not look as if it was going to be thrown away. He worked out some very complicated business for it, which involved running around the set until he fell over a deckchair, taking off his white hat with its false top whipped off to show the bloodied part, dying upside-down over the chair, then slowly putting the bloodied hat on his bottom. It looked so convoluted and melodramatic that he finally abandoned it, and just ran and fell over.

The Brighton audience was as quick as ever to take offence at the bad language in the play, and one night someone got up and shouted during the last scene, 'Do you realize this is a social occasion?' Ralph turned round and walked down to the front of the stage and looked out into the auditorium, holding his gaze for what seemed like an eternity to the rest of the cast; then he just wandered back and got on with the scene. After the uproar over *What the Butler Saw*, and the general exodus during *Home*, a solitary heckle from the audience was not likely to throw him.

The London critics saw it as much more than 'a social occasion', indeed as a major statement on a society in decline, performed by a strong cast. John Barber in the *Daily Telegraph* thought that Ralph dominated the play with a superb performance as 'a self-deprecating entertainer who pretends to be an old duffer but in fact is a skilled eccentric. His sparring with a cruel interviewer, whose impertinence he fends off with epigrams and bursts of engaging candour, is one of the highlights of the evening.'

J. W. Lambert in the *Sunday Times* went further.

Sir Ralph's portrait of this man, a burnt-out case from birth, seems to me a total triumph. The big frame moves with a puppet-like angularity, plays at a babyish physical incompetence. But the head turns like an old stag's, the eyes, widening and narrowing, are always watchful — and the voice takes on a score of colours just as the phrasing, the pauses, the downright breaks are themselves a miracle of characterization.

Helen Dawson echoed this in the *Observer*.

Ralph Richardson's performance is, quite simply, a joy. He radiates knowing innocence. Tut-tutting when criticized, rolling his eyes in affected alarm, he delivers his lines so that they hang in the air, imprinting themselves on the memory. At the close of the first act, he stands silently, alone on the stage, and a brief cantankerous look changes to one of ominous distress. The face seems to pale. It is rare to see an actor of his years performing at this voltage.

His fellow-actors could hardly fail to register that high-voltage performance too. Penelope Wilton still treasures the experience of its power.

He had an amazing energy, a quality I've noticed in all the great actors, and it was the energy of the character always. When he wasn't very well at one point in the run, there was talk of cutting the matinees, but he wouldn't hear of it. 'No, that's the thin edge of the W, the thin end of the wedge.'

There was not much room backstage at the Royal Court, and his dresser Hal helped him with a quick change in the dark towards the end of the play. Then he and Penelope Wilton climbed up some very rickety steps behind the set to make their entrance together. She was concerned that he always had one button undone, and said to him, 'Sir Ralph, do you want me to do that up?'

'Yes, please.'

I said to him once, 'Can't Hal see whether that's done up or not?'

'Yes, he can, but I like you doing it.'

So I did it up most nights, but it made me laugh terribly.

During a run the off-stage routine settles into a regular pattern, as the same characters assemble every night at the same point to make their entrances, and while they wait they often ask each other what they have done during the day.

Penelope Wilton was standing with Sheila Ballantine one night, and they were both nonplussed by Ralph's response to her question.

'What have you done today?'

'Oh, today my brother died.'

So I was sorry I'd asked.

'I didn't know him very well, we were separated when we were children, and he died in a fire.'

So I was completely devastated, at twenty-two you don't know what to say. So I said, 'I'm terribly sorry.'

'Yes.' Then there was a pause. 'Still, it won't happen again.'

We nearly laughed because it was such a funny thing to say.

Ralph had only met his two brothers again when they were all young men, and their long separation in those formative childhood years prevented him from re-establishing close relations with them. But his seemingly flip remark which nearly convulsed the two young actresses reveals that detachment from conventional sympathies that contributed to his reputation as an eccentric. He similarly stopped two actors in their tracks by his unexpected response to a more public tragedy – the massacre at the Munich Olympics in 1972. His colleagues in *Lloyd George Knew My Father*, James Grout and Simon Cadell, were standing with him in the wings talking about the disaster of the sharpshooters failing to knock out the terrorists at the airport, and how dreadful the whole affair was, and Ralph's only comment then was, 'Yes, damn bad shooting', which terminated that conversation. He only seemed to be emotionally engaged with those whom he knew well, which was strange in a man of such an imaginative temperament, whom few could excel in conveying the depths of human sympathy in his acting.

After its run at the Royal Court *West of Suez* transferred to the Cambridge Theatre for a respectable run, but it was really too large for the play to make its full impact, and sometimes audience attention flagged. In one scene Ralph had an exit-line, 'Well, I think I'll go in for a bit now', and if it was a sluggish audience he would look down at his youngest daughter sitting by his feet, and murmur, 'And I might not come back', making it difficult for her to contain her laughter.

The Osborne play was not a comedy, although laughter is the emotion with which its company recalls its leading player. His next play was, by an author with a highly successful track record in the light comedy field – William Douglas-Home. The play was *Lloyd George Knew My Father*, and the laughter it engendered continued for over two years, with Ralph playing opposite three leading ladies before he had finished with it.

When the impresario Ray Cooney asked him who he would like to co-star with him he thought for a moment, and after murmuring, 'Edith couldn't do it now,' he proceeded logically to the leader of the next generation – 'Peggy, I might give Peggy a ring.' She agreed, although many people were surprised to see them both in such a lightweight vehicle. When Robin Midgley was invited to direct it he thought it 'one of the slightest pieces I'd ever read'. But Ralph perceived another dimension beneath the surface text, and his enthusiasm outweighed Peggy Ashcroft's nervousness about whether she ought to be appearing in such a play; at least it did until Ralph had another of his last-minute doubts on tour in Oxford.

Robin Midgley was soon enthused by Ralph's keenness to get to work. When he went to see him in Chester Terrace, Ralph said, 'I know just the chap who should design it,' and got out a book of Turner paintings. 'This is the chap we need to design it.' This example inspired the designer, Anthony Holland, to produce some drawings to show how light could change the feeling in a room.

Midgley found working with Ralph wonderful, but disconcerting in many ways, not least when the actor said, 'I like to creep up on a scene and take it by surprise.' He never started rehearsing a scene where he was asked to, he would chat a bit and then slide into it. At one point the director had to say to the actor: 'I'm finding it hard to find how we're pitching the play, because you are determining it.'[5]

Ralph played a retired General, Sir William Boothroyd, whose wife resolves to commit suicide if the Ministry of Transport goes ahead with a plan to route a bypass through the grounds of their park. Her threat arouses great interest and concern in everyone except the General, who seems indifferent as his wife calmly decides on her coffin and headstone.

The youngest member of the company was Simon Cadell, then twenty-two years old, and overawed by the man who had acted with both his mother and his grandmother. He was soon christened 'the boy' by Ralph, and was taught one lesson very quickly.

When I got too close to him, within two feet of him on the stage, he said, 'Oh no, no, no, too close, you're in my bubble.' I understand it now totally. He knew that, unless one was playing an intimate scene with somebody, space on the stage is terribly important; and if two characters who are not being passionately intimate get too close, the audience definition between the two disintegrates, and he called it his 'bubble'. It was in no sense ungenerous.[6]

This consciousness of necessary space is consistent with one of Ralph's definitions of the actor's art: 'Acting is like blowing up a balloon, you've got to blow the balloon up until if anyone came near it with a needle it would burst, but nobody dares to come near it with a needle.'

Even at this stage in his career, he could be subject to sudden deflation. Quite late on in rehearsals Robin Midgley rather sharply reprimanded him, 'For God's sake, Ralph, don't be so sentimental!' Ralph almost completely seized up, and was unable to work properly for the rest of the day.

The first preview was in Oxford, and by this time everyone was a little nervous about whether it was going to work, including the director. 'The opening night was packed, and the audience howled from the opening moment, Ralph manoeuvred every laugh as if he'd been playing it for months. Peggy was so surprised she walked into every laugh, and came off bubbling like a schoolgirl.'

Ralph may have had his doubts beforehand, but when he was on-stage in full flight he seemed able to cope with any difficulty. At one preview his voice had got a bit husky, and he could not clear his throat properly. His dressing-room was only about ten feet from the main stage exit, and in the middle of his scene with Simon Cadell, he calmly walked over to the exit and called, 'Hal, Hal,' and came back into the scene. He gave his dresser time to run down to the wings and went back up to the exit and said, 'Hal, Listerine, Hal', came back and carried on with the scene, went off into the wings for a gargle, and came back on. Simon had actor-friends out front that night, and when they came round afterwards he gasped, 'Did you see what Richardson did in the first Act?'

'No, what? We just thought it was a character we hadn't seen.'

'The boy' was even more grateful for the master's aplomb when his own mind went a complete blank one night. As the young journalist Simon Green, he had to say at his first encounter with the General, 'My grandfather was in the Indian Army too, sir.'

Ralph used to step back, lift his arm out to the side and drop it back in one of his strange gestures, and say, 'Oh, what was his name?'

'Duggan.'

Another step back. 'Did you say Duggan? I knew your grandfather.'

About two months into the run the answer unaccountably came out 'Boothroyd', the name of Ralph's character, instead of 'Duggan'.

The General took an extra step back, 'Don't you mean Duggan?'

'Yes, sir.'

Another strange arm-gesture. 'Dirty Duggan?'

'Yes, sir, yes, sir, yes, sir.'

(The 'Dirty Duggan' elaboration remained, and is in the published text.)

The mortified young actor went to the No. 1 dressing-room in the interval to apologize.

He sat in his huge white towelling robe, slightly stained with 5 and 9 make-up, with R.R. embroidered on the breast-pocket.

'I'm terribly sorry, Sir Ralph, I don't know what happened.'

He looked at me with those extraordinary eyes, and he said, 'Oh, it's all right, it's just a question of concentration, you know, and we're all going to be here for an AWFULLY LONG TIME.'

And they were – the audiences flocked to see them. Many of the critics thought the playing transcended the play, giving it a greater weight than it deserved. A. E. Matthews had had a comic triumph in an earlier play by this author, *The Chiltern*

Hundreds, but Felix Barker in the *Evening News* thought that that was now eclipsed.

> I shall not quickly forget Sir Ralph's horrified amazement at discovering a mouse in a hat-box in which he keeps his military memoirs. But he immediately gives it a saucer of tea. Sir Ralph's performance may have overtones and the same endearing absurdity as Matty's immortal Earl of Lister. But his dottiness is forged out of a more restrained and precise artistry.

Irving Wardle in *The Times* described 'Richardson popping a letter into an envelope as if knocking a nail in', and Milton Shulman admitted in the *Evening Standard* that 'whether he is involved with rambling, irrelevant anecdotes about friends who thought they were camels, or misinterpreting a stone-mason for a social Mason, Ralph Richardson, as the senile old General, makes us forget through sheer comic technique the emptiness of this very contrived play.'

The demonstration of that technique drew the professionals like a magnet. One of the highspots was the scene where Lady Boothroyd is talking about the masons who will make her gravestone, while her husband persistently thinks she means Freemasons. That late, great comedian, Eric Morecambe, went to see the show twelve times, because he thought it was the most perfectly played piece of double-talk that he had ever seen. The cast could see him sitting in the fourth row, 'with that wonderful face lighting up like a child'.

Some critics thought the ending too soft, when Lady Boothroyd tells the General that although the motorway cannot be stopped she has changed her mind about suicide, because she loves him too much. But Harold Hobson thought his colleagues had missed Ralph's reaction. 'Sir William sits immovable, and his face, in which every muscle is frozen, is half turned away from her. The words make no more impression on him than the spray of a wave on a rock.'

When she says she has never looked at any man but Sir William, Hobson noted that his quiet reply, 'You looked at Tim Carson all right', was spoken with passionate venom. The *Sunday Times* critic had detected that extra dimension which Ralph sensed from the beginning, and which the director says was 'so understated it was very easy to miss'. The latter particularly admired the way in which Ralph never varied his performance, either in England, Australia or America.

Ralph attributed this to the author: 'He decides on a certain beat, which is to do with the construction of sentences so far as commas, semi-colons and full-stops are concerned. He builds a beat which is absolutely unvarying through the part.' The same, he said, applied to David Storey.

He had one little trick which aided that consistency. He never just stepped on to the stage, as many actors do; several lines before his cue he would walk round in a circle, and then on-cue continue to walk and step on to the stage in character. The effect he created in *Lloyd George Knew My Father* prompted a friend of Simon Cadell's to tell him, 'When he first walked on it was almost as though he happened to be passing this room, and you were terribly lucky that he had decided to come in; and that was before he had opened his mouth; now, that ability for an actor is beyond price.' When he walked on at the beginning he tapped a barometer before he spoke, and immediately riveted the audience's attention.

After four months Peggy Ashcroft handed over to Celia Johnson who, knowing her old partner's hatred of re-rehearsing, arrived word-perfect, and then apologized to Robin Midgley for one tiny word-fluff. Her sensitivity and her own brilliant comic timing allowed her to stamp her own mark on Lady Boothroyd, while still perfectly complementing Ralph's Sir William.

His total command of this part, and of the stage as a whole, is hard to reconcile with the occasional insecurity he revealed he still suffered from at this time.

> I was in difficulties about acting when I went on the stage and I'm still worried and uneasy – maybe a little less. When one gets to middle age, one does learn a little, but the essential insecurity remains. You observe and learn many techniques, and the possibility, as a painter, of having more colours in your palette. I know very much more about what you can do with the human body on the stage than I did fifty years ago, but I've also observed many more eloquent actors. As you discover new advantages, you also notice more dangers, and it about, I think, balances itself out. When I was young they'd say, 'Would you go on tonight as Orlando?' And I'd say, 'Oh yes, just give me the part.' And on I bounded. Because I didn't know the dangers.[7]

He set great store by the routines of the theatre, and his own rituals of preparation before, and relaxation afterwards. In a long run, like the William Douglas-Home play, he would regularly entertain individual members of the cast in his dressing-room to a post-performance drink. Simon Cadell's night was usually on a Wednesday.

> The litany of the drinks was that you'd go in, Ralph would be sitting in his dressing-gown in the little make-up area, and I'd say, 'Good evening, Ralph.'
> 'Hello, boy, drink?'
> 'Yes, Ralph, please.'
> 'Gin?'
> 'Yes, please.'
> 'Hal, gin for the boy.'
> And Hal would bring a beautiful cut-glass tumbler, and a

bottle of Gordon's, and would hand it to Ralph, who would fill the tumbler up with a staggering amount of gin, and then he'd say, 'Tonic?'

'Yes, please, Ralph.'

'Hal, tonic for the boy.'

And Hal would bring a bottle of tonic, and Ralph would put the tiniest splash in the glass in a very quick gesture. Ralph had a glass of this same concoction in front of him, and he'd raise it and drink his first tumbler as though it was lemonade – straight down in one. Then the second one was poured for Ralph while you were still taking the first sip of what was virtually pure gin, and always when he lifted the second glass to his lips he used to go: 'And now for the pleasure', and take the tiniest little sip.

As the run of the play continued with Celia Johnson the *Evening News* commented, 'They will have to run a bulldozer through the Savoy to get rid of this one', but in the end it was the actors who decided to call it a day. When Celia felt she had done it long enough and said she was leaving the cast, Ralph announced publicly, 'I've had two leading ladies shot from under me and I can't take any more.'

So *Lloyd George Knew My Father* came off in the West End, but then Ralph agreed to take the play to Australia on a twelve-week tour, with his wife playing opposite him, and a supporting Australian cast. He travelled out via Iran, so that he could visit the great historical sites. On arrival in Melbourne he gave everyone the most terrible fright by fainting at the airport. His wife confided to Robin Midgley later that she believed he was going to die, and she naturally refused to let him rehearse.

Derek Glynne had arranged this tour, and when Ralph began to recover he prevailed on his stars to meet the press and confirm that the play would open as planned, as bookings had stopped with the news of Ralph's collapse. At the press conference Ralph looked pale and ill, until one enterprising Australian journalist said they had a motor-bike outside and asked if they could perhaps get a photograph of Ralph with it. This seemed to give his spirits a lift, and he sat astride it for the photographers; before anyone could stop him he revved it up and roared off round the block, with his anxious wife running after him.

This little escapade was well reported, and the box-office picked up business again. The public were more enthusiastic than the press, but this concerned Ralph much less than it did Derek Glynne.

We got a couple of reviews from young would-be reviewers who wanted to make their name in Australia, and took the play apart, and all Ralph said to me next morning was, 'What are they going on about, dear chap? It's just a simple little play, I came to do a simple little play, and I did it.'[8]

Audiences dipped again at one stage of the tour, and Ralph wrote to Derek Glynne, now back in London:

I have a hope that we may be doing
a little better here – but next
week the dreaded Russian Ballet company
to compete against us – if I could
only learn to DANCE by next
Tuesday perhaps we could compete!
We hope that we may see you in
Sydney and if that will be so could
I ask you a favour?
We plan to return by boat over the
Pacific and I would like to have
my BINOCULARS to observe the

mermaids – they are not heavy,
if you were coming I would
have them sent to your home.
Hotel life is all very well but
I am a little homesick for
home – it is always like that
isn't it.
            EVER.
                    affectionately
                    Ralph

He was still not quite done with General Boothroyd. The following year he and Mu led a tour to Toronto's O'Keefe Centre, and Washington's Kennedy Center, where one critic compared it favourably with *The Cherry Orchard*. He refused to take it to New York, saying that the play had 'too English a humour' for Broadway.

Then it was time for another major change of scene. After three successes in new plays by English authors, he turned again to Ibsen, which brought him at last back to the Old Vic, now the home of the National Theatre.

CHAPTER NINETEEN

1974–1975

BY THE time he was seventy Ralph had played nearly as many different roles on stage, but only one of them, Peer Gynt, was written by Ibsen. He had also played in *Brand* and *When We Dead Awaken* on the radio, and *Hedda Gabler* on television; those four parts had been spread over a period of twenty-five years. Now, within the space of only six years, he did three more, beginning with Dr Rank in Patrick Garland's film of *A Doll's House*. It had a starry cast – Anthony Hopkins as Torvald, Claire Bloom as Nora, Edith Evans as the Nurse, Denholm Elliott as Krogstad, and Anna Massey as Mrs Lindstrom. This was the second film Hopkins and Richardson had worked in together, and this time the younger man found him very preoccupied and remote: 'I only learned from Mu that he liked my work, apart from saying on one occasion, "You're awfully natural in this, you young chaps are awfully good in it."'

It was a different order of naturalism that Sir Anthony now associates with Sir Ralph: 'He had a mannered style, but it was so real, it was a true revelation of the human condition. Only a handful of actors could do that, and Richardson was one of them. His powerfully eccentric style reminded me sometimes of Wilfrid Lawson.'[1]

Patrick Garland was impressed by Ralph's detailed preparation, one aspect of which he only observed by accident.

I came back early from lunch-break one day to think about the next scene and look at the script, and came in very quietly at the back of the stage, to discover Ralph standing there all by himself in full make-up with his stick, looking at where the lights were positioned, and though they were dark he was checking where the key light was; which I thought was extraordinary, and very crafty, and I was very impressed with that.

Garland tried, and failed, to get Ralph to give some special charge to his last line to Torvald – 'Thanks for the cigar.' He met the same response as Olivier had in *Richard III* – 'Yes, I see' – but then at each take he delivered the line as he had before.

Ralph demonstrated the power he could turn on at will when they were all lunching one day at a restaurant where the waitresses wore an Edwardian uniform of long black skirt, white blouse and long white apron. The waitress serving the film company table was a very pretty girl in her early twenties, and Patrick Garland suddenly observed Ralph switch on the charm.

It was quite discernible, Claire Bloom noticed it just as much as I did, he was exuding that strange mixture he had of an extreme sensuousness and male gallantry, and there was something absolutely exquisite about it as he gave her his order, 'Oh, my dear young girl . . .', and she blushed to the roots of her hair as she sensed this enormous charm. It was very palpable, I can't forget it, it showed his powers.[2]

The emotional chemistry in the film is powerful, but it was released at the same time as another screen version of *A Doll's House*, starring Jane Fonda, so critical attention was divided and it never really attracted the audience it deserved.

Dr Sloper in *The Heiress*, with Peggy Ashcroft as his daughter Catherine, directed by John Gielgud, Haymarket, 1949. 'Every word spoken as if it were a note in music, resonant, reverberating, echoing down the corridors of interminable years of sorrow.' (Houston Rogers/Theatre Museum, V&A)

Above: David Preston in *Home at Seven*, with Campbell Singer as the Police Inspector, directed by Murray Macdonald, Wyndham's, 1950. 'Sir Ralph is the Wordsworth of our actors in that he sees poetry in the commonplace.' (Houston Rogers/Theatre Museum, V&A)

Below: Macbeth, with Margaret Leighton as Lady Macbeth, directed by John Gielgud, Stratford-upon-Avon Memorial Theatre, 1952. 'Richardson haunted the tragedy like a sleepwalker (an odd transference here) with a look of fixed astonishment.' (Angus McBean/Shakespeare Birthplace Trust)

Volpone, directed by George Devine, Stratford-upon-Avon Memorial Theatre, 1952. 'He looks like a corpse dressed up for a party.' (Angus McBean/Theatre Museum, V&A)

Sir Ralph and Lady Richardson opening the new theatre in Nairobi, Kenya, in 1952.

Opposite page: Timon of Athens, directed by Michael Benthall, Old Vic, 1956. 'All Shakespearean viciousness of phrase is transferred into a threnody, a lamentation.' (Angus McBean/Theatre Museum, V&A)

Victor Rhodes in *The Complaisant Lover*, with Phyllis Calvert as his wife, Mary, and Paul Scofield as her lover, Clive Root, directed by John Gielgud, Globe, 1959. 'Ralph was an actor of rhythm – he had a beat, a pulse inside him which dictated to him; and playing opposite him one had to learn to respect that rhythm.' (Angus McBean/Theatre Museum, V&A)

Opposite page: Jim Cherry in *Flowering Cherry*, directed by Frith Banbury, Haymarket, 1957. 'Those critics who hold that he excels in portraying the Average Man cannot, I feel, have met many Average Men.' (Angus McBean/Theatre Museum, V&A)

Sir Peter Teazle in *The School for Scandal*, with Anna Massey as Lady Teazle, directed by John Gielgud, Haymarket, 1962. 'It may well be said that Sir Ralph belies the text: my reply is that he transcends it.' (Angus McBean/Theatre Museum, V&A)

Dr Rance in *What the Butler Saw*, with Stanley Baxter and Coral Browne, directed by Robert Chetwyn, Queen's, 1969. 'It seemed as if the gallery wanted to jump on the stage and kill us all.' (Angus McBean/Theatre Museum, V&A)

Above: Shylock in *The Merchant of Venice*, with David King, directed by Glen Byam Shaw, Haymarket, 1967. 'His Shylock had an antique Jewishness.' (Houston Rogers/Theatre Museum, V&A)

Below: William in *You Never Can Tell*, with Celia Bannerman and James Hunter, directed by Glen Byam Shaw, Haymarket, 1966. 'While most actors play it as a waiter whose experience has made him a philosopher, he makes him a philosopher in grain, who has somehow found himself a waiter.' (Angus McBean/Theatre Museum, V&A)

Above: Doing conjuring tricks as Jack in *Home*, with John Gielgud as Harry, directed by Lindsay Anderson, Royal Court, 1970. 'Behind the perfect collaboration and masterly skill of their duets one senses a lifetime's friendship and trust as well as a lifetime's experience.' (caricature by Clive Francis)

Below: Hirst in *No Man's Land*, with John Gielgud as Spooner, directed by Peter Hall, National Theatre, 1975. 'These two great actors are the best double-act since Laurel and Hardy.' (Anthony Crickmay/Theatre Museum, V&A)

On his BMW motorbike in 1974. 'I don't like those full-face helmets, you can't see the floor when you're coming out of the garage.' (Hulton Deutsch)

Above: A relaxed moment with Laurence Olivier. (Mary Evans)

Below: 'José's sharp beak and sharper temper frightened everybody except his indulgent owner.' (Hulton Deutsch)

During a break in filming *Invitation to a Wedding* in 1983, entertaining the crew with the story of how he smuggled his parrot in a hatbox on to the flight from Madrid to Heathrow, drugged with a cocktail of brandy and zambuca. When it woke up and screeched the stewardess fetched the captain, whose remonstrations were cut short by Sir Ralph threatening to report him to the Chairman of British Airways, and demanding another slug of brandy to put José back to sleep. (Graham Attwood)

1, CHESTER TERRACE,
REGENT'S PARK,
N.W.1.

19 JUNE 83

Dear Laurie,

It was so kind of you to come to the play and to have with bottles of splendid port was heroic! Then I had a PRESS telegram on the night as well! Thank once again for cheering me up when you rang up and gave a sum up that as really for me as I would be very upset if Peter Hall were to mess with me as this really put on a play for me. I am funny we did not get the cross of Lindsay Anderson because I'd be an any cross to get an artist on the podium.

LOVE to you and
MARY
EVER   R

Letter showing his distinctive flowing calligraphy and columnar layout, which may have been determined by his tunnel-vision later in life. (Reproduced courtesy of Laurence Evans)

His last stage role – Don Alberto in
Inner Voices, directed by Mike Ockrent,
National Theatre, 1983. 'He conveys
totally a man unsure whether he is
dreaming or waking; and it is precisely
because he seems half-motored by
dreams, that his final condemnation of
base humanity carries such force.'
(Alastair Muir)

Very soon afterwards Patrick Garland interviewed Ralph for a BBC television documentary to mark his seventieth birthday, and pressed him on his working relationships. His eyes twinkled as he launched into the Richardson philosophy.

'I don't have a lot of time for living authors. Modern playwrights gave me a great deal of trouble, until I hit on a revelation, and everything's all right now. You see, when I'm doing a play by my old friend Bernard Shaw, or Jack Priestley, or Mr Ibsen, or indeed Mr Shakespeare, you don't have these fellows standing up every few minutes and telling you what to do, you don't have a peep out of them. All these modern authors, they're always there interfering and changing their minds and making you say things, I couldn't get on with that at all; until I suddenly thought to myself, 'As I have no trouble with dead authors, why do I have trouble with living ones? If I imagine they are dead too it should be all right', and so I consider them all like dead playwrights, and do you know, I've never had a peep out of them since.'

'You don't have a very high opinion of playwrights?'

'No, not much.'

'And directors?'

'Not them, either!'[3]

This may have been said with a smile, but his wariness of directors was something they all noticed, from the nervous and inexperienced up to the most confident and distinguished. Peter Hall was very aware of it. 'Ralph was very suspicious of directors; he believed, with some reason I think, that most of them were thinking more about their own preoccupations than the needs of the actor.'

Ibsen provided the bait with which Peter Hall lured Ralph into coming to the National Theatre, with the title-role in *John Gabriel Borkman*; and his acceptance reactivated the question that had been in many minds since the opening of the National Theatre at the Old Vic in 1963 – why had its first director, Laurence Olivier, not taken the opportunity to be reunited with his partner from those brilliant Old Vic seasons at the New Theatre?

Since neither of them would discuss the subject publicly, and deflected questions from any persistent journalist, the rest of the theatre world was left to speculate on whether Olivier had not invited him, or Richardson had turned him down. Did the former not wish to share the glory, or the latter not want to come back with less than equal status?

Peter Hall believes that the decision was Ralph's,

> that's the mystery – he was asked constantly, and Larry was livid that at the very beginning of my time at the National Ralph came, when Ralph had not been there with him. The fact that Ralph had become a very close friend of mine Larry couldn't bear. Richardson was always helping me, and on my side, and they were quite difficult times I think between Ralph and Larry. But the Ralph/Larry tensions go right back to the New in the Forties, and the fact that they never worked together again in the theatre was by Ralph's design.[4]

But, as so often in the Olivier–Richardson relationship, it was a little more complex than that. Olivier never offered his old partner anything that appealed to him, so the invitations were seen by Richardson as little more than a token gesture.

Not that it was exactly easy for Olivier's successor to gain the Richardson talents. His very first attempt to work with Ralph had got off on the wrong foot. In 1963 he tried to persuade him to come to the Royal Shakespeare Company and revive his Falstaff, and found that this was not the easiest of tasks perched on the pillion of the Norton riding round Hampstead Heath. When they reached a private road Ralph urged him to have a go on his own. 'So he put me on the Norton, and showed me how to do it, and I fell off it. I thought to myself then, "He'll never trust himself to a man who falls off his Norton." And he didn't come and play Falstaff, I was always trying.'

Peter Hall is nothing if not tenacious, however, and when he took over as Director of the National Theatre ten years later he immediately set out to woo the triumvirate of Gielgud, Ashcroft and Richardson, the last two of whom had never appeared there during Olivier's time. Ralph was excited by the prospect of playing Borkman, and asked for a meeting in June 1973 to discuss it, before he left for the Australian tour of *Lloyd George Knew My Father*.

In his published *Diaries* the director recorded:

> Ralph stamped up and down reading notes he had made on Borkman. He said it must be a whirlwind, a volcano, a typhoon – go straight through with no stop. Be cataclysmic. He also said he had had a chat with John and he thought all of them should get behind me at the National. It was, he said, an exciting idea that next year at the Old Vic I was going to, as he put it, stack up productions in the air, like aeroplanes awaiting a landing on the South Bank.[5]

But the runways were not ready in time for the landings as planned, because the new building was bedevilled by one construction delay after another. Ralph's first two plays at the National opened in the Old Vic, a stage he had not graced since his 1956 *Timon of Athens*.

The Peter Hall regime had got off to a shaky start in 1973, and he suffered attacks in public and in private by the press, politicians, and the Olivier loyalists who felt their hero had been shabbily treated over the succession. So a lot hung on Ralph's arrival and the success of his first appearance.

Peter Hall had previously directed all the great Richardson
contemporaries, but he was still a bit overwhelmed by this
first experience of Ralph.

> He shared with Edith Evans a capacity in rehearsal to create
> something so completely, from a standing-start, that it was
> almost frightening to watch it. It was completely real, and
> then he would come straight down out of it, and say, 'Oh no,
> no, no, I don't think that's very good, do you?' Whereas most
> actors when they rehearse, there's a sense of 'when I play this
> on-stage it will be more or less like this', with Edith and
> Ralph it wasn't, it was absolutely the thing itself, which I
> wouldn't say about Peggy or Larry. So it made rehearsing with
> him a very interesting experience, because since he never did
> anything false it was terribly difficult to refuse what he did,
> and you almost didn't like to interrupt. I remember having
> that feeling, thinking I can't stop this because he's not Ralph
> Richardson, he's Borkman.[6]

(In 1974 Ralph had revived his old practice of playing the
part first on the radio, so he was clear about his interpretation,
although it took him much longer to become as confident
about knowing the text.)

Peter Hall found that his function as a director became
more editorial – rather than trying to help the actor find the
interpretation and the performance, he was having to pick
and choose between the rich variety he was being offered,
saying, 'No, I don't want that, I love that but I don't want
it.'

Ralph saw *John Gabriel Borkman* as an ironic comedy, and
the comic seam he mined surprised those who only associated
the author with darkness and gloom. He also championed the
playwright against the charge that his plays were museum-
pieces with little modern relevance.

Every year Ibsen is getting more and more appreciated in this country. There is still a long way to go. These plays set in a foreign country and seemingly to be about local events are, in fact, very universal and about very universal feelings. This is becoming more and more recognized. They are semi-poetic plays too.

The inner depths and the poetry were given their full weight by his partners. His two leading ladies were Wendy Hiller as the embittered Mrs Borkman, and Peggy Ashcroft as her sister Ella Rentheim, thrown over by Borkman years before to make a marriage that would further his career. They were both trusted colleagues and friends from earlier success-es, and Wendy Hiller was happier to be creating a relationship on-stage from the beginning, rather than stepping into someone else's shoes as she had done in *Flowering Cherry*. 'We started as equals this time, and as he found Ibsen more difficult to learn than I did, I could help him, hearing his lines, and this brought us much closer together in friendship.'[7]

Ralph's difficulty with learning Borkman's lines began to worry both actresses, but neither of them relished the idea of telling him, so they approached Alan Webb, who was playing Borkman's elderly clerk, Foldal, and who was a contemporary of Ralph's. They told him he must have a word with him, that he really had to go away and learn it properly. Alan Webb did not quite know how to broach the subject either, but eventually plucked up the courage to say, 'Isn't it a funny thing, Ralph, when you get to our age I find that sometimes I forget my lines?'

'Oh, if I worried about that, cocky, I'd never get on the stage.' So that was the end of that conversation.

But he was grateful to those who helped him through the most difficult passages. Wendy Hiller was fortunately able to prompt him unobtrusively, and at a party during the run Ralph came up to her and raised his glass: 'To the best prompter in the business.'

Peter Hall sometimes found himself in the same position as Frith Banbury two decades earlier, with Ralph not wanting to be given lots of notes.

> I still have a vision of him, after we'd just had a run-through of *Borkman* on the stage of Her Majesty's, with all the actors sitting there, Wendy, Peggy, Alan Webb, and Ralph was in his raincoat with his white plastic motor-cycle helmet on his lap. It was clear he was ready to go, he didn't want to hear a lot from me.

The final stages of rehearsals were plagued with problems. Both Wendy Hiller and Alan Webb were taken ill, the latter so seriously that he had to be replaced by Harry Lomax. In their absence Peggy and Ralph rehearsed their scene sitting side by side on the sofa. She complained it was much too high for her to work on; her long-legged partner said it was just right. Peter Hall tried to defuse the situation by saying they would experiment with foam rubber to reach a happy compromise. Afterwards, as the actor left, he winked from under his motor-cycle helmet and whispered, 'Don't touch that bloody sofa.' Peggy later apologized to Peter Hall for adding to his problems at a difficult time.

The previews were uneven, and Ralph feared he was not getting a grip on the part. He changed his make-up for the last preview, sharpened the shape of his nose and added a moustache and two great sweeps of hair so that he reminded his director of 'a mad Toscanini'. When he went round to congratulate him on his courage just before the opening, Ralph told him that acting on any first night was going out on a tightrope, one was quite inclined to fall off, so one might as well do a pirouette into the bargain.

Far from falling off the tightrope, the following night was a triumph. Michael Billington told his *Guardian* readers that in seamlessly marrying the symbolism and realism of the play Peter Hall had pulled off the impossible. In reviewing a fine cast he reserved his highest praise for the central performance:

> He presents us with a man in love with his own image of himself: a Napoleon of commerce who greets visitors with a hand symbolically inside his greatcoat, an ageing Peer Gynt for whom other people are simply things in his dream. When his son bids him farewell for ever, he acknowledges his departure with an airy wave of the hand that makes you wonder if he ever apprehended his existence; yet Richardson is earthy enough to produce an astonishingly realistic cry of pain when death finally claims him. Richardson's Borkman is both moral monster and self-made superman; and the performance is full of a strange, unearthly music that belongs to this actor alone.

Irving Wardle in *The Times* also harked back to the *Peer Gynt* which had converted him to Ibsen thirty years before, and exulted that this Borkman 'recaptures the same exhilaration and ferocious joy that seized the New Theatre public in 1944. And again, its protagonist is played by Richardson.' He traced admiringly the development of the character from his first appearance 'as a beautifully manicured old dandy, sitting and keeping time with his feet to little Frida's *Danse Macabre*', through his gradual return to the world in the different rooms of the house and finally out into the snow, 'and Richardson performs this with steadily increasing madness, entering each fresh environment like a ghost amazed to be among the living, his voice searching for a conversation register while his eyes become fixed in a crazed gleam'.

The playing of the final scene up on the mountain inspired B. A. Young in the *Financial Times* to argue that Dame Peggy and Sir Ralph showed acting not often seen, 'because it is in a style that has gone out of fashion, speech that is larger than life, characters that are first and foremost characters in a drama'.

John Peter in the *Times Educational Supplement* believed the production to be historic:

> It gets an outstanding performance from Ralph Richardson which no one with the slightest interest in great acting can afford to miss . . . The terrible whisper of his final speech and his wolf-like cry of death bring to a spine-chilling end one of those truly great acting performances which can make theatre-going a major experience of life and dramatic criticism a privilege.

John Gielgud was particularly moved at the end by the strange death-rattle Ralph created. 'I shall never forget the noise he made when Borkman died, as if a bird had flown out of his heart.'

Harold Hobson tried to explain in the *Sunday Times* why 'Sir Ralph is in my opinion the most extraordinary actor in the world. Other great players have a wide range, but he is the only one who can be at both ends of the range at the same time.'

Ralph was not so easily convinced himself, and never felt that he had been wholly successful in carrying it off. This streak of self-criticism applied to everything he did, so Peter Hall believes.

> I don't think Ralph was ever happy with anything he ever did. His whole philosophy of acting was that you tried to do

it each night, you went and carved it each night again, and you got some of it a bit better, and some of it a bit worse, and on the whole it improved, but you never got it right.

But if Ralph had his reservations, his director had none: 'The fright I have when I see great acting is akin to the fear one has of madness. It's the person being possessed, becoming something else. Ralph could switch into that, and his truth could make other actors seem artificial – he was a great, great actor.'[8]

Each night the audience applauded a performance which ended on the heights, both dramatically and physically, as the curtain fell on Borkman and Ella at the top of the mountain. The problem for the actors was how to descend quickly enough to join the others for the curtain call. The solution was simple, and one treasured by the rest of the cast as each night they watched Sir Ralph and Dame Peggy tobogganing down the mountain on their bottoms like a couple of schoolchildren before quickly dusting themselves down to take a measured and dignified bow. (Ralph squirrelled away all experiences for some future dramatic use, and pulled this one out of his mental filing-system for a memorable screen-image in his last film.)

John Gabriel Borkman stayed in the National Theatre repertoire for two years, at last making its debut in the new Lyttelton Theatre on 11 March 1976. But before then he notched up another great National success, re-forming his double-act with John Gielgud in a new play by Harold Pinter – *No Man's Land*.

CHAPTER TWENTY
No Man's Land – 1975–1977

HAROLD PINTER wrote *No Man's Land* with no particular actors in mind to play the parts, and sent the script off to Peter Hall at the National Theatre. They approached John Gielgud first, who to their surprise opted not to play 'the posh part' of Hirst, but the man he picks up on Hampstead Heath, the seedy, down-at-heel Spooner. When the three of them talked about the casting of Hirst they discussed various actors, until suddenly Gielgud said, 'Have you thought of Ralph?' They had indeed thought of him, but Pinter said, 'I've heard he's having a little difficulty with his lines.'

'Oh no, no, I'm sure that's absolutely no problem. The point is, I feel that I do need an actor playing opposite me who has, in these parts, even more authority than I do. There's only one actor I know who has, and that is Ralph.'[1]

That settled it, and the script was sent off to Richardson. This conversation took place during the difficult run-up to the opening of *John Gabriel Borkman*. After the first night of that play Peter Hall threw a small supper party at his flat in the Barbican, and brought author and actor together for the first time. They hit it off from the moment they met and shook hands, and matched greetings.

'I am holding a poet in my hand.'

'I am holding a great actor in mine.'[2]

Their conversation a little later impressed the author even more; he was aware of what an arduous role Borkman was, and had thought it must have taken all of Ralph's attention up until the opening.

> I was alone with him at a certain point, and he stood against the door and quoted from Hirst in *No Man's Land*, which he remembered in a rather original way, and to a certain extent he continued like that. He never asked me questions about it. He continued to address me as 'the poet'. 'Ah, here comes the poet.' I think he rather saw the play in those terms.[3]

(Happily there was no occasion to drop the sobriquet 'poet' later, as there had been with Graham Greene.) If he saw the play in poetic terms, his director thought he was well-equipped to find that quality and bring it out. 'He brought so much to a line that sometimes he made it resonate and become poetry, in the sense that it became ambiguous and rich, whereas in another actor's mouth it wasn't.'

The ambiguities in a Pinter text are not just in the words, enigmatic and mysterious though they often are to both actors and audiences, but also in the pauses that are his trademark. The author has been known to complain that some actors have only played two dots instead of the three he wrote, and this was a precision that was new even to these two great professional performers.

Peter Hall understood this, and took his time in rehearsals.

> I'm absolutely a stickler for saying what the man wrote, and when we did *No Man's Land* the pauses induced terror in John and Ralph, because they both belonged to a theatre where if there was a silence someone had dried, and it was terribly difficult to get them to understand what a Pinter pause was about – that you went on acting through it, and it wasn't just

a great big hole. They both panicked, but I rehearsed *No Man's Land* for a fortnight, and then sent them away for a fortnight to learn lines before we went on, which was one of the luxuries that the National Theatre could provide.[4]

Ralph approved of this sensible approach. 'I think Peter Hall is a very excellent new kind of director, he doesn't fiddle about.' During the run of the play he expanded on what he wanted from the director.

It is what you want from the conductor, the beat. But it must be one's own instincts, it's no good anybody showing you. If you're painting a picture it's no good someone leaning over your shoulder to say, 'I think that cow's a bit too red.' I'd say, 'Go away, shut up, I haven't finished the picture, it won't show up against that green.' And that's just what some irritating directors do. These details should be left to the cook. Having engaged a cook you don't want to come into the kitchen when he's stirring up the soup, and say, 'If I were you I'd put in a little more pepper', he'd throw you out of the kitchen. I don't say the chef shouldn't be told the menu that should be designed for the feast, but don't bumble in the kitchen as some directors do, thank goodness not Johnny, and thank God not Mr Peter Hall.[5]

The physical demands made of Hirst were taken in his stride. He had to do several falls on-stage, and this prospect worried his director, but his fears for the safety of his seventy-two-year-old star were put at rest when they came to the first one in rehearsal. Ralph just said, 'Now, this fall, what would you like? I could do this,' and he flung himself forward, 'Or this,' and hurled himself sideways, 'Or this,' and threw himself backwards. They then worked out a slightly different effect for each of the falls, and as a precaution during the run very thick foam rubber was put under the carpet where he fell, but Ralph cheerfully rehearsed without such cushioning.

He dropped with such skill that it fooled everyone. At the very first preview the entire audience froze when he collapsed the first time, and there was an audible gasp as they all feared momentarily that it might be the actor rather than the character who had fallen down. After the reviews came out, and commented on the brilliance with which he fell, it still created a shock-effect in audiences. Even another practised physical actor like Nicky Henson says, 'I was convinced I was there the night Ralph died, it was one of the best stage falls I've ever seen, everybody gave such an intake of breath.'[6]

It also deceived one of the actors on-stage with Richardson. When the play went to America later Michael Kitchen said to the author,

> 'I'm terribly worried about Ralph's falls, I can't believe he's not going to do himself serious damage.' I remember saying to him, 'That's the *last* thing you need to worry about. You worry about yourself.' Because Ralph could fall till kingdom come, it was very graceful, and he didn't need any kind of education about how to fall. When I played the part twenty years later I had to deal with these falls myself, and after a couple of weeks of falling my elbow was really quite inflamed, until after experiment I finally managed to find a way of falling without hurting either of the two things you had to look out for – the elbow or the knees.[7]

Harold Pinter was not the only other person to find it much more difficult than Ralph made it look. When Norman Claridge, Ralph's understudy, had to stand in for him at one rehearsal, he broke his glasses, broke his deaf-aid, and cut his head open.

While everyone else was so impressed by Ralph's collapses,

unaware that he had found the trick sixty years earlier on
Shoreham beach, the actor himself got a little impatient with
what he saw as undue attention being given to what was just
a bit of routine business for him. He complained to Peter
Hall, 'Well, they come round, you know, and they say, "Oh,
those falls," or "Oh, those blue socks," they never say, "Oh,
Hirst!"'

The director knew that for him the words and the speech-
rhythms were all-important.

> He was one of the few English actors of our time who
> pronounced every single letter – Ralph didn't say 'Where?',
> he said 'W-h-ere?', there's an 'h' in it. He was shaky on his
> words in the early days of the run, but not through the run
> once he'd got hold of them. It wasn't that he didn't know
> them, I think the nerve-level as you get older becomes more
> difficult to control. In rehearsal he'd say, 'Now what are you
> doing, de-dum, de-dum, de-dum, de-da,' and the other actor
> would look at him in horror, but the rhythm was right.[8]

That was nothing to his own horror at any late changes
suddenly introduced by anyone else. Harold Pinter had been
unable to attend as many of the rehearsals as he usually did,
so he came to the first full dress-rehearsal with keen anticipation. The director and the designer, John Bury, were the
only two others present in the auditorium. It was an experience
he would not have missed for anything.

> In the middle of the first Act, while Ralph was pouring a
> drink, with his back to the audience, John suddenly sat on a
> stool by the bar, which he'd never done before, and Ralph
> stopped dead, with the bottle in his hand, paralysed, turned
> very slowly and looked at him, and said, 'Are you going to do
> that, Johnny?'

John jumped up as if stung by a wasp, and said, 'No, no, no, I don't know what came over me, I've no idea why I sat down then, I know I shouldn't really do that at all, I should be miles away, I should be over there.'

Ralph ignored all these protestations, and turned to the auditorium, which was dark, and said, 'Pete.' [A diminutive of his name Hall hates, which he only ever permitted to Peggy Ashcroft and Ralph Richardson.]

'Yes, Ralph.'

'Didn't rehearse it this way, did we?'

'No, Ralph, I think John was just improvising at that moment.'

And Ralph turned to John and said, 'Oh, is that what you were doing, Johnny?'

'I think I should really play this from far left, as far left as possible.' John went to the curtains and nearly disappeared out of the window, and Ralph suddenly turned and said, 'Shall we go on?'

And I then knew exactly what John Gielgud was talking about, over this question of authority. Ralph had absolute authority. It was an extraordinary few minutes on the stage. It was a very odd thing for John to do, because he is equally scrupulous and punctilious, but it was just one of those things, he probably felt tired for a moment or two. But Ralph was quite rigorous and precise about every detail, of where the glass was and so on.[9]

At the first preview he was not happy with his own performance. 'I knew where the ducks were but I fired at them either too late or too early. Took off the occasional tail-feather, but brought none down.'

His marksmanship was much more accurate on the opening night, and the director thought it was the best all-round performance yet. At the party afterwards Gielgud told the playwright that he now thought Pinter had to be played like Congreve or Wilde, with a consciousness of the audience, and a manipulation of it which was precisely the same as for high classical comedy. In the beginning he had thought it would be like playing Chekhov, where the actors must ignore the audience, but it was not like that at all.

Irving Wardle in *The Times* found echoes of both T. S. Eliot and Samuel Beckett, although it was 'palpably the work of our best living playwright in its command of language and its power to erect a coherent structure in a twilight zone of confusion and dismay. And it receives a production of burnished precision from Peter Hall.' He welcomed the 'reunion for the masterly partnership last seen at work in David Storey's *Home*. With that play, you could give full attention to the music of Gielgud's viola blending with Richardson's bassoon. In this case, the game is too intricate for that kind of relaxation.'

In the *Guardian* Michael Billington sought to capture the essence of these two portrayals:

> Ralph Richardson's Hirst, contrasting a peppery, ramrod-backed power with chilling geriatric collapses and exits on all-fours, has precisely that other-worldliness that makes this actor such a magician; and John Gielgud's Spooner, with the creased, tobacco-breathed quality of the kind of Forties Bohemian you meet in BBC pubs, is superbly sly, mellifluous and ingratiating.

Frank Marcus made another comparison in the *Sunday Telegraph*, asserting that Spooner

> must be numbered among Sir John Gielgud's most sublime comic creations ... Sir Ralph, knocking back whisky incessantly, is a rock-like presence with a robot walk, military

bearing but, like the Captain in *Dance of Death*, prone to sudden falls. These two great actors are the best double-act since Laurel and Hardy.

The demand for tickets was too great to keep the production sharing the repertoire with other plays at the Old Vic, so it transferred for a long run at Wyndham's Theatre. Ralph welcomed the prospect of developing his understanding of it.

It takes off a good deal of the tedium if you are playing in several layers of time at once. Acting can get very tiring if you've solved the crossword puzzle. If you've got everything right you go on repeating it. I've never given myself a good notice for a performance in this play. This is not very satisfactory to me but in another respect it makes it more exciting.

John Gielgud was amused by his old friend's occasional vagueness, as when he congratulated a stagehand instead of the understudy one night, but not convinced that it was always entirely genuine. 'He appeared to be very dreamy, and yet he was extremely watchful and observant and not much got past him. But he rather enjoyed pretending to be very vague and not having to greet people who bored him, or he didn't particularly want to spend time with.'[10]

The prospect of seeing what Peter Hall called 'the Old Lions' playing together was so appealing that the play ran well into 1976, and in November went to the Longacre Theater in New York. Broadway was not quite sure what to make of the play, but it recognized great acting when it saw it, and the critics were ecstatic. Peter Hall flew over for the opening, and was cheered to be told by Ralph that he wanted to stay with the National Theatre for the rest of his life.

Harold Pinter was directing something else in New York

at the time, so with the agreement of the director and the cast he kept a watchful eye on the production. This was not just a formality.

> I actually gave Ralph a note, I took my life in my hands, because he had changed his performance. He'd become extremely aggressive in the first Act, so that he was tending to bark everything at Spooner. I asked to have a drink with him, and said, 'Ralph, I think you've lost something, first of all you've become very, very aggressive, secondly by doing so what you're tending to lose is the privacy, and the secrecy of the man, the inaccessibility of him. Spooner keeps trying to get at him and finds it very difficult, because he won't give anything away. I think you're being too defensive, rather than that withdrawnness you actually had, those recesses of secrecy which you had.' He said, after a long pause, 'Take your point,' and slapped his knee. And did, he acted on it. He listened very carefully, but he clearly wasn't used to it.

That was nothing to the astonishment he produced in the author when he was arranging a big charity evening at the Duke of York's Theatre on behalf of International PEN, of which Harold Pinter was a member. Together with Christopher Hampton and Ronald Harwood, he had edited a selection of writings to be read by

> a wonderful array of actors, including John Gielgud, and I asked Ralph if he'd like to take part in it. He said, 'What is it, old chap?'
> 'It's to do with Writers in Prison, there are a lot of writers in prison, and the money goes to the fund for their families.'
> He said, 'Oh, I don't know about that.'
> 'Why, don't you like the idea?'
> 'Got to have a bit of law and order, old boy.'

Which left me totally open-mouthed, so I just changed the subject. It was one of the most extraordinary things, because it was so totally unexpected – he seemed to be saying that was exactly where writers belong.[11]

At last *No Man's Land* reached the theatre for which it had originally been intended. In January 1977 the Old Lions padded on to the stage of the Lyttelton Theatre, where their double-act had lost none of its power to entrance an audience. The newly appointed chairman of the Arts Council's Drama Panel, Richard Hoggart, saw *No Man's Land* there for the first time, and was particularly struck with their rapport:

They seemed neither to be playing *against* nor *to* each other, but *with* each other – in concert with each other. They constantly modulated their voices, their timbres, so as to match, and contrast, and set off one another. So there was a succession of brilliant vocal and verbal passages, like two pianos or two violins. They knew each other's characteristic pauses, and respected them so that they could have their full effect; as they also did with their characteristic lifts and drops. They never milked a line to the other's disadvantage; clearly they enjoyed each other's acting and brought out each other's special styles and stances. The language of the play was of course very interesting. The way it was *bodied out* was just as interesting – a joint virtuoso performance of the highest quality.[12]

Not everyone was quite so sensitive to the heights they could reach. When it came to making the Granada TV recording of the play, the television director was so overwhelmed by what he saw on the monitors at the first take that he took some convincing by Peter Hall that the actors could play it even better than that, if he would take the time to do a second take. In fact the whole recording would have benefited by having more time. Some of the camerawork was clumsy, there was an occasional very obvious boom-shadow, and the author was not alone in thinking that somehow 'it became artificial on the screen; but at least it was a record'.

There had been a lot of discussion about how much of the strong language would be permitted on television. Harold Pinter dug in his heels and said he would not cut any of it. The Granada management supported him, and said they would fight it through the Independent Broadcasting Authority. Only Ralph expressed a quiet doubt about the wisdom of this stand, muttering to Peter Hall: 'What about the American sales? Is it worth losing all that lovely money for the sake of saying fuck?'[13]

No Man's Land had been a major part of Ralph's life for two and a half years by the time he committed his performance to videotape in early 1978. There had been a gap between ending the run at Wyndham's and opening in America in late 1976, during which there was a revealing interchange between Ralph and the man who had become his agent in 1970, Laurence Evans.

When they renewed their professional relationship, a quarter of a century after their days together with the Old Vic at the New Theatre, Ralph invited Evans to lunch at the Athenaeum and said frankly,

> Now, I want to explain my financial situation, because I've spent the morning with my accountants, and they've said to me, 'You don't have to change your lifestyle, you don't have to sell the Bentleys, Mu can go on buying her clothes, you have nothing at all to worry about for the next three weeks.' So it was putting me on the spot.

Since then Ralph had never stopped working. In the theatre he had done *Home, West of Suez, Lloyd George Knew My*

Father, and *No Man's Land*; he had appeared in nine films, many of them in small parts, but two of them – *Eagle in a Cage* and *A Doll's House* – were substantial or leading roles; and three television plays – *Hassan*, *She Stoops to Conquer*, and *Home*.

So on the face of it, it was quite understandable that at the end of the six-month run of *No Man's Land* at Wyndham's, Ralph should say to his agent, 'Now, look, when the play closes Saturday night, Mu and I are going round the world for three months, and you can say NO to everybody, not available, won't be working for at least six months, you needn't even tell me, just say No.'

'Are you sure, Ralph?'

'Yes, Mu and I are going round the world for three months, I don't want any interruptions, I don't want to hear from you.'

The play closed on Saturday night and on Sunday the Richardsons went to Brighton and stayed at the Royal Crescent Hotel, their regular home when visiting or playing in that town. On Tuesday morning Laurence Evans was telephoned by Ralph, who said in an indignant voice, 'Look, do you realize I'm out of work?'[14] The round-the-world trip was never mentioned again; after a week's break at the Royal Crescent they returned to London, and Ralph took the next job.

For Harold Pinter the rewards of having Sir Ralph and Sir John create Hirst and Spooner were as thrilling as for David Storey when they breathed life into Jack and Harry in *Home* – with exactly the same penalty.

> While it was one of the richest things that ever happened in my career – that production and those performances – it also did something else. It frightened the life out of every other actor in the world, so that the play wasn't done here again for ages. People just wouldn't touch it, because after Richardson

and Gielgud set such an extraordinary standard of performance, what could you do? In 1990 I asked Michael Gambon to
play Hirst; we'd worked together a number of times, and I
thought he'd make a wonderful Hirst, and he thought about
it and said, 'I can't do it, I simply can't do it, the memory of
Ralph is much too strong. You'll have to wait another twenty
years.' He admired Ralph so much that it rendered him unable
to play the part. The same thing applied in America, until
Christopher Plummer and Jason Robards revived it in 1994.

Peter Copley had much the same experience when he
played Hirst at Leicester some years later. 'I just couldn't get
the image of Ralph out of my mind, sitting so big and four-
square in the chair. I suddenly thought to myself, "Why am I
sitting here like this, trying to look big?"'[15]

In the end, the only way Harold Pinter could get his play
revived in London in 1994 was to play Hirst himself (with
Paul Eddington as Spooner, thus completing his double of
both the original Gielgud parts within twelve months). Pinter
tried hard to push the memory of how Ralph had played it
from his mind, very conscious that it would be fatal to attempt
an imitation, but he admits to repeating one of his tricks.

I copied one thing from him, which I thought couldn't be
bettered, which was the opening of the whole play. As the
lights went up he was pouring a drink, and I clunked the
glass with the bottle, which shut the audience up before they
knew where they were. 'As it is?' comes the line, and he
always used to do that, and it's a great opening.

Ralph's next opening was also scheduled to be at the
National Theatre, in another William Douglas-Home play,
The Kingfisher, but now some fairly bitter theatrical politics
forced him to choose between the play and the institution.

CHAPTER TWENTY-ONE
1977–1978

THE LONG and happy run of *Lloyd George Knew My Father*
had encouraged Ralph to commission a new play from the
author. William Douglas-Home came up with *The Kingfisher*,
and Peter Hall was keen to stage it at the National Theatre
for a brief run there before transferring it to the West End.
But the commercial managements had begun to jib at having
their natural fare poached from them by the subsidized sector,
and then competing with them on their home ground. The
press picked up this theme and questioned whether the
National's subsidy should be used to mount try-outs for
Shaftesbury Avenue, so that West End royalties could then be
pocketed by the directors under contract to the National.

The fact that in this case the person involved was likely to
be the Director himself, Peter Hall, made the latter feel it was
not worth laying himself open to even more critical fire. He
had already endured more than most men in his position from
his political paymasters, union militants and some newspapers,
on top of all the problems he was experiencing in his attempts
to get the new building open and functioning. So he relinquished his option on *The Kingfisher* and, as expected, there
was little difficulty in finding a theatre – the Lyric – or the
right people to put it on. Ralph asked Lindsay Anderson to
direct it, and arranged lunch at Marcel's in Sloane Street to

introduce him to the author. Anderson had recently directed *The Cherry Orchard* at Chichester with Celia Johnson, and all three men thought she would be perfect for this play. She was not initially enthusiastic, but succumbed to Ralph's persuasiveness.

The plot was a simple one, as so often with this author, and its dynamics lay in the tensions, spoken and unspoken, between the characters. After her husband's funeral Evelyn calls on an old love, Cecil, now a best-selling novelist, who had proposed to her many years before, when she had turned him down. Her visit reawakens his feelings for her and he seizes the chance to repeat his offer of marriage, to the annoyance and apprehension of his long-serving and devoted manservant, played by Alan Webb.

The director had looked forward to the experience of working with three such old pros, but it was not quite what he expected. 'The play went really very well, and effortlessly; I think there could have been a little bit more effort about it, but it was enjoyable.'[1] By 'effort' he meant being open to suggestion, but he found to his surprise that this time both the elderly lovers were unresponsive to his direction. Backstage at a preview he grumbled to the lighting director Joe Davis: 'They've got me licked.'

Ralph surprised another distinguished director on the pre-London tour – Richard Eyre, then in charge at Nottingham.

> I went round before the first night to welcome him and say how honoured I was he was playing at the Nottingham Playhouse. I knocked on the dressing-room door and he called, 'Come in.' I was rather taken aback to see him with a stick of lake in his hand, putting it under his eyes, giving himself lines (as young actors have to do). He must have observed my surprised look, because he waved the stick of Leichner at me and explained – 'Aah, I'm playing an old character, you see.'[2]

The self-confidence of these three old-stagers was severely tested on the opening night in London. Half an hour before curtain-up parts of the West End were blacked out by a fire in a power-house, including the end of Shaftesbury Avenue where the Lyric Theatre stood. Some of the audience stayed jammed in the dim foyer as the May evening was darkened by teeming rain, the rest sought temporary refuge in the nearby pubs. Celia Johnson sat calmly playing patience in her dressing-room, while Ralph read a book by candle-light. The blackout lasted a couple of hours, and the curtain did not rise until nine o'clock.

When it finally did, the audience felt its long wait was worth it, as *The Times* critic recognized: 'The play is so much a celebration of the actors, that what happens hardly seems to be the matter of the play.'

Jeremy Kingston in the *Financial Times* admired the playing, from 'Celia Johnson, roguishly revealing the details of a past love and becoming bewitchingly drunk on crème de menthe', and from Alan Webb: '"The barometer seems set fair," he remarks in a voice of deepest gloom when the septuagenarian courtship is going well.' But he hinted at the fragility of the piece when he turned to the third member of the cast.

Sir Cecil is a little interested in what his Evelyn has done this past half-century, but not if it interferes with the schedule for finishing his next chapter. She is the missing section of the book of his life, and this artificial attitude would make him a fatally unreal old buffer if Ralph Richardson lost his grip for a moment on the winning performance he gives.

(Ralph was perfectly aware of what he was handling – a couple of years later when Michael Denison and Dulcie Gray told him they were going to do the play, he responded, 'Ah, gossamer on a tightrope.')

The *Telegraph* reviewer's pleasure had a sting in the tail for the author:

> At curtain-call, Home's evening of civilized banter leaves us pondering . . . whether dreams can ever be brought to reality, whether love is one thing and marriage quite another . . . and whether we shall ever see these peerless artists in more rewarding roles.

Michael Billington also attacked the play in the *Guardian*, before going on to say,

> the acting, however, beguiles. Richardson, whether doing that famous feathery spring across the stage, letting his hands play over his loved one's head as if about to produce a rabbit from it, or screwing a glass into someone's hands like Humphrey Bogart, is his irresistibly magnetic self.

His comic effects were both inspired and rooted in his interpretation. Simon Cadell was struck by the way

> he opened his jacket and looked at the lining one side, then opened the other side as if to check it was the same patterned lining, which of course it was, but it was the most arresting piece of business as a revelation of the character's thinking.[3]

The production could have run much longer than it did, but after six months Celia Johnson decided she did not want to extend her contract, and Ralph refused to do it with anybody else. The projected tour to New York collapsed because Lindsay Anderson could find no leading lady acceptable to Ralph.

So Ralph returned to the National Theatre, which everyone now hoped was at last beginning to emerge from the deeply troubled years of getting the new building open. Ralph had been totally supportive through that difficult time, and Peter Hall was very touched when he telephoned him the morning his knighthood was announced, in 1977: 'Congratulations, after what you've been through they should have made you a Viscount!'

Earlier in his career Ralph had entrusted himself to Sir Barry Jackson and then to Binkie Beaumont. Now he said he wanted to put himself in the hands of Sir Peter Hall. 'He did say to me, "I'm an old horse put out to pasture, and I'm here, jolly good, anything you want, what do you want me to do?" But that was a bit of an act, I think.'⁴

The first thing they settled on was Firs in *The Cherry Orchard*, which started rehearsals at the beginning of December 1977. When Peter Hall asked the actors to talk about their characters and how they should look, Ralph said, 'Well, I've been watching these old buggers recently, I think I'd like something in the shoulders to make me look a bit older' (his conviction that he had to make up to look old was still as strong as in *The Kingfisher*).

Nicky Henson was playing Yepikhodov, and was very nervous at the prospect of acting with his hero. He had met him as a small boy, when he had been taken to Smallie's birthday parties every year because his father, Leslie Henson, was an old friend of Ralph's. Now he was aware of Sir Ralph sitting on the edge of his seat watching him and scowling a lot, and he thought, 'Oh God, he's thinking, there's Leslie's son, he's rubbish, and he can't do it.' Good directors are acutely sensitive to actors' feelings, and Peter Hall observed his reaction, came over and said quietly, 'He's not scowling, he's concentrating, he's just seeing if you're doing anything that's of use to him.'⁵

When they reached the end of the play Ralph walked through his final scene, not acting it but doing a running commentary on it, rather as he had, to Basil Dearden's frustration, when filming *Khartoum*, but this time his director was entranced.

> Now I come through the door in my slippers. Good heavens, there's nobody there, they've all gone. So I go off to the window and look out. Can't see anything. So I go over to the sofa feeling very tired now, sit down, drop my stick, too tired to take it up. So I lie back, want to put my legs up, but I can't, I'm too tired. Then I die . . .

Ben Kingsley, who was playing Trofimov, watched him lie there for what seemed 'a very long time. Then he suddenly sat up and asked, "Will that be OK?"'

It was Ralph's seventy-fifth birthday during the early rehearsals, and Peter Hall arranged to have a birthday cake and champagne brought in. The entire cast gathered in a circle around Ralph to sing 'Happy Birthday'. Ben Kingsley squirms with embarrassment whenever he is on the receiving end of this song, but he was struck by the way in which Ralph stood in the centre of the circle and slowly rotated, looking each singer straight in the eye, one by one.

Kingsley, and others in the cast, felt they were in touch with a great acting tradition. In the hope that some of it might rub off, Trofimov and Varya (Susan Fleetwood) used to stand on either side of Firs in the wings, each stroking a shoulder. Ralph asked them, 'What are you doing that for?'

'For luck, Sir Ralph.'[6]

Dorothy Tutin played Ranevskaya, who shares many of Firs's scenes, and her enjoyment at playing opposite him was tinged with just a little apprehension.

> He had a slightly unstable way of playing the part, because Firs talks and chunters to himself, and Ralph talking to himself was just a delight, he loved all that. But you weren't

absolutely certain of the moment when he was going to come out with the line, which of course made everyone on the stage absolutely riveted to him, and made the audience absolutely riveted too.

There were two examples in this production of his insight into the other performances, and his diffidence about offering it to the actors concerned, that made both of them wish he had spoken earlier. The first involved Nicky Henson who, a little way into the run, stopped getting a big laugh and occasional round of applause on one of his lines. He tried to forget there had ever been a laugh there, and just played the scene.

I was walking down one of those numerous passages at the National, and Sir Ralph passed me and said, without looking at me, 'You're leaving the "d" off the word "and".' I'd never said anything to him, but he could see I was worried. I went into my dressing-room, opened my script, and there was no word 'and' in that sentence. So I checked back through it, and two speeches earlier there was an 'and' in there, and he was right, I'd been leaving the 'd' off that 'and' two speeches earlier which fed that laugh. I went on the next night, pronounced the 'd' on that 'and', got the laugh, got the round of applause, and as I turned there was Sir Ralph just turning his back. Obviously it had worried him.[7]

Dorothy Tutin's revelation came after the final performance, when she went to Ralph's dressing-room to say goodbye to him.

He poured me out the most enormous gin in a tumbler, mainly gin and a tiny dash of water, and we sat down and chatted, and he was terribly sweet. Suddenly he took hold of my hand – he had very beautiful skin, his hands were so soft – and he stroked my hand and said, 'You know, I thought you were rather good, but you missed something because, you see, she was absolutely rotten to the core.' It made my hair stand on end, and I wasn't able to speak for a while, because it was totally chilling. If anybody had told me that before I started to play Ranevskaya I know I would have got it right, because that's the kind of remark that when it's made to you everything turns around inside. I couldn't bear it that it happened after a whole tumblerful of gin, when I couldn't do anything with it now; I never got the chance to play it again.[8]

She was not the only one chagrined to feel their failure in *The Cherry Orchard*. In addition to Richardson, Tutin, Kingsley and Fleetwood, the Company also included Albert Finney as Lopakhin, Robert Stephens as Gaev, Judi Bowker as Anya and Helen Ryan as Charlotta – what their director called 'a completely staggering cast'. But as early as 3 January Peter Hall was beginning to worry that his production was destined for the wrong auditorium. After it opened he was convinced of it.

It was one of the best things I've ever done in the rehearsal room, it was magic, but when we got it into the Olivier it completely disappeared; I hadn't done a production for the Olivier, I'd done a little jewel, which would have been wonderful in the Cottesloe. It was dreadful, everything got lost, it simply disappeared. That was my fault.[9]

The critical reaction was mixed, with the overnight reviews in the daily papers being generally kinder than the more considered notices in the Sundays. Bernard Levin and Robert Cushman slammed the production, although Frank Marcus acclaimed it as a triumph. Some thought casting Richardson as Firs unbalanced the production; Michael Billington had feared in advance that he 'might be almost too mesmerically eccentric', but then acquitted him of any scene-stealing and admired his perfectly judged impression of 'age in unregarded corners thrown'.

Irving Wardle found his performance 'spellbinding' as this near-senile character 'ready to fall to ashes, as it does at the end'. John Barber admired the strong cast, 'with Ralph Richardson particularly fine as the ancient retainer Firs, who finds the modern world all chippety-choppety and dies on-stage at the end. A dreadful shiver then slowly possesses his body and the clatter of his stick to the ground is like a pistol-shot.'

After the end of this run, in which so many involved regretted that it never fulfilled their early high hopes of its potential, Ralph had a gap before rehearsals for *The Double Dealer* began. He chose to fill it with a play that had no potential at all, whose failure became the subject not of regret but of near-hysteria by the other actors, and of despair by its successive directors.

This was *Alice's Boys* by Felicity Browne and Jonathan Hales. Lindsay Anderson was first invited to direct it, following his two other successes with Ralph in *Home* and *The Kingfisher*, but when he read the script he thought it did not deserve to be produced, and said so. He withdrew, and Eric Thompson agreed to take it on. Few actors could resist the opportunity of appearing with one of their great heroes, and Gary Bond, Michael Gambon and Michael Jayston now all say that they only accepted their parts for that reason. They were the three young Secret Service agents who discover a murder and call in their chief, Colonel White, played by Ralph.

Their motives for agreeing to act in this play are perfectly explicable; the mystery is why its star ever thought it would work. Lindsay Anderson believed that Ralph was attracted by the thought of doing embroidery on the stage, which hardly seems sufficient reason. The other actors struggled to make sense of their parts. Michael Gambon did not get very far.

> After the read-through we had what was laughingly called a text-analysis discussion, while we sat around discussing the text of this pile of rubbish. My only contribution was I thought my character might be gay. Ralph didn't like that at all, he said, 'Oh no, you're not.'[10]

A jocular aside by Ralph to a reporter in the second week was only too prophetic.

> Rehearsals at the moment? The ship is steering north into a lot of icebergs. Someone dropped the key of the engine room overboard last night and the waters are shark-infested so no one dare go in and pick it up. It's all quite normal, old man. Absolutely disastrous. Always is. We get muddled up in rehearsals. We get too near, can't see the proper perspective.[11]

The absurdities of the plot, and the banalities in the dialogue, made it difficult for the cast to take the play seriously, and this became impossible on the pre-West End tour, not least because of Ralph's inability to remember his lines properly, or the names of the other characters.

Michael Jayston's character was called Dan, a name often transposed by Ralph to one of the others, and one night he addressed all three of them in succession as 'Dan'. Other transpositions made it difficult for Jayston to keep a straight face. After the corpse was discovered the Chief's line was: 'There's a black sheep in the family. And he's dead.' Once this came out as: 'There's a dead sheep in the family. And he's black.'[12]

The body was discovered when the Put-U-Up bed was folded up into the wall. The ASM had to play the body, and lying under the bed was uncomfortable. When he was picked up one night Michael Gambon said something under his breath and the corpse burst out laughing, adding a whole new meaning to 'corpsing' on-stage, and provoking mutters of disapproval from the audience. As word got round about a new mishap every night, the audience filled up with actors eager to catch this extraordinary theatrical disaster before it folded.

Ralph tried to repeat *The Heiress* salvage operation by firing the director, and Lindsay Anderson was approached again, now as a matter of some urgency to protect Ralph's reputation. He saw a preview at Richmond and agreed to try to help. His predecessor had been too frightened of his star to direct him, even over such details as Ralph's refusal to take his hat off in the drawing-room. The first thing the incisive Anderson said when he took over was, 'For God's sake, Ralph, take your hat off.' Ralph then wore a toupee instead.

But the inadequacies in *Alice's Boys*, unlike *The Heiress*, were not only in the direction; they were rooted in the script, and despite a couple of weeks' re-rehearsal under Lindsay Anderson this vehicle was beyond repair. Ralph's uncertainty with his lines continued. Gary Bond remembers him saying on-stage to the girl prompter, 'My dear, you must learn to speak up more clearly.'

As Michael Billington put it in the *Guardian*:

Even the great Richardson is left fixing his Ancient Mariner eye on vacancy and searching for some line on which to exercise his springy, arching tones and yeasty inflexions: it is like seeing a famous conjuror asked to juggle without his Indian clubs or coloured balls.

The critics unanimously savaged the play and wondered what on earth had induced Ralph to touch it. Towards the end of its brief run Ralph remarked to Michael Gambon, 'In the old days nice intelligent people used to come to the theatre, now they send their cooks.' Soon they stopped doing even that, and it closed at the Savoy after only a couple of weeks. *Alice's Boys* has become a legend among collectors of Ralph Richardson stories, including the one so often quoted:

> On tour one night Ralph walked down to the front of the stage and asked, 'Is there a doctor in the house?' A man stood up in the stalls and said, 'Yes, I'm a doctor.' Ralph looked at him mournfully and said, 'Doctor, isn't this a terrible play?'

All the actors who tell this story swear they were told it by one or other of the cast in *Alice's Boys*; the cast themselves deny it ever happened during that play. Ralph himself told a slightly different version. Without identifying the play he said he once heard someone in the stalls cry out, 'Is there a doctor in the house?' Receiving the answer 'Yes' from the dress circle the first man said, 'Doctor, isn't this a terrible play?'

If Ralph ever in fact said it of *Alice's Boys*, he would have been more than justified in doing so. Fortunately he was quickly released from his penance, and returned to the National Theatre for all but one of his last half-dozen plays.

CHAPTER TWENTY-TWO
1978–1979

BY THE time he was in his seventies Sir Ralph was more than a great actor, he was a national institution. He had become a great character, with a reputation for eccentricity and unpredictability. Some of that was natural and instinctive to him, some of it was more calculated. Certainly his public appearances and utterances were carefully chosen. Those close to him saw how thoroughly he prepared and rehearsed his apparently 'impromptu' speeches at awards ceremonies and other theatrical occasions.

He gave infrequent interviews to the press and broadcasters, and then only after pleading by his managements, anxious for some pre-publicity for a play or a film. It was actually written into his contract, before the Australian tour of *Lloyd George Knew My Father*, that he had to give interviews to the Australian press before leaving England, to boost the advance box-office, since there was no time to build an audience in each city.

When he did appear on television he was the delight of viewers and the despair of interviewers. However well they prepared their questions, he never gave anything away, and something unexpected always seemed to happen. Sitting in the television studio at Lime Grove with Derek Hart, for his appearance in the BBC 'Great Acting' series in 1965, the glass of water on the table beside him suddenly exploded of its own volition into a thousand fragments, to the consternation of everyone except the actor. The make-up artist, Julie Cruttenden, rushed in to find Sir Ralph still sitting there, calmly brushing splinters of glass off his jacket; all he said was, 'My goodness, what a surprise,' with a benign smile, as everyone else leaped about in horror at what might have resulted.

Russell Harty invited him on to his London Weekend Television chat-show in 1975, and found himself being mischievously wrong-footed as Ralph wandered around the stage, pretending to admire the non-existent views of the riverscape out of the false windows on the set, talking to the studio audience, and then asking so many questions of Harty about his job that there was little time left to talk about himself, the ostensible reason for his appearance.

In 1978, during rehearsals for *The Double Dealer* at the National Theatre, he agreed to go on the Michael Parkinson show, which was televised by the BBC on a Saturday night. The format here was to have more than one guest, and it must have seemed a good idea at the time to have Ralph preceded by the motor-cycle racing champion, Barry Sheene. But when he joined him on the set all he wanted to do was to share motor-bike experiences, and for aficionados of the sport he asked the young champion some very informed questions. (Nicky Henson heard some bikers in a pub the next day saying, 'Hey, did you see Sheeney on the box last night, wonderful, wasn't it? What about that old bugger, wasn't he great?' They had no idea who he was, but admired his rapport with their racing hero.)

Parkinson kept trying to change the subject, at one point smiling through gritted teeth, 'This is like an evening-class on motor-bikes.' He finally gave up trying and took them both over to a gleaming racer standing at the other side of the studio, which Ralph sat astride and exchanged experiences of wheel-wobbles and their attendant dangers.

The young man who took his life in his hands every time he went on the track was concerned that his more elderly fellow-biker only ever wore an old-fashioned open-face helmet, instead of the new-style full-face helmet that also protected the jaw. On the Monday after their encounter, Ralph came into rehearsal with a box which had been left at the stage door for him; when he opened it he said, 'Ah, how sweet.' There was an accompanying note from Barry Sheene, who had sent him a top-of-the-range full-face Bell helmet, very smart, costing about £250. Nicky Henson, another keen motorcyclist, said, 'Gosh, that's wonderful, Sir Ralph.'

'What a sweet young man.'

> The next day he came in with the biggest shiner you've ever seen.
>
> 'Gosh, Sir Ralph, what happened?'
>
> 'I don't like these full-face helmets, you can't see the floor when you're coming out of the garage.'
>
> And he'd driven straight into the side of the garage wall, because he was used to looking down, and of course you can't see anything.[1]

One Richardson throwaway line to Parkinson was: 'Actors never retire, they just get offered fewer parts.' As a good Company man at the National he was quite prepared to play smaller parts, although there were some concessions he was not prepared to make. He still designed his own costumes; in *The Double Dealer* everyone else was dressed in the period of Hogarth, but Ralph insisted on wearing a full-bottomed wig. The designer, Tanya Moiseiwitsch, was an old colleague from their days at the New Theatre, and did not object to his ideas, because Lord Touchwood was supposed to be old-fashioned anyway.

Peter Wood has a particular gift for directing Congreve – his *Love for Love* with the Olivier Company had been a great triumph in 1965, when the minor part of Tattle became something exceptional in the hands of Sir Laurence. Now he found Sir Ralph pulled off the same trick as Lord Touchwood.

> When in doubt, Ralph just substituted a piece of Ralph. Where Ralph had the advantage, that if a part is a big jigsaw and you were missing two or three pieces of sky, Ralph would just put in pieces of Ralph all along. He was very wonderful as Touchwood, except by that time he did have memory problems. He'd remember the laugh lines, and of course his timing was excellent. He'd throw away a line, he and John both had that great gift, flick something off to leg with the lightest strokes, which would bring the house down. Nobody has the breath now to deliver those flick lines.[2]

Director and actor had put *Carving a Statue* behind them and forged a much closer relationship than they had managed previously, but Peter Wood still smiles when asked if that meant he would take direction.

> You mean, where did he take it? He took it to the back door! They're all the same, you have to prove yourself. You had to do something for them that was better than they were doing for themselves, and if you didn't, forget it! Ralph belonged to a great elect, and they really were a great elect. No one shall say that they were easy to handle, but then no one shall say it was easy for them to handle themselves.[3]

In this play the director did prove himself to Ralph's satisfaction, at least as far as the overall production was concerned. He devised a dance to some tinkling music which brought all the characters on at the beginning, and then again for the curtain-call. They warmed-up backstage, much more energetically than Ralph's usual pacing around; Dorothy Tutin played Lady Plyant, and recalls, 'We used to start off doing the twist, he was absolutely wonderful, and I'd tap him on the shoulder, and we'd set off dancing on to the stage.'

The convoluted plot involves deceit, seduction and disguise, and if Ralph was at a loss for one of Congreve's lines to unravel the plot he would sometimes fall back on Shakespeare. 'Give me the ocular proof,' he cried one night, which made perfect sense in the scene, except to those members of the audience who waited in vain for Iago's response at that point.

Robert Stephens played Maskwell, the double-dealer of the title, in a brilliant display of deviousness that was much admired by Ralph. The whole of the scintillating cast were inspired by Peter Wood to give the audience what B. A. Young in the *Financial Times* called 'a fountain of sheer enjoyment'. The director was saddened only by Ralph's self-deprecation.

> He said, 'You know', sitting upstairs in his full-bottomed wig and dreadful ultramarine costume, 'I think you've hit the bull's-eye fair and square in the centre with this one. How I wish I could say that as Lord Touchwood I had done the same.' That kind of thing took the breath away.[4]

Ralph settled into the routine of the National Theatre and sought no special privileges, with the sole exception of bringing in Hal, his own long-time dresser. He became a familiar sight in the canteen, and when Michael Gambon and other actors observed he nearly always had sausages they did the same.

He was kindness personified to the young. On her first day as an ASM Jane Suffling walked into the canteen, not knowing a soul, and sat down next to an old man in his carpet slippers, who said he hadn't seen her before, was she new? She told him it was her first day and she felt a bit lost. 'Oh, that must be terrible for you, let me show you round.'

So he took her to the rehearsal rooms, the scene dock, the wig room, and all the backstage operational areas. The next day at lunchtime she was with a small group of new colleagues when she passed her kindly guide of the day before.

'Hello, how are you getting on?' he asked her.

'Fine, thank you.'

Her new friends looked at her, impressed. 'How do you know him? Where have you worked with him before?'

'I haven't, I only met him yesterday, and he showed me all over the building.'

'Don't you know who he is?'

'No.'

'That's Sir Ralph Richardson.'

Characteristically he had not mentioned to her who he was,[5] and he obviously enjoyed not being recognized for once, especially knowing that his temporary incognito could not last. A lesser man might have taken umbrage but Ralph was never that kind of self-regarding star; and Jane Suffling still recalls this first meeting with more pleasure than embarrassment because of his great charm.

Their work together on *John Gabriel Borkman* and *No Man's Land* had brought Ralph and Peter Hall close together,

and ever after he was very supportive of what I was going through at the National, he became a friend and we used to lunch about every six weeks. He loved taking me to lunch at the Athenaeum – 'Let's go and see the bishops snooze!' I had really intricate conversations with him, about the theatre, about acting, about women, about relationships, about religion, about death; if you could actually get him one-to-

one, but he would never do it in public, never. He also had
that gentleness of his generation, instead of saying someone
was terrible, it was always done by understatement – 'Not
much of an actor, don't think too much of that writer, do
you?' Never cruel. We had a sort of father–son relationship
over the last ten years of his life; I was very close to him and I
loved him very much.[6]

He was not alone in that. Many of the figures who appear
in these pages used the same word to describe their feelings
for Ralph, but few people were able to tell him so to his face,
it always made him uncomfortable and embarrassed. When
Bernard Levin persisted in trying to tell him he was much
loved in a television interview when he was eighty, Ralph said
he did not understand what he was talking about. He just
would not discuss it.

It was an emotion that was much too important to him to
be exposed off the stage. On-stage was a different matter.
After a preview of Harold Pinter's *Betrayal* he told Peter Hall
that he thought it was a beautiful play, beautifully performed,
except that he was unconvinced by the playing of the last
scene, where the affair begins. He said, 'We've all been in
love. Love is a very big bomb. It must go off.'[7]

The special quality of that feeling for Ralph was privately
observed by Nicky Henson at an *Evening Standard* Drama
Awards Lunch in the early 1970s.

The awards were given, and halfway through Sir Ralph was
presenting an award. He got up and as he went on to the stage
the whole place rose and he had one of those twenty-minute
Sir Ralph ovations. At the end there was a Lifetime Achievement Award for Sir Laurence; he too got a wonderful ovation,
but not the same, which was kind of embarrassing. Then we
all climbed into buses to go down to a screening of the film of

Sleuth, and I happened to be sitting behind Sir Ralph. Sir Laurence came down the aisle and got level with Sir Ralph, who raised his arm in greeting, and Sir Laurence turned to him and said, 'My God, they do love you, Ralphy.'

And I went cold, because it was one of those things I shouldn't have heard, and it was obviously so hurtful to Sir Laurence, after all he'd achieved, that Ralph was the one they loved.[8]

The nature of theatre work means that actors strike up relationships for the duration of a play or a season, and then may not work together again for years, but Ralph was always keen to have a few familiar faces around him. When he was cast as the Master in Tolstoy's *The Fruits of Enlightenment* he asked for Joyce Redman to join him as his wife. She had been in the Olivier Company at the National, but this was the first time she had appeared with Ralph since their great seasons at the New thirty years earlier; another old friend from those days who also reappeared was Peter Copley.

Christopher Morahan was the director. He had come a long way since their association on the ill-fated *Macbeth*, but he still had some problems with the staging of this play. Peter Copley saw that Ralph was as preoccupied as he always had been with the mechanics of his first entrance.

He had to sweep into this living-room through double-doors, and Ralph had obviously indicated he needed to work this out, so Christopher Morahan had got this frame with two swing-doors from props, and we spent a very long time on this first entrance, when he had to come on with two friends. He tried coming on himself opening the two doors, then said, 'No, that's not right in my own house, maybe I can open one door, ah I'll open that one, not well-placed, let's try the other one.' Then he tried it with the butler (me) opening it, and this went on and nothing was satisfactory. Finally Ralph said, 'I don't see how I can get on-stage at all.'

I could see Christopher getting tighter and tighter, but always charming; by this time they'd been an hour doing this, and the resolution was that it was impossible.[9]

It was eventually resolved with the help of the butler. The main problem was that Tolstoy was not a real playwright. The translator, Michael Frayn, admitted recently that he really ought to have taken far more liberties with the text to make it workable,[10] as he did so brilliantly on Chekhov later with *Wild Honey*. The cast never felt that *The Fruits of Enlightenment* was a real play, or quite understood whether it was about master–serf relationships in Russia, or spiritualism, or whether it was a comedy or a drama. This made for some difficult rehearsals, and a few tensions.

Selina Cadell had been cast as Ralph's daughter, and she was terrified that anyone might think she had only got into the Company because her godfather had arranged it. Her reaction rather amused Ralph and she would catch him watching her, and tapping his pipe.

The worst thing he did to me was in rehearsal when the director was running late one day. Ralph was getting restless and tapping his leg. I was sitting a long way from him with my newspaper, and he suddenly said, 'What did you have for supper . . . last night?'

Everyone looked at me, and I was caught, like a rabbit in the headlights. So I just whispered, 'Pork chops.'

'Do you cook them . . . yourself?'

'Yes.'

Christopher glowered at me, because he couldn't really rebuke Ralph.

'Were they nice?' Louder each time.

'Yes, very nice.'

Christopher was now getting really impatient. 'Could we just concentrate on the scene?'

I don't know how Ralph did it to this day, but somehow I just knew I had to ask him what he'd had for dinner the night before. So eventually I whispered, 'What did *you* have for dinner, Sir Ralph?'

'Oh, I'm so glad you asked,' at the top of his voice, 'I had some curry, I had curry, my wife Mu's not a very good cook, I added a little bit of this and a little bit of that, and in the end it was quite delicious, oh Christopher my boy, are you waiting for me?'

It was terribly difficult for me to endure, but it was in a nutshell the way Ralph behaved sometimes.[11]

Christopher Morahan knew that he was dealing with someone of special qualities, who worked in his own way, which was a result of much study in advance.

I had no feeling that his preparation for the parts in advance of rehearsal was in any way a hindrance to discovery, or hindered other people at all. He wanted to get things right, and had a painstaking concern for detail, and rather like a pointilliste painter built it up through the observation and execution of little things, a miniaturist who worked on such a scale that what you saw was gigantic. One thinks of Seurat or Pissarro. That pursuit of perfection, I would guess, if it evaded him, dispirited him. If those dots didn't join up, as at Stratford in 1952, it must have been distressing, but on the occasions when I worked with him at the National the dots all joined up.[12]

Joyce Redman summed up her old partner's concern for detail with a homelier analogy. 'Ralph with a part was like a dog with a basket, they go round and round, one way then another, before they get in and settle down.'[13]

This production was heading for a very big basket – the Olivier Theatre, whose concrete walls were not much help to the actors trying to reach the back of its large auditorium. So Selina Cadell was eternally grateful for her godfather's advice.

> One wonderful day he said to me, 'Come and sit by me and bring your script. You know, I think you're really rather good. Have you got a pencil?'
>
> 'Yes, yes,' and I rummaged hastily in my bag.
>
> 'No, no, a *red* pencil.'
>
> 'I don't think I have got a red pencil.'
>
> 'Oh, you should always have a red pencil. Never mind now, let me tell you why. Take your first line and just put a red line under the last word, and then in every sentence that you say just underline the last word, and that will remind you to lift the inflection on the last word, and that's the secret of making sure you're heard in the Olivier. Take Joyce [Redman], for example – playing with Joycey is like playing tennis, biffing the lines back and forth to each other.'
>
> He was such a great technician, and I've told so many students that piece of Ralph's advice because it's so simple, and so effective. You always heard every word of Ralph's, right to the *end*. That 'd' was fantastic.[14]

(As Nicky Henson had found in the previous play.)

The lucky recipients of the fruits of his lifetime's experience treasured these insights into their craft, knowing they were the few who shared in his private knowledge. For he never spoke publicly, or at length, about his style of acting, except with self-deprecating modesty. It is possible to catch a glimpse of his own deep understanding of theatrical genius when he spoke of those he admired. In November 1979 he was Chairman of the Foyle's Literary Luncheon to mark the publication of *An Actor and His Time*, Sir John Gielgud's latest volume of theatrical memoirs. After wittily introducing the guests of honour in alphabetical order, so that the Ambassador from Italy took diplomatic precedence, he turned to his old friend and recalled his early successes at the Old Vic and the plays they had done together.

His description of Gielgud's mastery of verse-speaking could only have come from another great Shakespearean.

> When John Gielgud played these parts he sketched out the beginnings of his own method of speaking Shakespeare's romantic and dramatic verse — which I might call the long, melodic phrase. He had a singular success with this invention of his; the marvellous sweep and magic which I cannot possibly reproduce. But one example comes in Clarence's dream speech from *Richard III*. This is a speech which has sixty lines and only eight full stops. It is a speech with a multitude of detail and tiny little effects. How did Gielgud approach this? With a generous sweep, he would take one great armful of verse, right up to the first full stop. He would hold it there and then take another, with not one tiny particle ever being lost. He would take a whole verse and pour it into a casket, then gently shut the lid of the casket and pass it to the audience. This was a demonstration of his method of speaking long poetic phrases.[15]

That is also a brilliant description of the breath-control that Ralph demonstrated so effortlessly on his own recordings of the poetry of Keats, Blake, Marvell and Shakespeare.

Ralph's next play was also directed by Christopher Morahan in the Olivier — Ibsen's *The Wild Duck*. For Irving Wardle in *The Times* the tone of the production was set by Sir Ralph, 'first seen spryly threading his way through the guests and making his exit with an appalled questioning look at his son who studiously ignores him'.

John Barber began his review in the *Daily Telegraph*: 'The tone is unduly sombre, the comedy is repressed, and the general effect is low-key and, almost incredibly, undramatic.' But he too picked out for particular praise the performance of Old Ekdal and of the actor playing his son Hjalmar, Stephen Moore.

> It is one of the beauties of Christopher Morahan's production that Ekdal is so convincingly the son of his pottering, useless old father, given a masterly performance by Ralph Richardson. Richardson's desiccated clerk still retains the traces of a military bearing, and fragments of the dashing huntsman who once shot nine bears. But life has broken his spirit, and the actor suggests not only senile sentimentality but a man's fuddled effort to cling to his former dignity and manliness.

But overall it was not much liked by the critics, who Peter Hall thought were 'criminally unfair' to the production. Its director thought it was one of the most rewarding things he had done, and also one of Ralph's best. 'His performance as Old Ekdal was very rich and exquisitely conceived, and done with very great grace and generosity to those people round about him.[16]

One of those was Michael Bryant, who watched Ralph 'always looking for the lighter side, which of course made the tragedy so much more poignant'. One of his regular difficulties produced a few unintended lighter moments. 'He got mixed up with foreign names, for instance I played Gregers Werle in *The Wild Duck*, and he would always call me McGregor Whirly, which finished us all.'

Ralph described Michael Bryant's performance as 'very delicate, like a fly's wing'; the two men got on well, helped not a little by their shared interest in motor-bikes (all these biking enthusiasts at the National Theatre were quickly dubbed 'Hall's Angels'). Ralph was riding a 750cc BMW at this time, and he was envious of the other man's new 1000cc BMW sports model.

> He said, 'May I sit on it?'
> 'Certainly, of course.'
> And he sat on it, and the sports model was a bit lower than his, and he went 'Brmm, Brmm', just like a child. Before that, I had Moto-Guzzis, and he called them 'Gookeys' – 'Are you on your Gookey today?'

Michael Bryant was intrigued by this great interest in the latest machinery from a man who 'was an Edwardian actor, with Edwardian pronunciations, like EDWAHDIAN, both his manner and his manners were somewhat Edwardian'. But, like many fellow-players before him, he knew he was in the presence of a singular talent.

> He was unquestionably a great actor. When he went on-stage, bang! Your eyes went straight to him, and you just couldn't stop looking at him. You could never be sure what he was going to do next on-stage, you could never be sure how he was going to play something, he always had surprises for you, and I think they surprised him as well.[17]

The biggest bunch of surprises came with the production of Ralph's last great leading role with the National Theatre – Kitchen in David Storey's *Early Days*. He had played four supporting parts in succession on the South Bank, and brought something remarkable to each of them. But Dorothy Tutin, who acted with him in two of them, felt he had done justice to the parts, but not to himself.

He wasn't a small-part actor, he really wasn't. He'd play these small parts with graciousness and charm, but when he had a big part he was really like a horse with the bit between his teeth. He was a different man when he was doing *Early Days*. Suddenly he came on the stage and he looked ten years younger, he looked like an actor who knew he'd got the audience in the palm of his hand, and could do absolutely anything, and he did. He was just wonderful, and I thought how wasteful it was for him to fiddle around with small parts, because he was a giant of an actor.[18]

Before this horse did get the bit between his teeth and enter the race there was an awful lot of shying at the jumps, until everyone wondered whether he would ever take off over the first one.

CHAPTER TWENTY-THREE
Early Days – 1980–1982

DAVID STOREY declined several other offers to put on *Early Days* after Ralph Richardson first turned it down, and the script eventually ended up at the National Theatre, where it had been sitting on the shelf for three years, before a happy coincidence persuaded Ralph to reconsider it. He had been in touch with Lindsay Anderson in Los Angeles, asking whether they could do something together again, and the director wrote back, in his customary red ink, to urge that they did the Storey play. 'Why not? You're going to end up doing something, some rubbish, and there is no point; you know perfectly well David is a proper writer, you've worked together, let's do it.'[1] (Ralph said he thought the letter must have been dropped in the swimming-pool before posting, because he thought it was covered in blood when he first opened it.)

The very day the letter arrived, Peter Hall telephoned to say, 'Why don't we do *Early Days?*', and the author believed that both messages arriving on the same day appealed to Ralph's sense of superstition. Once he had said yes, however, the problems began. In the absence of the director in California, Ralph began to worry at the script in a way that Frith Banbury would have recognized from his pre-rehearsal problems with Ralph on *Flowering Cherry*. This time Ralph went direct to the author, ringing him up on Easter Sunday, and disarmingly opened by saying, 'I've been reading your play, it's much improved, this version.' At this stage not a word had been altered. But Ralph had some changes in mind.

'Can you come round and discuss the text, Lindsay says we shouldn't, but he won't mind us just talking a little bit, will he?'

The Sunday telephone call became a routine.

'I'm very worried about the end.'

'What about the end?'

So I went round and reassured him about the end.

Next Sunday, 'I'm very worried about the middle.'

'I thought it was the end.'

'No, no, the end is fine, beautiful, it's the middle I'm worried about.'

I went round and reassured him about the middle.

The following Sunday, 'I'm very worried about the beginning.'

'I thought it was the middle and the end.'

'No, no, the middle and the end are no problems at all, it's the beginning.'

So when I'd talked about the beginning, and that was all right, I thought, 'I wonder if he will ring up on Sunday.'

Next Sunday he rang to say, 'I wonder, I've just got a few wheezes about our play, could you come round? I'd like to talk about them, I don't think Lindsay would mind.'

So I went round, and what he'd done was he'd actually started transposing sections of the play. He'd started doing what I intuitively had tried to do with *Home*. He was trying to find a narrative structure which he could fasten on to; there wasn't really that narrative structure there but he'd elucidated one from the text, and by shifting scenes around he'd constructed a kind of narrative, and was delighted with it. We sat side by side, and he'd got it all marked out in his script. I went through it with increasing despair as to how I could tell him, so I thought the best thing was just to be bold about it. I went through each one, and I said, 'Look, if you do this, we're turning the play into a very conventional narrative, which once done will appear to have very little content, and you're going to make the play extremely conventional.'

A very long silence.

'Right!' And he crossed them all out, with a big gesture, 'Wheezes no good! Right, now then, what shall we do next?'[2]

What he in fact tried to do next very nearly sank the production before it even got into rehearsal.

'I've decided, before I sign my contract, I'm going to learn the whole play by heart. Then I know I can do it.'

'You'll never do it, Ralph.'

'No, no, I've talked to Peter Hall, before I sign the contract I want to learn it. In fact, I've learned it. Would you like to hear what I've learned?'

'Sure. This isn't the way to go about it, but if you feel that's what you want to do, I'll come round.'

So on Sunday I went round, and we sat side by side in his study. He started off from page 1, and he got to about page 5. 'Well, that's it, that's as far as we'll go. What do you think?'

And I foolishly said, 'Well, that's very, very good.'

'Nothing missed out, it was all there?'

'Well, there were one or two . . .'

'There were?'

'Just one or two.'

'One or two, three or four?'

'Well, a few.'

'Ohh.' And he started weeping, in a very quiet way, without sobbing, but tears came into his eyes. He'd obviously put such enormous effort into doing this.

'I'm sure this isn't the way to learn it, Ralph, you can only learn it in rehearsal, with the moves.'

But he persevered with it, and kept ringing up to report progress. 'I've got to page 17 . . . to page 23 . . . page 27.'

The next time he rang he said, 'I'm on page 17.'

'But you were on page 27 last week.'

'I was? Are you sure?'

'Yes, Ralph, I'm sure you were.'

'Oh God, I'm going backwards. It's hopeless.'

When Lindsay Anderson returned he was alarmed by all this; unlike Noël Coward, he discouraged actors from attempting to arrive word-perfect on the first day.

I'd much rather they don't know the play when we start, and at the first day of rehearsal Ralph didn't particularly want to be directed, didn't want what I call 'to work on the play' properly, and I had to speak rather firmly. It's always difficult when you get a senior and much-respected actor, and this can be very bad for the actor, because you do get to a point when they're so distinguished and respected that they don't get directed, and that anything they do will get applauded. This is something I've never gone along with, and I don't think it is good for the actor anyway.[3]

The first day reduced him to despair, as Ralph insisted on trying to rehearse without the book, when all the other actors had it in their hands; he could not remember a line, and would either peer over their shoulder at their copy or have to be prompted. Every time he was urged to use the book he insisted that this was the way he wanted to do it. That evening the director rang the author. 'I can't direct him, you'll have to talk to him.'

'What about?'

'Well, you'll have to frighten him, obviously I don't frighten him, but you do, so you'll have to say something to him. He can't learn it this way, he'll have to go on the book.'[4]

It is hard to imagine that the soft-spoken and mild-mannered author 'frightened' Ralph more than the naturally acerbic director, but it is clear that despite his flip remark about preferring dead writers he did have enormous respect for playwrights like Pinter and Storey.

The latter girded himself for a showdown on the second day, and sat himself in a chair opposite the one Ralph used at the beginning of the play, almost in his eyeline. They were in a windowless and claustrophobic rehearsal room in the basement, and Storey noticed with some trepidation that Ralph arrived looking very wound-up. He made straight for him without a word, swept past, took off his hat and coat and put them on the next chair, went and sat on his chair, clapped his hands, and said, 'Beginners.'

The rehearsal began. Every few moments he caught the author's eye, who knew from their experience in *Home* that something was going on in his mind, which would be revealed in due course. It was not long in coming. As the director got up to talk to the other actors in the scene, a letter he was writing fell out of his script on to the floor at Ralph's feet; he was not being addressed, and he was visibly irked at being so deliberately ignored.

Storey watched with rising apprehension.

Ralph bent down, had a glance at the writing, Lindsay went on talking to the actors and just took the letter out of Ralph's hand, his face going whiter and whiter, as it did when he was suppressing great anger, talking more and more calmly as he put it back, turned and walked back to his position. I could see that something pretty awful was going on in Ralph, his face went absolutely livid. There was a great banging on the chair, and Ralph cried out, 'I'm not used to being addressed like a fucking schoolboy, Lindsaaay, I don't like this fucking headmaster act' (but saying this to me, not to Lindsay), 'in fact I've come absolutely to the end of it.'

He got up and walked towards me. I thought, 'Should I hit him first, or will he hit me first?'; then he swerved and walked right round the room, in a long loping stride, shouting, 'I've had enough of this fucking schoolboy act, I don't like being addressed by a fucking headmaster.'[5]

(Ralph never swore like this unless he was under very great stress — his wife remembers him at one Christmas lunch at Claridge's threatening to flatten Lindsay if he used another four-letter word in front of their son Charles, then aged nineteen.[6])

They all watched this astounding performance, as Ralph came back, picked up his hat and coat, put the hat on, flung the coat over his shoulders, and swept out of the room.

Total silence, and Lindsay stood up. I could see he was very, very angry, absolutely seething with rage, very white and very quiet. When I got to him I saw there were tears in his eyes, he was very distraught. I put my arm on his shoulder, and walked down the room with him, saying, 'It'll be all right.' Lindsay said, 'Nobody's ever walked out on me before, no, I'm wrong, Bob Shaw walked out on me once in *The Long and the Short and the Tall*, and he came crawling back after half an hour. I don't see Ralph crawling back after half an hour.'

'Look, just quieten down, I'll go and find Ralph, shall I? It's not the end of everything, and if it is we'll pack it in.'

As they turned at the end of the room, they saw that it was deserted, everybody else had fled. The director grunted, 'Rats, do you think?' After a while the stage manager returned to say she had located Ralph, he had not left the building yet, so the author set off in search of him, and opened the door to find Ralph standing there.

'I'm pissed. I've had a Pernod – wrong time of day.' He clapped his hands, 'That's the end of it. Acting over.'[7]

Somehow Storey managed to mediate between his two highly charged colleagues, until the one was saying that perhaps he had been misunderstanding the actor, and the other that perhaps he had been a bit over the top, 'and me saying that working without the book was a difficult way to work; but it lanced the boil, and I think it was all to do with his insecurity in taking on what he basically saw as a solo performance'. (A view he sustained throughout – when Peter Hall travelled down to Bath with him on the tour he remembers him saying, 'Very lonely play, this!'[8])

It was only many months later, after the play had transferred to the Comedy Theatre, that Ralph confessed to the author that his diffidence and insecurity at the beginning had been to do with the fact that he liked to share a play with at least one other leading actor; he had always resisted being out on his own. In *Early Days* all the other actors really had just supporting parts, while he embarked on a series of what were in effect monologues.

His character, Sir Richard Kitchen, was a retired politician who had missed becoming Prime Minister by giving one misguided speech and one indiscreet interview. He took his bitterness out on his family and his staff, and talked to the spirit of his late wife, who may have been driven to an early death by his disgrace.

Storey came to the conclusion that Ralph had a very rich inner world, which only found its outlet in acting, and when he had trouble with a text he internalized it in a way which made sense only to him.

> In the middle of a line he'd suddenly get up and say, 'What does this line mean? Is this where the rabbit sees the stoat?'
>
> I'd say, 'Well, in a curious way it probably is.'
>
> 'Yes, I've got it.' And he went back to his seat.
>
> Once, when we were rehearsing on the huge stage of Her Majesty's, I was sitting in the front seat of the stalls, and he was acting way up-stage; we were having a difficult time that week, and I could see him eyeing me across the depth of the stage, and he suddenly came forward to where I was sitting, held up his arm and said, 'I am a rabbit, this is a blade of grass, and I am completely hidden behind it.' And the way he said it I thought, 'He is, he was.' Somehow his arm was a blade of grass and it completely hid his figure in some extraordinary way, it was just like seeing the horse in his house.[9]

The play was set in the garden with the house in the background, and the designer was Jocelyn Herbert who, fortunately for this production, had struck up a happy working relationship with Ralph ten years earlier on *Home*. She felt this play needed something more than just a naturalistic setting, 'so I had these gauzes painted with some rather abstract trees on them, and when Ralph saw this he said, "Where's the house? There's nothing there." He was rather terrified when he saw the model, but I think he liked the actual set in the end.'[10]

That was still some way off. The dress-rehearsal was a total disaster – Ralph could not remember a single line, and it had to be abandoned. Up until this point everyone had despaired in turn – actors, designer and director. Only the author had not lost faith in it, but now he suddenly thought: 'My God, what do you do when you have an audience and no play, what happens next?'

As he sat there alone in the stalls, watching the technicians at work and thinking it was all now going to be in vain, a door into the auditorium opened and a figure came in. As it crossed in front of him he recognized the silhouette as Ralph's. His wig had slipped round so that the fringe was over his left ear, and he slumped into a seat.

> I thought, 'Should I cough?' or indicate he was not alone; suddenly his head came back and he shouted up to the ceiling, 'Oh, for a cup of hemlock!'
>
> That's when I thought, 'Oh God, he doesn't think it's going to work.' I coughed to indicate he wasn't alone, and he slapped his knee. 'Oh well, that wasn't a very successful run-through, was it? Well, never mind, it's just like a lighthouse, the light keeps going on and off, or a tangled ball of wool at my feet, I can't find the end to unravel it.'

At the end of the evening, having had no dress-rehearsal, director, designer and author walked along the Brighton seafront to their hotel, all now convinced that the opening was going to be a nightmare. They took their seats the following night in various degrees of dread. Storey sat between Lady Richardson, who said she had taken half a heart-pill, and the composer Alan Price, who seemed paralysed, laid out like a plank across the seat rather than in it. The theatre was packed as usual for a Richardson first night in Brighton, the lights went down, the music came up, the lights came up on the stage for Ralph's entrance, and nothing happened. The music flowed on and faded away, and still nothing happened.

The author, who had been transfixed with rising alarm through this lengthening non-appearance, now gave up.

I suddenly didn't care any more, I thought, if he does or doesn't take his entrance it's a wonderful moment. And then in the far distance it sounded just like a horse, a galloping of some animal coming at a great pace, then suddenly this great figure came bursting from the back of the stage; he'd reminded me of a horse when I'd first seen him, but it was a front view this time. His eyes were bolting, it was just like some pirate king or Attila the Hun, a great raging figure of fury and intensity, and I suddenly saw this man absolutely *loves* acting. There was an enormous, rapacious appetite to act, his nostrils flared, and he dried, he couldn't remember a single word; and he stared, and his hands did extraordinary things, and he started a speech which in fact we'd cut out many, many months before. It was the stuff he'd been learning on his own, and panic had brought it back, which then became interspersed with the bits he was supposed to do.[11]

As he gathered confidence his improvisations to plug the gaps in his memory reached heights that terrified his fellow-actors. At one point he had a four-line verse with alternate rhymes – A, B, A, B – he had forgotten the first line so he made one up, then he made the second line up. His third invented line rhymed with the first, and then the fourth line off the top of his head rhymed with the second line. The other actor in the scene stood there with his eyes popping, because he had to follow this with a rhyme too, and he could not believe what he was hearing – a total invention that rhymed and scanned perfectly.

Not all his inventions at later performances were as inspired. He had one interchange with his daughter, played by Rosemary Martin, after she defends her husband.

'You have a false image of him, Father. My life isn't bound up with Arthur's the way my mother's was with you.'

'Promiscuity with him is like a disease: it hangs around him like the air he breathes. Scent, perfume, lotion, cream. The man is like a fetish. What does he do with all these women?'

After it opened in the Cottesloe Ralph continued to struggle with this speech, and once he launched into: 'The man is like a scent, talcum powder, Lifebuoy soap, Lux toilet soap, the man is like a . . .'

The author stood in the wings looking over Ralph's shoulder at Rosemary Martin's face, watching her trying to say 'fetish' with her eyes.

And he began quivering, I thought he was going to have a heart-attack, his neck got redder and redder, with his whole shoulder-blade shaking, and he was towering above her as he struggled . . . 'The man is like a croissant!'

And she had to repeat the line. I went down afterwards and said, 'That was a wonderful invention there, Ralph, fetish becoming a croissant.'

'Well, I think Gerald Flood's face does look like a croissant, I've always thought so.'

The first night at the National Theatre went very well, and afterwards Peter Hall took them all off to a restaurant. Lindsay Anderson was delayed, and David Storey found himself sitting opposite Ralph at the end of the long table. The actor's adrenalin was pumping, having sailed through with many inventions and transpositions.

Ralph said, 'Do you remember the second day of rehearsal?'

'I do.'

'Somebody has to take a very large stick to Lindsay. He

always wants to be top dog, and there are no top dogs around here.'

He stared at me for a long time. 'There are just people like you and me – beasts!'

Yet, despite their arguments and fights (none of which were ever quite as fierce as in this play), Ralph and Lindsay had a great deal of respect for one another; and on more than one occasion, in despair with a director he frightened too easily, Ralph was heard to say, 'We could do with the cross Lindsay, he's a cross I'm prepared to bear.'

When *Early Days* opened the critics were divided. Ned Chaillet, with his *Times* column headed 'Pale Shadow of Old Court Days', thought Ralph's performance entertaining enough to cover up the play's thinness, 'but when he speaks the line: "If they paid me enough my memory might start coming back", he shares it with the audience as a joke which could refer to his performance.'

Michael Billington's headline in the *Guardian* was 'Richardson's Triumph', and he enthused, 'Given that this is a tone-poem rather than a conventional drama, it is hard to see how it could be better done'. He praised the writing, the setting, the music, and 'Anderson's calm, still production'. But

the real triumph belongs to Richardson. All the familiar mannerisms are there: the legs-apart, croquet-game stance, the right hand hitting the left in a *quiet* slap, the widening of one eye in thunderstruck amazement. But he also brings to the part a wonderful sense of practical mischief ('It's men of integrity I can't stand. You never know where you are with them'), and sporty outrageousness through which a feeling of life's meaninglessness constantly breaks. Richardson has a genius for jaunty sadness and ebullient despair; and his great moment here comes when, envisioning his dead wife, he flings out his arms to greet her with a cry of 'Ellen, Ellen' like a man embracing a ghost. This is vintage acting: the result of a lifetime's experience.

John Barber gave the play an unreserved welcome in the *Daily Telegraph*: 'It is as good to have this accomplished playwright back in the theatre as it is to see Sir Ralph triumph in his *pièce d'occasion*.'

The audiences thought so too, and the Cottesloe was packed out every night for eight weeks, in an unusual break from the National's pattern of running several plays in repertoire. After a North American tour it moved to the Comedy Theatre, where its first night was very nearly its last. Richardson had always refused to take a solo bow at the end, but this time the applause was so prolonged that the rest of the cast urged him forward. By the time he eventually and very reluctantly stepped forward the curtain was beginning to fall, weighted at the bottom with a huge beam, and it was only inches above his head when he was grabbed and pulled back, as it thudded at his feet. Had it fallen on his head it could well have killed him.

A stream of visitors made their way backstage during the run, including a colleague from the National Company, Robert Stephens. His girlfriend was wearing a very becoming red dress, with a low-cut neckline and a short skirt, and a pearl necklace. As Stephens entered the dressing-room, he knelt with an extravagant gesture, saying, 'Hail the greatest living actor in the English-speaking world, Hail!' Ralph got up, stepped over his kneeling figure, put his hand on his companion's necklace, and said, 'What a wonderful necklace, my dear.'[12]

Over the years Ralph perfected his own way of greeting

visitors, backstage or anywhere else – he would grip with both hands, neither drawing in nor pushing away, but firmly holding the person at a certain distance. It was perfectly warm and friendly, but succeeded in discouraging any kind of theatrical over-intimacy.

He also had his own way of saying farewell, which Simon Cadell experienced several times. After *Early Days* Ralph said to him, 'Ah, he dreams well, doesn't he, Storey?' and then reminisced about acting with Simon's grandmother, Jean Cadell, at the Birmingham Rep. 'He was almost in mid-flow, I'd been there about ten minutes, I'd had my shocker, and suddenly without any warning at all, he said, "Oh no, I've got to go now," and Hal appeared, my arm was taken, and before I knew it I was out of the room, with Hal saying, "Bye." '[13] A variant on that formula, experienced by many visitors, was 'I'll have to let you go now.'

David Storey became very close to Ralph during that run at the Comedy, and went round afterwards on many nights; echoing Peter Hall's experience, he soon realized that any intimate confidences would be exchanged only between the two of them on their own; even the presence of just a third person put up Ralph's shutters. After one shaky performance he said to Storey, 'You know, in this profession, you need the skin of a hippopotamus, on top of that you need the skin of an elephant, and around that you need the skin of a rhinoceros, and only then will you be able to survive.'

But even tête-à-tête there was a part of Ralph he was not prepared to expose. 'One late-night chat he said to me, "Don't mention self-pity or loneliness to me, we're all alone, cut it out." It was suddenly a very powerful evocation of his own solitariness – he was a very solitary fellow despite him being so very sociable.'[14]

Lindsay Anderson was also keenly aware which areas were off-limits. 'He liked to discuss after the performance how it had gone, and what he had done, so in that way Ralph had a craftsman's feeling about his acting; but the secret thing that there always is about acting, which is what comes out of the soul, he wouldn't or perhaps couldn't talk about.'

The television recording of *Early Days* was delayed, when Granada declined to take it as part of their regular arrangement with the National Theatre, and when it finally went into production with an independent company Lindsay Anderson was unavailable to direct it, so he suggested another alumnus of the Royal Court, Anthony Page.

Page jumped at the first chance of working with Ralph since *West of Suez*, and quickly discovered how seriously Ralph was taking the rethinking of his performance for the more intimate medium. A young would-be director asked permission to come and watch quietly at the back of rehearsals and Anthony Page agreed.

Ralph noticed almost immediately, beckoned me and said, 'Who is that?'

'It's someone who admires you, Ralph, and wants to learn about theatre.'

'I think this is the most precious time, when we can make fools of ourselves, it's really better if we don't have people watching that.'

He'd picked up like an animal that there was a stranger there, and so I had to go and say, 'Please leave.' When he was rehearsing he was opening himself up to discover how best to do it.[15]

But he was not too keen initially on opening himself up to his director, who kept pressing him: 'What's the character thinking now, I can't really make out, and I don't think the camera will be able to tell?' He had to show what the old man was really thinking – whether he was tricking people, whether he really thought he saw his wife at the end. Ralph admitted to Anthony Page that it was very rare for him to discuss things in that kind of detail, he usually liked to keep all that to himself.

> He said that he always found his own private secret path through a role, which he didn't like to tell the director. When he'd done *No Man's Land*, he kept it quite secret both from Harold Pinter and Peter Hall; but I was forcing him to reveal it by trying to freshen him up on this.[16]

He felt most vulnerable at the end, in his death-scene, and had begun to resist his director's suggestions, so the author went down on to the studio floor to talk to him.

> He saw me coming a long way away, he kept eye-contact until I got near him, and said, 'I know what you're going to say, but despair is out!'
> He was too tired (we'd been doing the play for months and he'd got quite worn out), the final end of someone dying was out.[17]

The television setting was much more realistic than in the theatre, no gauze screens but a cedar tree, a lot of bushes, a wall, and a view across hedges to distant meadows and hills. Ralph objected to the place set for him to die, he wanted a place of mystery, with a feeling of ghosts floating about, and he decided it would be much better under the cedar tree. So at quite a late stage it had to be re-plotted and re-lit, but Anthony Page was keen to accommodate his wishes.

> He was so strong about that and convinced by his instinct, and I knew him quite well by then so we did shoot it there. When we actually took the death, where he thinks he sees his

wife waiting for him in heaven, he started doing the most wonderful take of it (part of which is in the final edited version), and then he suddenly stopped. I think it was getting too real for him, I think it frightened him how real it was; we went back and did some more takes, but it never quite got that feeling again.[18]

Not perhaps for the director, who had caught that glimpse into the character's soul, but the wider audience was entranced by the revelations the actor did provide. Sylvia Clayton in the *Daily Telegraph* was bowled over by 'the living quicksilver of this unique actor', and by his voice 'which has within it a kind of music of doubt ... For me this was the virtuoso performance of the year.'

Peter Ackroyd used the identical phrase in *The Times*.

Since his is very much a virtuoso performance, the camera does not detract from it but rather brings it to a different level of intensity. It moves slowly towards his face so that the slightest movement of his eyes, or his mouth, can be seen to add a dimension to his words. And it is in his extraordinary control of such things that Sir Ralph reveals his mastery.

The play was transmitted in August 1982. As Sir Richard Kitchen he had the poignant line at the end: 'I have discovered the key to life, and nobody wants to use it.'

As Sir Ralph Richardson his key to happiness was to carry on working, and as he approached his eightieth birthday he showed little sign of slowing down, or any desire to put his feet up in what most men of his age would have seen as a long-overdue retirement.

CHAPTER TWENTY-FOUR
1982–1983

RALPH HAD a gift for friendship that he kept to the end of his days, and he was as happy to make new friends as he was keen to cherish old ones. Often these were outside his own profession, like Sir Georg Solti, whom he first met when they got into the same elevator in a New York hotel. Ralph once complained in a BBC lift, as everyone politely avoided his eye, 'The trouble with being famous is that nobody speaks to you in the lift.' With two famous men in the same one, neither of them had any such inhibition, and their conversation led to a late-blossoming friendship enjoyed by both men and their wives. Sir Georg thought him 'a typical English eccentric, but always the most enchanting man. I didn't find him unpredictable, I think because he respected musicians. He was not musically educated, but he liked the noise it makes.'[1]

Ralph always took great pains to find an unusual gift for special occasions. For the conductor's seventieth birthday he brought a small jar made out of agate, with a card simply inscribed:

21 Oct 81

A BIRTHDAY SALUTE

'AND SHE COMES IN SHAPE NO BIGGER THAN AN AGATE STONE'

ROMEO AND JULIET

By the time Angela Huth got to know Ralph he was in his eightieth year, and never in her wildest dreams had she thought he might star in her first play. Because she had not anticipated such good fortune she soon found herself in a real dilemma. *The Understanding* won a play competition at the Salisbury Playhouse, but then the director left. So she approached Roger Smith, who had just had a success directing Nell Dunn's *Steaming*. He loved the Huth play and said he would like to do it. In her pleasure at his enthusiasm she promised him he would be the director, whatever happened. When she went to see the producer Michael White he told her the play needed big names, so they sent it first to John Gielgud, who turned it down.

Ralph was next on the list, and within hours of receiving the script he rang to say he would do it. Producer and author met the actor at Claridge's. She thought Ralph was dressed as if he was going to a wedding.

What was so stunning and moving and awe-making was that he'd already learned practically the whole part. He quoted great chunks at me, and I just sat there with my mouth open; by the time we got to the coffee, which in Ralph's case was tea, poured into his saucer to cool, he was suggesting he designed the programme as well. The great discussion was how we should do this play, where we should do it, and who should be in it. He wanted Celia Johnson, and it was he who finally persuaded her to be in it; she felt her part wasn't quite big enough and wanted me to write it up a bit, which I did slightly.[2]

Celia had really wanted to spend the summer in her garden, and was feeling very tired, but once again she was unable to resist her old partner's pleas. However, there was an immediate problem with them both over the question of the director. Ralph wanted Anthony Page, and when Angela explained she had already made an arrangement with Roger Smith, his response was: 'Who's Roger Smith?' He was not at all pleased, and nor was his co-star. The author now found herself facing 'the most awful dilemma of my life – either I broke my promise to Roger, or I risked losing Ralph and Celia'. Her attempts to keep all three on board faltered at their first meeting when the director hardly opened his mouth. He was far too overawed by his leading players to direct them, and while they could, and did, in effect direct themselves, they could hardly direct the others.

When the director did assert himself it was even worse. He insisted on using the designer he had had for *Steaming*, Jenny Tiramani, to the author's dismay.

She was a very nice working-class girl, who said to me, 'I expect I'll manage, because I can look up in a book what a drawing-room looks like.' She also designed the clothes, and when the three old actresses put them on and showed Ralph he said, 'I'm not having any of those, they look like three cooks on their day out!' He was quite right. In the end Celia went out and bought her own in Henley on the morning the play opened. The set was rather grand, but lots of things were wrong, like the antimacassars on the sofas that no one in that sort of drawing-room would have had. It didn't have anything in it, not a book, or any invitations on the mantelpiece; I kept asking for candles, and books, and some things to indicate a room that had been lived in for forty-five years, not a hotel-suite.[3]

That faded, lived-in look was important. All that time Leonard had lived there with his uncomplaining wife Eva, her sister Acton, with whom Leonard had been platonically in love for the last forty years, and a third sister, Lydia, who had joined the family ménage ten years before. When Eva dies, Leonard and Acton are free at last to marry, but now he is undecided, until a young girl, Kate, arrives to help out with the domestic chores and disrupts the household.

The long-unconsummated love between Leonard and Acton was sensitively played by Ralph and Celia, and the pre-London audiences in Richmond and Brighton were enchanted. The week of previews at the Strand Theatre coincided with the Falklands War, which hit theatre audiences everywhere, but at the very last preview on the Saturday night the two stars received a standing ovation. On the Sunday Celia was at home playing bridge, and that evening her son-in-law, John Grimond, rang Angela Huth to say, 'I'm terribly sorry, Celia died at lunchtime.'

Michael White told Ralph, who after he had recovered from the initial shock said, 'I'm not going to open with the understudy.'

To Angela Huth's distress the off-stage saga now over-whelmed her delicate creation.

We tried every old actress we could think of, but none were available, in the end we settled for Joan Greenwood, who wasn't really quite right for the part, but she learned it in two days, and had only five days' rehearsal. By this stage Roger wasn't even able to tell her where she was to come in from. We opened the night after the sinking of the *Belgrano*, and Joan had bronchitis. Ralph's first entrance was in funeral clothes, the whole audience gasped, thinking of Celia, and it was rather doomed.

Most of the critics helped to doom it. Michael Coveney condemned it in the *Observer* as 'a catalogue of fluffs, bumps, awful direction by Roger Smith, average design by Jenny Tiramani, and a distinctly out of sorts performance by Richardson'. J. C. Trewin began his notice in the *Birmingham Post*: 'Not a good title; and really an indifferent play'. Rosalie Horner dismissed it in the *Daily Express* as 'so old-fashioned it virtually creaks'; but Milton Shulman fastened on to that very quality in the *Evening Standard* to praise its 'old-fashioned virtues of cultured conversation, civilized attitudes and wry humour'.

In the *Daily Mail* Jack Tinker thought it had 'a worth and value quite beyond its own apparent weight', and put his finger on why the opening night had failed to live up to its promise:

> Of course, the tragic death of that fine actress Celia Johnson casts its long shadow over this autumnal evening. The players still seem stricken by the blow. Though Joan Green-wood has stepped gallantly into the breach, there is a strange incompleteness about the production. Even though her voice is toothsome and inviting, as if strained through soft, warm toffee, Miss Greenwood strikes only intermittent responses from Sir Ralph, who appears to be listening for messages which never arrive at quite the moment he expects them.

His distress at losing one of his favourite leading ladies, this time for ever, finally proved too much for Ralph, according to Angela Huth.

> Ralph was marvellous for about a week, then post-depression about Celia set in. After eight weeks we called it off, and Ralph was terribly upset. 'About another 100 performances and I'd begin to get the measure of the part.' It really died when Celia died.

For all the disappointment and sadness she suffered over the production of her first play, Angela still treasures the brief but rewarding friendship with Ralph that it brought her. Her last meeting with him is forever etched in her memory. A few months after *The Understanding* closed, she went to lunch with some friends who were entertaining the Queen Mother, and they all went on to John Gielgud's house for tea. They were met in the garden by Sir John and Sir Ralph.

> As we walked up to the house we paused as John showed the Queen Mother a couple of tortoises. She said, 'I wonder how tortoises communicate with each other, do you think they speak to each other?' Ralph said, 'Oh, Ma'am, would you like me to try to find out?' and he leaned over the wire and made as if to listen to the conversation of the tortoises, it was a very charming scene.
>
> Then we went into the dining-room for tea, which looked like a banquet for a hundred people, and there were only six or seven of us; profiteroles done up in pyramids, with strawberries and sugar all interlaced falling down, fifteen different kinds of sandwiches, cakes and biscuits. Mu was at the end pouring tea, and I had the good fortune to be sitting opposite the Queen Mother, who had Ralph on one side and John on the other. They were competing with anecdotes to

entertain her, and she was dazzlingly happy, turning from one to the other of the old knights. I thought I can't really believe this, it's just the most memorable tea of my life, nothing whatever will ever, ever surpass it. After the Queen Mother had gone, Ralph came up and just patted me on the shoulder and said, 'Pity about that play, it was a wonderful play.' Then he drove off, and that was the last time I ever saw him.[4]

Angela Huth was the last in that line of English play-wrights – Priestley, Sherriff, Bolt, Storey, Osborne, Douglas-Home and Pinter – who had reason to be grateful that the Richardson magic had enveloped their creations. Directors and actors might, and did, share that admiration, although one or two of them experienced the competitive streak in Ralph that occasionally showed itself, and revealed the inner drive that had taken him to the top of his profession.

After the actress's death a number of people decided to raise money for the Celia Johnson Memorial Theatre at St Paul's Girls' School, and a gala evening at the Aldwych Theatre had Ralph at the top of the bill. Simon Cadell was also appearing, in a short play by John Mortimer about Holst, once the music teacher at St Paul's. Jeremy Irons had been a friend of Simon's since their days at drama school together, and he was now a rising star, following his double screen success in *Brideshead Revisited* and *The French Lieutenant's Woman*. He was eager to meet Ralph, so Simon went round to the dressing-room to ask, 'Ralph, Jeremy Irons would love to meet you, can I bring him in?'

He was sitting at his dressing-table at the left end of the long narrow dressing-room, looking at Celia's poems that he was going to read, and said, 'Yes, bring him in.' To the right of the door was a long sitting area with a mantelpiece at the end, and when Simon returned moments later he found Ralph standing there with his back to them.

So I ushered Jeremy in and said, 'Ralph, I'd like you to meet Jeremy Irons.'

As I left Ralph turned to Jeremy and said, 'Hello, so . . . you're . . . the young . . . tiger.'

I could see in his eyes as he said it – 'You haven't met one of the big boys, I'm an old tiger.' And I understood why Jeremy came out of that room, about ten minutes later, looking ten years older and about six inches shorter.[5]

Ralph's ability to surprise, which was one of his great qualities as an actor, could be disconcerting in the extreme off the stage. When the preparations were being made to celebrate Lord Olivier's seventieth birthday, the General Manager of the Theatre Royal at Brighton, Melville Gillam, was deputed to go and see Ralph to discuss the plans. American friends were to be flown over, the food was to be brought from Claridge's, and it was to be a big occasion. He asked Ralph what he thought, was it a good idea?

'Yes, I think it's a very good idea. Or . . . you could wait until he is seventy-one.'

He was just as cagey about celebrating his own eightieth birthday in 1982. He was persuaded to take part in a televised conversation with Bernard Levin for the BBC, most of which was filmed on the stage where he had triumphed as Peer Gynt, Falstaff and Cyrano de Bergerac – the New Theatre, now renamed the Albery.

He reminisced happily enough for a while about his youth, of buying forty-two volumes of Shakespeare at sixpence each from a barrow at Brighton, of his few months at art school where he regretted he never got as far as the life class, and then he pulled his usual role-reversal trick of getting Levin to tell him a story about Montgomery, and started asking him about his life as a critic. He talked a little of the mechanics of acting, and the problem he had had with coughers in *Cyrano*.

'You're trying to write something on a nice white sheet of paper, which is your script or your part, and someone continually throws ink on it, it's very annoying indeed, you get more angry than you should.'

This memory of a thirty-six-year-old irritation seemed to unsettle him, and to his interlocutor's consternation he looked off-screen to his right, at one of the camera crews, saying, 'These chaps need a drink.' Suddenly he was on his feet, putting on his hat and coat and picking up his stick, indicating that they had talked quite long enough. Levin desperately tried to detain him by getting him to demonstrate how as Falstaff he had carried off Olivier as the slain Hotspur, even lying down on the stage to play the corpse, but Ralph just twinkled down at him, saying he could not remember now, and then he was off. He always knew how to make an exit, and he had long mastered the art of controlling its timing.

Part of his reticence was a product of his genuine belief that he had not achieved all he should. He told *The Times* for its eightieth birthday profile,

> People might think of me as an eccentric old actor, keen on motor-bikes, but I know my worth. I know how good Olivier is and I know how good Gielgud is. It is just that, in all my eighty years, I haven't achieved much. Those people have been building bridges: I haven't. I have been lucky. I know how much is talent and how much is luck and I'm not such a damn fool that I don't know exactly where I stand. They can build me up as they like, but it's just flattery. That's not false modesty. That's a fact, I am sincere in that.

Just in case anyone may have missed the point that he felt he had been favoured by good fortune, which he never took for granted, he spelt it out again in an article he wrote for the

Observer on his birthday, under the headline 'Recollections of a Lucky Man'. 'Oh yes, I've been lucky up to now, *up to now*. Nobody knows tomorrow! If I push along into AD 1983 I'd like to pluck a leaf from the Italian laurel Eduardo de Filippo, a dreamy foliage, this one, for the National Theatre.'

Before he plucked that leaf in the theatre, he had a couple more dates with the film cameras. One was memorable, and much-hyped, because it brought together on screen the great triumvirate of actor-knights, Gielgud, Olivier and Richardson, in *Wagner*. The film starred Richard Burton in the title-role, and was directed by Tony Palmer. It overran its planned length and its budget; a truncated version was seen briefly in the cinema, and a longer serialized version on television. For most critics and viewers the only moments of value featured the three knights, and there was a division of opinion as to which of the three had scored most points against the other two. Ralph much enjoyed working with his two old friends again, although he complained for long afterwards that he had not yet been paid for this performance.

He and Gielgud had fun together again in *Invitation to the Wedding*, he as a bishop on a motor-cycle, and Sir John in a stetson with an American accent, but the film did not make much of a splash.

Ralph's last film did, however. *Greystoke* set out to tell the story of Tarzan of the Apes as Edgar Rice Burroughs originally conceived it, shorn of all its Hollywood excrescences. It was directed by Hugh Hudson, who had made the Oscar-winning *Chariots of Fire*, and he was very keen to get Ralph to play the eccentric old Earl of Greystoke, grandfather of the Tarzan-figure. In an early conversation he found a common bond in their love of the work of the writer W. H. Hudson (no relation), who wrote a string of books about life in the Argentinian pampas of the last century. Hudson's favourite novel for both of them was *Far Away and Long Ago*; Ralph as usual had read all of them, and gave the director a couple that he had not yet read.

The film had two script-writers. The first was Robert Towne, who wrote the earlier scenes where the child grows up with the apes, but he only sketched out the return-to-civilization part, so Michael Austin developed those scenes, and Ralph wanted a number of changes, which the director rapidly incorporated.

> We wrote this character with Ralph, and rightly so he changed it all. He wrote his own dialogue, he's got his own poetry in it, and you can feel it, the dialogue absolutely belongs to that man, slightly dotty dialogue in his own rhythm, that strange rhythm of performing, of delivering lines. I should say it was about seventy per cent him. There's a very good scene when they are riding on the estate by the wall, when he talks about land, 'Land is the lifeblood of this family', that's all Ralph's dialogue, the ambivalent dialogue about the wall keeping them out but keeping him in, those ideas were written but he rephrased them all.[7]

One of the most moving scenes in the film is when he first sets eyes on his long-lost grandson, brought home from the jungle. As the coach rolls up the drive the Earl of Greystoke comes out to greet him, followed by staff and friends. The leader of the expedition to Africa, Sir Evelyn Blount, was played by John Wells, who stood next to Ralph and overheard him, just before the cameras turned over, repeating to himself sotto voce, 'I think he's going to be a monkey, I think he's going to be a monkey.'[8]

This enormously impressed Wells as Ralph's way of concentrating and preparing his reaction for when the carriage door opened and Christopher Lambert looked out. The emotion with which he then played the scene caught even the director by surprise. 'I didn't realize how he was going to react, that he was going to express himself like that, it was incredibly moving; every time I see it I cry, even me and I know it intimately, I was there when it was done.'[9]

Other surprises were used to brilliant comic effect. In the scene where Sir Evelyn Blount goes in to the Earl with his breakfast for a serious discussion about the inheritance, he finds him shaving at the mirror. Suddenly, in a move he had never rehearsed, Ralph dipped his shaving-brush in his coffee-cup, an inspired stroke of eccentricity wonderfully in character for the part. It was also his idea to drink his soup out of the bowl at the dinner-party, which shocks his guests but puts his jungle-bred grandson at ease when he is mystified by all the cutlery.

Ralph only appears in a few scenes, but the depth and truthfulness of his playing mean that he effortlessly dominates the film. Towards the end there is a big Christmas-party scene where he announces his grandson's engagement, when he surprised and delighted his director again.

> I love the way he took over the scene, it should really have been Tarzan and the girl's scene, because they're getting married. He took it over, naughty really, but OK; and one wanted him to take it over, because he was the dominant factor really, you can't avoid him in those moments.

After his announcement, as the dancing gets under way, the old Earl drifts upstairs, and in a joyful celebration of his own he spies a large tea-tray and decides to toboggan down the stairs as he did as a boy. This exit was Ralph's invention. In the original script he has a heart attack and falls down the stairs, but in Ralph's version it is the whim of sliding down the stairs that kills him, happy in the knowledge that there is now an heir to carry on the line. It made for a much more poignant death. A stunt-man was used for the actual slide, although Ralph was quite game to go down himself, if the director had let him. But he did insist on driving the pony-trap himself, despite Hugh Hudson's nervousness about the dangers for a man of his age.

His natural curiosity and professional interest led him to ask to go up to the set to watch when he was not called. He was fascinated by the scenes of the ape behaviour, and would stand amongst the foliage watching 'the monkeys', as he called them. The actors in the ape-suits simulated simian behaviour so accurately that even the real baby chimpanzees on the set were deceived.

The jungle location scenes, which were shot in the rain forests of Cameroon, did not involve Ralph, slightly to his regret, but he ensured that he was there in spirit with the director. 'Before I went to Africa, Ralph sent me a wonderful little piece of Roman glass as a present for my trip, with a note in Latin – 'Hail Caesar, Hail Africanus.'

John Wells was touched by his natural modesty when during a conversation one day on the set, Ralph said, 'Is there no end to your talents? Someone once said that to me. I was at the barber's, and he said, "Do you like it, sir?" I said, "Hand me your comb," and I combed my quiff forward, and the barber said, "Is there no end to your talents?" '[10]

Greystoke was not released until after Ralph's death, which inevitably gives his death-scene in it an extra resonance, but his performance in this screen-farewell would have been moving in any circumstances. Hugh Hudson dedicated the film to Ralph's memory when it was released.

His final stage performance was, as he wished, at the National Theatre, in the play he had mentioned on his eightieth birthday – *Inner Voices* by Eduardo de Filippo. Peter Hall found it, and thought it would appeal to him – it had a couple of features especially suited to the actor's temperament.

One was its use of fireworks, a lifelong passion of Ralph's. He had persuaded the National Theatre, when it moved into its new building on the South Bank, that curtain-up each night should be marked by the firing of a rocket from the roof to alert London to the event. It was known, naturally, as 'Ralph's Rocket'. After a while this was restricted to first nights only. (At the height of the IRA bombing campaign it had to be discontinued at the request of the police; Richard Eyre asked after the IRA ceasefire if he could now reinstate 'Ralph's Rocket', which was readily agreed.)

It was not Ralph's character in *Inner Voices* who had the pleasure of setting off the fireworks on-stage, but that of his dotty old uncle, though only he, perhaps, could have convinced the audience, as he did, that he was actually communicating with the fireworks. But he was required, as Don Alberto, to dream, and when he dreams of a murder it becomes so real that his accusations set off a chain of counter-accusations that provide the engine for the plot. Characters who dream were always Ralph's forte, and he invested Don Alberto with all that Richardson magic.

He experienced his customary trouble with foreign terms. In his mouth the *carabinieri* became 'the carburettors', and on occasion he got his Italian genders and names mixed up. He had an entrance line addressed to an old woman, 'Good morning, Donna Rosa,' in a scene that also included his brother Carlo, played by Michael Bryant, who remembers how one night 'Ralph swept in, in a very confident manner, took off his hat with a flourishing gesture, and said, "Good evening, Don Paxo," which stopped the play for a little while.'[11]

He also ran into trouble with his director again, this time Mike Ockrent. Ralph just could not get on with him, and did not approve of anything he told him to do. The author himself had played Ralph's part in the Italian premiere; Ockrent got hold of a video-recording of it – what Ralph called 'a veedo thing' – and asked if it would help if they both watched it. Ralph was appalled at the very idea, as should have been anticipated, and their relationship never recovered.

The *Sunday Telegraph* reviewer castigated 'the extraordinarily limp direction', but felt the evening was saved by the outstanding performances, by Michael Bryant as Carlo, Robert Stephens as Don Pasquale, 'and as Alberto, Ralph Richardson – well, extravagantly and incomparably, Sir Ralph once again shows himself to be the Merlin of our theatre.'

John Barber drew the same distinction in the *Daily Telegraph*:

> In Mike Ockrent's production, the story proceeds like a sleep-walking tortoise ... However, Ralph Richardson gives a haunting central performance as the aged informer who in all honesty denounces the family next door for murdering a missing man, and then realizes he dreamed the whole thing. When he recants, the police think he is lying. With drooping moustache, a burning eye and 'a constitution not worth tuppence', the old man speaks quaveringly of the ever-present ghosts of the dead, every feathery word threatening to be his last. Spry and obsessed at first, and eager to trap his suspects, he ends a wreck as the wickedness of the world sinks into his consciousness – the acid that will soon destroy him.

This climax was the highpoint too for Michael Billington in the *Guardian*:

> He conveys totally a man unsure whether he is dreaming or waking; and it is precisely because he seems half-motored by dreams, that his final condemnation of base humanity carries such force. It is a rebuke from the Heavens; and it puts a memorable seal on an erratic evening.

In the *Observer* Robert Cushman pinpointed not only the key to this performance, but also part of the secret of this actor's genius.

> Richardson, of course, is perfect casting. No actor, for a start, can get more out of the vital word 'dream'; none can so delicately kick himself for foolishness that may be wisdom after all; and none can pass so effortlessly from a world of his own to the crispest of everyday comic timing.

During the run his offbeat sense of humour was almost too much for Michael Gambon, who had made him a little silver box in his workshop for a present.

> When I went to see him in *Inner Voices* he opened it for me and showed me this tablet in it, like a Redoxon Vitamin C, a great big tablet, grey with dirt, it was years old. I said, 'What is it?'
> 'That tablet was given to me by a doctor in the war, when I wasn't very well, and I've never taken it.'
> 'Shouldn't you take it now?'
> 'No, I want you to take it.'
> 'I'm not taking it.'
> 'I think you should, you don't look very well.'
> You know how formidable he was, he poured me a glass of soda water and gave me this tablet, and I swallowed it. He went hysterical with laughter, he loved that. He said it was prescribed in 1940.[12]

It was some hours before the unwilling patient recovered his equilibrium, and his fear of unimaginable side-effects subsided.

It was that ever-present sense of humour, as much as his deep sensitivity, that so endeared him to Sir Peter Hall.

My favourite memory of him is that I never met him, or saw him, without my spirits rising, because he was so funny. He really was a very, very funny man, he thought life was very funny. He enjoyed so many things that we all enjoy and made no secret of it – books, and food, and wine, and living. To me he was the father you always wanted and perhaps never had, that you could say anything to about your problems – he would listen, and be wise.[13]

For most of the last eight years of his life the National Theatre was home to Ralph, and when *Inner Voices* was scheduled to go on a regional tour he was planning to go with it, true to that lifetime belief he shared with Phyllis Calvert in 1960, that without touring the theatre would die.

But this was one tour where the great trouper was forced to disappoint his public. Early in October 1983 he suffered a series of strokes of increasing severity, and was taken into King Edward VII Hospital in Marylebone. According to those close friends Michael Meyer and Peter Hall, his end was very Roman. When he asked the doctor, 'I want a straight answer to two questions, shall I live, and if I do what will I be like?', the doctor answered, 'You will live, but you will be in a wheelchair for the rest of your life.'

'Thank you,' said Ralph, turned over and died within two days, on 10 October.

His death came so quickly that it caught everyone by surprise. At 5.30 p.m. that Monday, Laurence Evans received a call from Mu to say that Ralph had died half an hour before, and asking him if he could take care of the announcement to the press. He called the Press Association and gave them the bare announcement. A few minutes later they rang back to ask, 'How are you feeling?' He said, 'Awful,' and burst into tears on the telephone, and so did his secretary in the office.

The wires were immediately humming as the newspapers

began calling round for tributes. Sir John Gielgud was one of the first to be telephoned, and was much too upset to comment. Sir Peter Hall could only manage the briefest of public statements: 'He was one of the greatest actors who ever lived – I am sure of this. He was also a great man – tender, warm and funny. And he was a great friend.' Later that evening he put together a longer, private message to the National Theatre Company.

In Nottingham the cast of *Inner Voices* were beginning to get made-up for the evening performance. They all of course knew that Ralph was in hospital, but had no idea of the seriousness of his condition, so when Michael Bryant answered the telephone to hear a voice say, 'This is *The Times*, do you have any comment on the death of Ralph Richardson?' he was so shaken and outraged that he slammed the receiver down with an oath. That night, for the first and only time, the fireworks refused to go off properly on-stage.

All the actors gave a very heightened performance. Robert Stephens had taken over Ralph's part, and at the end stepped forward to announce his death, to an audible gasp from the audience. He made an emotional speech and then asked for two minutes' silence in remembrance of the great actor. All the audience stood, as the actors whipped off their mafiosi-style fedoras. Michael Bryant's wife Judy stood next to Hal, who had come up to dress Robert Stephens as Don Alberto, and watched Diana Boddington 'trying to carry on through a sea of tears'.[14] There was an unspoken feeling throughout the Company that an era was gone.

At the National Theatre in London the leading actor made a speech from each of the three stages – Sir Michael Hordern in the Olivier (*The Rivals*), Paul Jones in the Cottesloe (*The Beggar's Opera*), and Martin Jarvis in the Lyttelton. Jarvis was playing Hector in *The Trojan War Will Not Take Place*, and was surprised to receive a visit in the interval by its director,

Harold Pinter, who said tersely, trying to contain his emotion, 'Martin, Ralph's dead. I think you ought to make an announcement.' He had only acted with him once, but had come under his spell, like so many of his colleagues.

I spent the rest of the interval thinking about what I would say. When I saw him in *Inner Voices* he looked about ten feet tall, as if he had follow-spots, which of course he didn't. I couldn't take my eyes off him.

As we finished and took the curtain-call I stepped forward and put my arm up to call for silence. 'Ladies and gentlemen, I have some very sad news to tell you. Our very great colleague, Ralph Richardson, has died this evening.' There was a sad explosion of air and a great cathartic groan, it was an extraordinary sound. I asked for us all to share a minute's silence in remembering him, and we all stood there on-stage. Then I stepped back and the audience applauded as the curtain came down.[15]

Peggy Ashcroft heard the news on her way to see *Measure for Measure* at Stratford-upon-Avon. Daniel Massey was playing the Duke, and was surprised when she appeared in his dressing-room with Ian McKellen before the performance.

She said, 'You know Ralph has died?'

I was completely bowled over. I was getting ready to go on, and they said, 'You'd better make an announcement at the end, as the leading man in the company you'd better make a speech.'

We got to the end of the show and I stepped forward and said, 'Many of you sitting here tonight will not know the sad news that I have to tell you, that one of our great actors, Ralph Richardson, has died.'

And I couldn't get anything else out, I couldn't speak

because there was an audible, visceral, I don't know what to call it really, everybody contributed something audible, of pain. At the end of a very short speech I quoted Ralph, 'Silence is the paper on which the actor writes', and said, 'Perhaps you will stand with us for a minute.'

It was a great privilege to do that, but what I divined absolutely at that moment was that he was loved, genuinely loved.[16]

If the news was hard for audiences to bear, it was harder still for those who had grown close to Ralph Richardson over the years. Robin Midgley heard it on the car radio, and had to pull into a layby, where he sat for half an hour, just thinking about Ralph during *Lloyd George Knew My Father* and their meetings since. He says, 'It was just like the death of Kennedy, we can all remember where we were when we heard Ralph had died.'[17]

For Simon Cadell it was on location for *Hi-de-Hi* the following morning. 'I was coming down the stairs and Su Pollard was standing at the bottom and she said, "Oh, Simon, your friend Ralph Richardson has just died." I had to carry on filming the comedy series – it was the most terrible morning.'[18]

In a mark of respect reserved as a tribute for the greatest in the profession, all the theatres in London dimmed their lights on the Tuesday night. The funeral Mass was said on the Thursday in Sir Ralph's favourite church in Walton Street, and the ceremony was attended by family and close friends. The following day, his burial in Highgate Cemetery was attended only by the immediate family.

He was two months short of his eighty-first birthday, and it was sixty-three years since his imagination had been set aflame by the sound of Sir Frank Benson's sword scraping the stage.

EPILOGUE

BY NOON on 17 November 1983, Westminster Abbey was packed, and could have been filled five times over, so great was the demand for tickets to the memorial service of thanksgiving for the life and work of Sir Ralph Richardson.

The front of the programme bore a quotation from John Bunyan: 'And I awoke, and behold it was a dream.'

After the opening hymn the Dean, the Very Reverend Edward Carpenter, spoke the Bidding Prayer.

> In this ancient Abbey Church where Ann Oldfield, David Garrick and Sybil Thorndike are memorialized, we meet together as members of his family and admirers, to thank God for so rare a person as Ralph Richardson. We think of him as one of the great and outstanding actors of his time who held the mirror up to nature; plumbed the depths of our earthly experience; played many parts across the years always with sympathy never with cynicism, thereby laying bare the mysteries of our human condition in its frailty and in its grandeur, in its perfidy and in its purity. We give praise to God for the most kindly, the most lovable and the most human of men. We rejoice that if his death, as Johnson said of Garrick, 'eclipsed the gaiety of nations', yet his influence will live on to inspire in future generations of actors a like integrity

and seriousness in the practice of so noble and so essential an art.

The two Lessons were read by actors from the next generation. Albert Finney spoke the passage from Revelation beginning: 'I saw a new heaven and a new earth'; and Alan Howard read from Corinthians on 'faith, hope and charity'.

The Address was given by Lord Olivier, who began: 'Ralph started to be my hero in 1926, and has been my closest friend for nigh on sixty years.' He recalled with humour their time together with Barry Jackson, in the Navy, and at the Old Vic, and ended with this peroration:

> In these latter years, he and John Gielgud have partnered each other with the happiest and most brilliant results. Various combinations of two of the three of us have also been witnessed over the last fifty years or so, but most strangely indeed, it was not until two years ago that the triple pleasure was achieved of being all together – three minor roles in a film made in Austria. Such an agreeable companion as Ralph did not lack for friends, either in personal, professional or universal popularity. His friendship for me, and mine for him have been, I must conclude, the steadiest influences of my life.
>
> Wise, strong, gentle, shrewd, understanding – I loved him – not this side idolatry but right in the core of it. A Golden man, take him for all in all – we shall not look upon his like again.

After the prayers for all actors and actresses, for the welfare of all animals, and the Blessing by the Dean, the last spoken words of the service came from Sir John Gielgud, who read from Bunyan's *Pilgrim's Progress*. Irene Worth knew how hard the occasion was for him, and was moved, like many others, when his voice broke on those last lines: 'So he passed over, and all the trumpets sounded for him on the other side.'

The Abbey choir picked up this theme with the Purcell Anthem 'Sound the Trumpet', and after Robert Tear had sung Giordani's 'Caro mio ben' the whole congregation rose for the final hymn, 'Jerusalem'. Few of them were able to sing properly since, as Michael Gambon recalls, 'everyone was weeping, it was the most powerful Memorial I've ever been to'.

As the congregation streamed out of the Abbey to the pealing of its bells, some may have recalled those lines by the Earl of Rochester which Ralph chose to head his own last birthday memoir:

> LOVE AND LIFE
> All my past Life is mine no more,
> The flying hours are gone:
> Like transitory Dreams giv'n o'er,
> Whose Images are kept in store
> By Memory alone.

The dreams Ralph Richardson brought to life still live on in the memories of all who saw them.

NOTES

PROLOGUE

1. Bryan Forbes, *That Despicable Race* (Elm Tree/Hamish Hamilton, 1980).

CHAPTER 1

1. 'Acting Is Partly Dreaming' (BBC2, 22 April 1972).
2. *Sunday Times*, 26 June 1960.
3. 'Acting Is Partly Dreaming'.
4. *Sunday Times*, 26 June 1960.
5. *Desert Island Discs*, (with Roy Plomley BBC Radio 4, 31 July 1979).
6. 'Acting Is Partly Dreaming'.

CHAPTER 2

1. *Sunday Times*, 3 July 1960.
2. Ibid.
3. 'Acting Is Partly Dreaming' (BBC 2, 22 April 1972).
4. *Sunday Times*, 3 July 1960.
5. Ibid.
6. Ibid.
7. Ibid.
8. J. C. Trewin, *The Birmingham Repertory Theatre, 1913–1963* (Rockliff, 1963).
9. *Sunday Times*, 3 July 1960.

10. Cantor Lecture, Royal Society of Arts, 3 March 1952.

11. Anthony Holden, *Olivier* (Sphere, 1988).

12. *Sunday Times*, 3 July 1960.

13. Sir Cedric Hardwicke, *A Victorian in Orbit* (Methuen, 1961).

14. Peter Copley, interview with author.

15. *Desert Island Discs*, (with Roy Plomley, BBC Radio 4, 31 July 1979).

CHAPTER 3

1. Hal Burton, *Great Acting* (BBC Publications, 1967).

2. Robert Speaight, *The Property Basket* (Collins, 1970).

3. Ibid.

4. Burton, op. cit.

5. Harcourt Williams, *Old Vic Saga* (Winchester Publications, 1949).

6. Elizabeth Sprigge, *Sybil Thorndike Casson* (Victor Gollancz, 1971).

7. Ibid.

8. Harcourt Williams, *Four Years at the Old Vic* (Putnam, 1935).

CHAPTER 4

1. *Sunday Times*, 10 July 1960.

2. Bryan Forbes, *That Despicable Race* (Elm Tree/Hamish Hamilton, 1980).

3. *Sunday Times*, 10 July 1960.

4. Anthony Holden, *Olivier* (Sphere, 1988).

5. *Sunday Times*, 10 July 1960.

6. Laurence Irving, unpublished memoir.

7. *Desert Island Discs*, (with Roy Plomley, BBC Radio 4, 31 July 1979).

8. Karol Kulik, *Alexander Korda* (Virgin, 1990).

9. Ibid.

10. Ibid.

11. Alan Coulson, *Films in Review*, October 1969.

CHAPTER 5

1. Karol Kulik, *Alexander Korda* (Virgin, 1990).

2. Sir Anthony Quayle, *A Time to Speak* (Barrie & Jenkins, 1990).

3. Harcourt Williams, *Old Vic Saga* (Winchester Publications, 1949).

4. Quayle, op. cit.

5. J. B. Priestley, *Margin Released* (Heinemann, 1962).

6. J. B. Priestley, *Daily Telegraph* Magazine, 1975.

7. J. B. Priestley, *Margin Released*.

CHAPTER 6

1. Sir Alec Guinness, *Blessings in Disguise* (Hamish Hamilton, 1985).

2. *Sunday Times*, 10 July 1960.

3. *Desert Island Discs*, (with Roy Plomley, Radio 4, 31 July 1979).

4. Sir Anthony Quayle, *A Time to Speak* (Barrie & Jenkins, 1990).

5. Dorothy Tutin, interview with author.

6. Diana Boddington, interview with author.

7. Joyce Redman, interview with author.

8. Harcourt Williams, *Old Vic Saga* (Winchester Publications, 1949).

9. Michael Meyer, interview with author.

10. Peter Howell, interview with author.

11. Peter Copley, interview with author.

12. Joyce Redman, interview with author.

CHAPTER 7

1. Peter Copley, interview with author.

2. Sir Laurence Olivier, *On Acting* (Weidenfeld & Nicolson, 1986).

3. *Sunday Times*, 10 July 1960.

4. Sir Peter Hall, interview with author.

5. Kenneth Tynan, *A View of the English Stage, 1944–1963* (Davis-Poynter, 1975).

6. J. C. Trewin, *Shakespeare on the British Stage, 1900–1964* (Collins, 1973).

7. Christopher Fry, letter to author.

8. Harold Hobson, *Ralph Richardson* (Rockliff, 1958).

9. Peter Copley, interview with author.

10. Sir Peter Ustinov, interview with author.

11. Donald Sinden, interview with author.

CHAPTER 8

1. Diana Boddington, interview with author.
2. Peter Copley, interview with author.
3. James Forsyth, *Tyrone Guthrie* (Hamish Hamilton, 1976).
4. Kenneth Tynan *A View of the English Stage, 1944–1963* (Davis-Poynter, 1975).
5. Peter Copley, interview with author.
6. Tarquin Olivier, *Laurence Olivier* (Headline, 1992).
7. Peter Copley, interview with author.
8. Sir Alec Guinness, *Blessings in Disguise* (Hamish Hamilton, 1985).
9. Peter Copley, interview with author.
10. Sir Alec Guinness, letter to author.
11. Tarquin Olivier, interview with author.
12. Sir Alec Guinness, letter to author.
13. Judy Campbell, interview with author.
14. Karol Kulik, *Alexander Korda* (Virgin, 1990).
15. Hugh Hudson, interview with author.
16. Patricia Bosworth, *Montgomery Clift* (Harcourt Brace Jovanovich, 1978)
17. Michael Meyer, interview with author.
18. Sir Anthony Hopkins, interview with author.

CHAPTER 9

1. Sir Tyrone Guthrie, *A Life in the Theatre* (Hamish Hamilton, 1960).
2. James Forsyth, *Tyrone Guthrie* (Hamish Hamilton, 1976).
3. Charles Landstone, *Offstage* (Elek, 1953).
4. Gillian Cadell, letter to author.
5. Ibid.
6. Sir John Gielgud, interview with author.
7. Michael Billington, *Peggy Ashcroft* (Mandarin, 1991).
8. Alan Coulson, *Films in Review*, October 1969.
9. Sir John Gielgud, interview with author.
10. Gillian Cadell, letter to author.
11. Harold Hobson, *Ralph Richardson* (Rockliff, 1958).

12. Donald Sinden, interview with author.
13. David Storey, interview with author.
14. Selina Cadell, interview with author.

CHAPTER 10

1. BBC Written Archives Centre, Caversham.
2. Max Reinhardt, interview with author.
3. 'Acting Is Partly Dreaming' (BBC 2, 22 April 1972).
4. Alan Coulson, *Films in Review*, October 1969.
5. Dame Wendy Hiller, interview with author.
6. 'Acting Is Partly Dreaming'.

CHAPTER 11

1. Gladys Varney, letter to author.
2. Bryan Forbes, *That Despicable Race* (Elm Tree/Hamish Hamilton, 1980).
3. Foyle's Literary Luncheon, 5 June 1951.
4. Sir John Gielgud, interview with author.
5. Ibid.
6. Sir Michael Hordern, interview with author.
7. Peter Howell, interview with author.
8. Sir Anthony Hopkins, interview with author.
9. Foyle's Literary Luncheon, 5 June 1951.
10. Sir Anthony Quayle, *A Time to Speak* (Barrie & Jenkins, 1990)
11. *Sunday Times*, 10 July 1960.
12. Cantor Lecture, Royal Society of Arts, 3 March 1952.

CHAPTER 12

1. Irene Worth, interview with author.
2. Ibid.
3. Tarquin Olivier, *Laurence Olivier* (Headline, 1992).
4. Sir Cedric Hardwicke, *A Victorian in Orbit* (Methuen, 1961).
5. Edward Hardwicke, interview with author.
6. Elizabeth Sprigge, *Sybil Thorndike Casson* (Victor Gollancz, 1971).

7. Frith Banbury, interview with author.

8. Ibid.

9. Sir Anthony Hopkins, interview with author.

10. Dame Wendy Hiller, interview with author.

CHAPTER 13

1. Phyllis Calvert, interview with author.

2. Paul Scofield, letter to author.

3. Phyllis Calvert, interview with author.

4. Paul Scofield, letter to author.

5. Piers Plowright, interview with author.

6. Alan Dobie, interview with author.

7. Sir Alec Guinness, letter to author.

8. Edward Fox, interview with author.

9. Alan Coulson, *Films in Review*, October 1969.

10. 'Acting Is Partly Dreaming' (BBC 2, 22 April 1972).

11. Katharine Hepburn, letter to author.

12. Daniel Massey, interview with author.

13. John Neville, interview with author.

14. Ibid.

15. Daniel Massey, interview with author.

16. Derek Glynne, interview with author.

CHAPTER 14

1. Barbara Jefford, interview with author.

2. John Powell, interview with author.

3. Irene Worth, interview with author.

4. Barbara Jefford, interview with author.

5. Sir Alec Guinness, *Blessings in Disguise* (Hamish Hamilton, 1985).

6. Sir Alec Guinness, letter to author.

7. Tom Courtenay, interview with author.

8. Peter Wood, interview with author.

9. Ibid.

CHAPTER 15

1. Charlton Heston, interview with author.
2. Judy Campbell, interview with author.
3. Keith Baxter, interview with author.
4. Felix Barker, interview with author.
5. Bryan Forbes, *That Despicable Race* (Elm Tree/Hamish Hamilton, 1980).
6. Judy Campbell, interview with author.
7. Daniel Massey, interview with author.
8. *Evening News*, 17 February 1967.
9. Frank Muir, interview with author.
10. *Evening News*, 17 February 1967.

CHAPTER 16

1. Ned Sherrin, *Theatrical Anecdotes* (Virgin, 1991).
2. John Powell, interview with author.
3. Sir Anthony Hopkins, interview with author.
4. John Lahr, *Prick Up Your Ears: Joe Orton* (Knopf, 1978).
5. Ibid.
6. John Tydeman, interview with author.

CHAPTER 17

1. Lindsay Anderson, interview with author.
2. Sir John Gielgud, interview with author.
3. Lindsay Anderson, interview with author.
4. David Storey, interview with author.
5. Sir John Gielgud, interview with author.
6. Jocelyn Herbert, interview with author.
7. Paul Moriarty, interview with author.
8. David Storey, interview with author.
9. Dorothy Tutin, interview with author.
10. Patrick Garland, interview with author.

CHAPTER 18

1. Michael Williams, interview with author.
2. Tom Courtenay, interview with author.
3. Anthony Page, interview with author.
4. Penelope Wilton, interview with author.
5. Robin Midgley, interview with author.
6. Simon Cadell, interview with author.
7. *The Times*, 1 July 1972.
8. Derek Glynne, interview with author.

CHAPTER 19

1. Sir Anthony Hopkins, interview with author.
2. Patrick Garland, interview with author.
3. Ibid.
4. Sir Peter Hall, interview with author.
5. Sir Peter Hall, *Diaries: 1972–1980* (Hamish Hamilton, 1983).
6. Sir Peter Hall, interview with author.
7. Dame Wendy Hiller, interview with author.
8. Sir Peter Hall, interview with author.

CHAPTER 20

1. Harold Pinter, interview with author.
2. Sir Peter Hall, *Diaries: 1972–1980* (Hamish Hamilton, 1983).
3. Harold Pinter, interview with author.
4. Sir Peter Hall, interview with author.
5. Interview with Martin Jenkins, BBC Radio 3, 10 May 1976.
6. Nicky Henson, interview with author.
7. Harold Pinter, interview with author.
8. Sir Peter Hall, interview with author.
9. Harold Pinter, interview with author.
10. Sir John Gielgud, interview with author.
11. Harold Pinter, interview with author.
12. Richard Hoggart, letter to author.

13. Hall, *Diaries: 1972–1980* (Hamish Hamilton, 1983).
14. Laurence Evans, interview with author.
15. Peter Copley, interview with author.

CHAPTER 21

1. Lindsay Anderson, interview with author.
2. Richard Eyre, interview with author.
3. Simon Cadell, interview with author.
4. Sir Peter Hall, interview with author.
5. Nicky Henson, interview with author.
6. Ben Kingsley, interview with author.
7. Nicky Henson, interview with author.
8. Dorothy Tutin, interview with author.
9. Sir Peter Hall, interview with author.
10. Michael Gambon, interview with author.
11. *Evening Standard*, 7 April 1978.
12. Michael Jayston, interview with author.

CHAPTER 22

1. Nicky Henson, interview with author.
2. Peter Wood, interview with author.
3. Ibid.
4. Ibid.
5. Jane Suffling, interview with author.
6. Sir Peter Hall, interview with author.
7. Sir Peter Hall, *Diaries: 1972–1980* (Hamish Hamilton, 1983).
8. Nicky Henson, interview with author.
9. Peter Copley, interview with author.
10. Michael Frayn, interview with author.
11. Selina Cadell, interview with author.
12. Christopher Morahan, interview with author.
13. Joyce Redman, interview with author.
14. Selina Cadell, interview with author.
15. Foyle's Literary Luncheon, 20 November 1979.

16. Christopher Morahan, interview with author.
17. Michael Bryant, interview with author.
18. Dorothy Tutin, interview with author.

CHAPTER 23

1. Lindsay Anderson, interview with author.
2. David Storey, interview with author.
3. Lindsay Anderson, interview with author.
4. David Storey, interview with author.
5. Ibid.
6. Lady Richardson, interview with author.
7. David Storey, interview with author.
8. Sir Peter Hall, interview with author.
9. David Storey, interview with author.
10. Jocelyn Herbert, interview with author.
11. David Storey, interview with author.
12. Ibid.
13. Simon Cadell, interview with author.
14. David Storey, interview with author.
15. Anthony Page, interview with author.
16. Ibid.
17. David Storey, interview with author.
18. Anthony Page, interview with author.

CHAPTER 24

1. Sir Georg Solti, interview with author.
2. Angela Huth, interview with author.
3. Ibid.
4. Ibid.
5. Simon Cadell, interview with author.
6. Edward Fox, interview with author.
7. Hugh Hudson, interview with author.
8. John Wells, interview with author.
9. Hugh Hudson, interview with author.

10. John Wells, interview with author.
11. Michael Bryant, interview with author.
12. Michael Gambon, interview with author.
13. Sir Peter Hall, interview with author.
14. Judy Bryant, interview with author.
15. Martin Jarvis, interview with author.
16. Daniel Massey, interview with author.
17. Robin Midgley, interview with author.
18. Simon Cadell, interview with author.

CHRONOLOGY
OF PARTS

PLAYS

DATE	PLAY	ROLE	THEATRE
1920–21			
(St Nicholas Players)			Brighton
Jan	*Jean Valjean*	Gendarme	
	The Farmer's Romance	Cuthbert	
Mar	*Macbeth*	Banquo and Macduff	
May	*The Moon-Children*	Father	
	The Taming of the Shrew	Tranio	
1921			
(F. R. Growcott Repertory Company)			Brighton
Jun	*Twelfth Night*	Malvolio	
	The Taming of the Shrew		
July	*The Farmer's Romance*	Cuthbert	
	Jean Valjean	Gendarme	
	Waterloo		
	Oliver Twist	Mr Bumble and Bill Sikes	
	Macbeth	Banquo and Macduff	
Aug	*A Tale of Two Cities*	Defarge, Stryver and Marquis	

1921–23		
(Charles Doran Company)		Tour
		1921
Aug–Sep	The Merchant of Venice	Lorenzo
	Hamlet	Bernardo and Guildenstern
	The Taming of the Shrew	Pedant
	Julius Caesar	Soothsayer and Strato
	As You Like It	Oliver
	Henry V	Scroop and Gower
	Macbeth	Angus and Macduff
	The Tempest	Francisco
	A Midsummer Night's Dream	Lysander
	Twelfth Night	Curio and Valentine
1922		
Jan–Jun	Macbeth	Banquo
	A Midsummer Night's Dream	Lysander
	Hamlet	Horatio
	Julius Caesar	Decius Brutus and Octavius Caesar
	Twelfth Night	Fabian
	The Taming of the Shrew	Vincentio
	The Taming of the Shrew	Lucentio
Sep–Dec		
1923		
Jan–June	Othello	Cassio
	The Merchant of Venice	Antonio and Gratiano

	Julius Caesar	Mark Antony	
1923			Abbey
(Earle Grey Company)			Theatre,
			Dublin
Jul–Aug	*The Rivals*	Sir Lucius O'Trigger	
	The Romantic Age	Bobby	
Sep–Nov			
(Charles Doran Company)			Tour
1924			
Jan–Jun	*Outward Bound*	Henry	Tour
Aug–Oct	*The Way of the World*	Fainall	Tour
1925			
Feb–Dec	*The Farmer's Wife*	Richard Coaker	Tour
1925–26			
(Birmingham Repertory Company)			
1925			
Dec	*The Christmas Party*	Dick Whittington	
1926			
Jan	*The Cassilis Engagement*	Geoffrey Cassilis	
Feb	*The Round Table*	Christopher Pegram	
	He Who Gets Slapped	Gentleman	
Mar	*The Importance of Being Earnest*	Lane	
	Devonshire Cream	Robert Blanchard	
Apr	*Hobson's Choice*	Albert Prosser	
	Dear Brutus	Mr Dearth	

May	*The Land of Promise*	Frank Taylor	
Jun	*The Barber and the Cow*	Dr Tudor Bevan	
Jul	*Oedipus at Colonus*	The Stranger	Scala
Aug	*Devonshire Cream*	Robert Blanchard	Tour
Nov	*Yellow Sands*	Arthur Varwell	Haymarket

1927
(Sunday performances)

Apr	*Sunday Island*	Harold Devrill	Strand
Jun	*The Warden*	John Bold	Royalty
Jul	*Samson and Delilah*	Sophus Meyer	Arts
Sep	*Chance Acquaintance*	Frank Liddell	Strand
Oct	*At Number Fifteen*	Albert Titler	Garrick

1928

Mar	*Back to Methuselah*	Zozim and Pygmalion	Royal Court
Apr	*Harold*	Gurth	Royal Court
	The Taming of the Shrew	Tranio	Royal Court
Jun	*Prejudice*	Hezekiah Brent	Arts
Aug	*Aren't Women Wonderful*	Ben Hawley	Royal Court
Sep	*The First Performance*	Alexander Magnus	Royal Court
Oct	*The Runaways*	James Jago	Garrick
Nov	*The New Sin*	David Llewellyn Davids	Epsom Little

1929
(Gerald Lawrence's Company)

			South African tour
Apr–Aug	*Monsieur Beaucaire*	Duke of Winterset	
	The School for Scandal	Joseph Surface	
	David Garrick	Squire Chivy	

1930

| Feb | *Silver Wings* | Gilbert Nash | Dominion |

	Cat and Mouse	Edward	Queen's
May	*Othello*	Roderigo	Savoy

1930–31
(The Old Vic Company)
1930

Sep	*Henry IV, Part I*	Prince Hal
Oct	*The Tempest*	Caliban
	The Jealous Wife	Sir Harry Beagle
Nov	*Antony and Cleopatra*	Enobarbus

1931

Jan	*Twelfth Night*	Sir Toby Belch
Feb	*Richard II*	Bolingbroke
Mar	*Arms and the Man*	Bluntschli
	Much Ado about Nothing	Don Pedro
Apr	*King Lear*	Kent

1931

May	*The Mantle*	David Regan	Arts
Aug			
(Malvern	*Ralph Roister Doister*	Matthew	
Festival)		Merrygreek	
	She Would If She Could	Mr Courtall	
	The Switchback	Viscount Pascal	

1931–32
(The Old Vic Company)
1931

Sep	*King John*	Faulconbridge
Oct	*The Taming of the Shrew*	Petruchio
Nov	*A Midsummer Night's Dream*	Bottom
Dec	*Henry V*	Henry

1932

Jan	*The Knight of the Burning Pestle*	Ralph
	Julius Caesar	Brutus
Feb	*Abraham Lincoln*	General Grant

Mar	*Othello*	Iago	
Apr	*Twelfth Night*	Sir Toby Belch	
Apr	*Hamlet*	Ghost and First Grave-digger	
Aug (Malvern Festival)	*Ralph Roister Doister*	Matthew Merrygreek	
	The Alchemist	Face	
	Oroonoko	Oroonoko	
	Too True to Be Good	Sergeant Fielding	
1932			
Sep	*Too True to Be Good*	Sergeant Fielding	New
Nov	*For Services Rendered*	Collie Stratton	Globe
1933			
Feb	*Head-on Crash*	Dirk Barclay	Queen's
May	*Wild Decembers*	Arthur Bell Nicholls	Apollo
Sep	*Sheppey*	Sheppey	Wyndham's
Dec	*Peter Pan*	Mr Darling and Captain Hook	Palladium
1934			
Feb	*Marriage Is No Joke*	John MacGregor	Globe
Sep	*Eden End*	Charles Appleby	Duchess
1935			
Mar	*Cornelius*	Cornelius	Duchess
Dec	*Romeo and Juliet*	Chorus and Mercutio	Martin Beck, New York
1936			
Feb	*Promise*	Emil Delbar	Shaftesbury
May	*Bees on the Boatdeck*	Sam Gridley	Lyric
Aug	*The Amazing Dr Clitterhouse*	Dr Clitterhouse	Haymarket

1937			
Nov	*The Silent Knight*	Peter Agardi	St James's
Dec	*A Midsummer Night's Dream*	Bottom	Old Vic
1938			
Feb	*Othello*	Othello	Old Vic
1939			
Feb	*Johnson over Jordan*	Johnson	New

1944–47
(The Old Vic Company at the New Theatre)

1944			
Aug	*Peer Gynt*	Peer	
Sep	*Arms and the Man*	Bluntschli	
	Richard III	Richmond	

1945		
Jan	*Uncle Vanya*	Vanya

(European tour of first three plays after VE Day)

Sep	*Henry IV, Parts I and II*	Falstaff
Oct	*Oedipus*	Tiresias
	The Critic	Lord Burleigh

1946
(New York tour with both double-bills and *Uncle Vanya*)

Oct	*An Inspector Calls*	Inspector Goole
Nov	*Cyrano de Bergerac*	Cyrano

1947		
Jan	*The Alchemist*	Face
Apr	*Richard II* (and director)	Gaunt

1948			
Apr	*Royal Circle* (and director)	Marcus Ivanirex	Wyndham's

1949			
Feb	*The Heiress*	Dr Sloper	Haymarket

1950			
Mar	*Home at Seven*	David Preston	Wyndham's

1951

| May | *Three Sisters* | Vershinin | Aldwych |

1952
(The Shakespeare Memorial Theatre, Stratford-upon-Avon)

May	*The Tempest*	Prospero	
Jun	*Macbeth*	Macbeth	
Jul	*Volpone*	Volpone	

1953

| Mar | *The White Carnation* | John Greenwood | Globe |
| Nov | *A Day by the Sea* | Dr Farley | Haymarket |

1955
(Tour of Australia and New Zealand)

| | *The Sleeping Prince* | Grand Duke | |
| | *Separate Tables* | Mr Martin and Major Pollock | |

1956

| Sep | *Timon of Athens* | Timon | Old Vic |

1957

| Jan | *The Waltz of the Toreadors* | General St Pé | Coronet, New York |
| Nov | *Flowering Cherry* | Jim Cherry | Haymarket |

1959

| Jun | *The Complaisant Lover* | Victor Rhodes | Globe |

1960

| Sep | *The Last Joke* | Edward Portal | Phoenix |

1962

| Apr | *The School for Scandal* | Sir Peter Teazle | Haymarket |

1963

| Jun | *Six Characters in Search of an Author* | Step-father | Mayfair |

1964
(British Council Shakespeare Quatercentenary tour of South America and Europe)

	The Merchant of Venice	Shylock	
	A Midsummer Night's Dream	Bottom	
1964			
Sep	*Carving a Statue*	Father	Haymarket
1966			
Jan	*You Never Can Tell*	William	Haymarket
Oct	*The Rivals*	Sir Anthony Absolute	Haymarket
1967			
Sep	*The Merchant of Venice*	Shylock	Haymarket
1969			
Mar	*What the Butler Saw*	Dr Rance	Queen's
1970			
Jun	*Home*	Jack	Royal Court (also the Apollo, and the Morosco in New York)
1971			
Aug	*West of Suez*	Wyatt Gilman	Royal Court (also the Cambridge)
1972			
Jul	*Lloyd George Knew My Father*	General Sir William Boothroyd	Savoy (also toured to Australia and North America)
1975			
Jan	*John Gabriel Borkman*	Borkman	National Theatre at the Old Vic

Apr	*No Man's Land*	Hirst	Old Vic (also at Wyndham's, the Longacre in New York, and the Lyttelton)
1977			
May	*The Kingfisher*	Cecil	Lyric
1978			
Feb	*The Cherry Orchard*	Firs	Olivier, National
May	*Alice's Boys*	Colonel White	Savoy
Sep	*The Double Dealer*	Lord Touchwood	Olivier, National
1979			
Mar	*The Fruits of Enlightenment*	The Master	Olivier, National
Dec	*The Wild Duck*	Old Ekdal	Olivier, National
1980			
Apr	*Early Days*	Kitchen	Cottesloe, National (also the Comedy, and North American tour)
1982			
May	*The Understanding*	Leonard	Strand
1983			
Jun	*Inner Voices*	Don Alberto	Lyttelton, National

FILMS

(INCLUDES FILMS MADE FOR TELEVISION)

DATE	TITLE	PART
1933	*The Ghoul*	Nigel Hartley
	Friday the Thirteenth	Schoolmaster
1934	*The Return of Bulldog Drummond*	Drummond
	Java Head	William Ammidon
	The King of Paris	Paul
1935	*Bulldog Jack*	Morelle
1936	*Things to Come*	The Boss
	The Man Who Could Work Miracles	Colonel Winstanley
1937	*Thunder in the City*	Manningdale
1938	*South Riding*	Robert Carne
	The Divorce of Lady X	Lord Mere
	The Citadel	Dr Denny
	Smith	Smith
1939	*Q-Planes*	Major Hammond
	The Four Feathers	Captain Durrance
	The Lion Has Wings	Wing Commander
	On the Night of the Fire	Will Kobling
1942	*The Day Will Dawn*	Lockwood
1943	*The Silver Fleet*	Jaap Van Leyden
	The Volunteer	Himself
1946	*School for Secrets*	Professor Heatherville
1948	*Anna Karenina*	Karenin
	The Fallen Idol	Baines
1949	*The Heiress*	Dr Sloper
1951	*Outcast of the Islands*	Captain Lingard
1952	*Home at Seven* (also director)	David Preston
	The Sound Barrier	John Richfield

1952	*The Holly and the Ivy*	The Reverend Gregory
1955	*Richard III*	Duke of Buckingham
1956	*Smiley*	The Reverend Lambeth
1957	*The Passionate Stranger*	Roger and Clement
1960	*Our Man in Havana*	'C'
	Oscar Wilde	Sir Edward Carson, QC
	Exodus	General Sutherland
1962	*The 300 Spartans*	Themistocles
	Long Day's Journey into Night	James Tyrone
1964	*Woman of Straw*	Charles Richmond
1965	*Dr Zhivago*	Alexander Gromeko
1966	*Khartoum*	Gladstone
	The Wrong Box	Joseph Finsbury
1969	*Oh! What a Lovely War*	Sir Edward Grey
	the bed-sitting room	Lord Fortnum
	Battle of Britain	David Kelly
	The Looking Glass War	Leclerc
	Midas Run	Henshaw
	David Copperfield	Mr Micawber
1971	*Whoever Slew Auntie Roo?*	Mr Benton
	Eagle in a Cage	Sir Hudson Lowe
1972	*Tales from the Crypt*	Satan
	Alice's Adventures in Wonderland	Caterpillar
	Lady Caroline Lamb	King George III
1973	*A Doll's House*	Dr Rank
	Dr Frankenstein: The True Story	Hermit
	O Lucky Man	Monty and Sir James Burgess
1975	*Rollerball*	Head Librarian
1976	*Jesus of Nazareth*	Simeon
1977	*The Man in the Iron Mask*	Colbert

1981	*The Time Bandits*	The Supreme Being
1982	*The Dragon Slayer*	Ulrich
1983	*Wagner*	Pfordten
	Invitation to the Wedding	Bishop
	Greystoke	Earl of Greystoke

FILM NARRATOR

1940	*Health for the Nation*	
	Forty Million People	
1949	*Rome and Vatican City*	
1950	*Eagles of the Fleet*	
1951	*Cricket*	
1966	*Chimes at Midnight*	
1978	*Watership Down*	

TELEVISION PLAYS

1939	*Bees on the Boatdeck*	Sam Gridley
1947	*Everyman*	Voice of God
1962	*Hedda Gabler*	Judge Brack
	Heart to Heart	Sir Stanley Johnson
1963	*Voices of Man*	
1965	*Johnson over Jordan*	Robert Johnson
1966	*Blandings Castle*	Earl of Emsworth
1968	*Twelfth Night*	Sir Toby Belch
1970	*Hassan*	Hassan
	She Stoops to Conquer	Mr Hardcastle
1972	*Home*	Jack
1975	*Comets Among the Stars*	Professor Macleod
1978	*No Man's Land*	Hirst

1979	*Charlie Muffin*	Sir Archibald
		Willoughby
1982	*Early Days*	Kitchen

RADIO

1929	*The City*
	Scenes from *Julius Caesar* (Schools)
	Twelfth Night
	Captain Brassbound's Conversion
1930	Scenes from *King Lear* (Schools)
1932	*Romeo and Juliet*
1933	*Macbeth*
	The Tempest
	Julius Caesar
1934	*A Midsummer Night's Dream*
1935	*Through the Looking Glass*
1936	*In Memoriam*
	The Tempest
1937	*Candida*
1940	*Johnson over Jordan*
1941	*Job*
1942	*The Shoemaker's Holiday*
	Dr Faustus
1943	*Don Quixote*
1944	*Peer Gynt*
1945	*Cyrano de Bergerac*
	Henry IV, Parts I and II
	Victory Programme
1946	*Moby Dick*
1947	*The Rubaiyat of Omar Khayyám*
1949	*Brand*

1951	*Home at Seven*
1953	*A Midsummer Night's Dream*
	The White Carnation
1958	*Noah*
1960	*Richard II*
1961	*Hamlet*
	Arms and the Man
1963	*The Ballad of Reading Gaol*
	The Merchant of Venice
1964	*A Christmas Carol*
1966	*Cyrano de Bergerac*
1968	*Heartbreak House*
1969	*When We Dead Awaken*
	Much Ado About Nothing
1974	*John Gabriel Borkman*
1976	*The Phoenix and the Turtle*
	The Passionate Pilgrim
1977	Programme on William Blake
1978	Readings from Andrew Marvell
1980	*Notes on a Cellar Book*
1982	*Little Tich — Giant of the Halls*

BIBLIOGRAPHY

Beauman, Sally, *The RSC: a History of Ten Decades* (Oxford University Press, 1982)

Billington, Michael, *Peggy Ashcroft* (Mandarin, 1991)

Bosworth, Patricia, *Montgomery Clift* (Harcourt Brace Jovanovich, 1978)

Burton, Hal, *Great Acting* (BBC Publications, 1967)

Casson, John, *Lewis and Sybil* (Collins, 1972)

Cottrell, John, *The Oliviers* (Weidenfeld & Nicolson, 1975)

Dean, Basil, *Mind's Eye* (Hutchinson, 1973)

Douglas-Home, William, *Old Men Remember* (Collins & Brown, 1991)

Edwards, Anne, *Vivien Leigh* (Simon & Schuster, 1977)

Findlater, Richard, *The Player Kings* (Stein & Day, 1971)

Findlater, Richard, *These Our Actors* (Elm Tree/Hamish Hamilton, 1984)

Findlater, Richard, *Lilian Baylis* (Allen Lane, 1975)

Fleming, Kate, *Celia Johnson* (Weidenfeld & Nicolson, 1991)

Forbes, Bryan, *That Despicable Race* (Elm Tree/Hamish Hamilton, 1980)

Forsyth, James, *Tyrone Guthrie* (Hamish Hamilton, 1976)

Gielgud, John, *Early Stages* (Heinemann Educational, 1974)

Gielgud, John, *An Actor and His Time* (Sidgwick & Jackson, 1979)

Guinness, Alec, *Blessings in Disguise* (Hamish Hamilton, 1985)

Guthrie, Tyrone, *A Life in the Theatre* (Hamish Hamilton, 1960)

Hall, Peter, *Diaries: 1972–1980* (Hamish Hamilton, 1983)

Hall, Peter, *Making an Exhibition of Myself* (Sinclair-Stevenson, 1993)

Hardwicke, Cedric, *A Victorian in Orbit* (Methuen, 1961)

Heston, Charlton, *An Actor's Life: Journals, 1956–76* (Allen Lane, 1979)

Hobson, Harold, *Ralph Richardson* (Rockliff, 1958)

Holden, Anthony, *Olivier* (Sphere, 1988)

Kulik, Karol, *Alexander Korda* (Virgin, 1990)

Lahr, John, *Prick Up Your Ears: Joe Orton* (Alfred A. Knopf, 1978)

Landstone, Charles, *Offstage* (Elek, 1953)

Meyer, Michael, *Not Prince Hamlet* (Oxford University Press, 1989)

Olivier, Laurence, *On Acting* (Weidenfeld & Nicolson, 1986)

Olivier, Tarquin, *Laurence Olivier* (Headline, 1992)

Priestley, J. B., *Margin Released* (Heinemann, 1962)

Quayle, Anthony, *A Time to Speak* (Barrie & Jenkins, 1990)

Roberts, Peter, *The Old Vic Story* (W. H. Allen, 1976)

Sherrin, Ned, *Theatrical Anecdotes* (Virgin, 1991)

Silverman, Stephen, M., *David Lean* (André Deutsch, 1989)

Sinden, Donald, *A Touch of the Memoirs* (Hodder & Stoughton, 1982)

Speaight, Robert, *The Property Basket* (Collins, 1970)

Speaight, Robert, *Shakespeare on the Stage* (Collins, 1973)

Sprigge, Elizabeth, *Sybil Thorndike Casson* (Victor Gollancz, 1971)

Tanitch, Robert, *Ralph Richardson: a Tribute* (Evans Bros, 1982)

Trewin, J. C., *The Birmingham Repertory Theatre, 1913–1963* (Rockliff, 1963)

Trewin, J. C., *Shakespeare on the British Stage, 1900–1964* (Collins, 1973)

Tynan, Kenneth, *A View of the English Stage, 1944–1963* (Davis-Poynter, 1975)

Tynan, Kenneth, *Show People* (Weidenfeld & Nicolson, 1980)

Ustinov, Peter, *Dear Me* (Heinemann, 1977)

Wapshott, Nicholas, *The Man Between: Carol Reed* (Chatto & Windus, 1990)

Wardle, Irving, *The Theatres of George Devine* (Jonathan Cape, 1978)

Williams, Harcourt, *Four Years at the Old Vic* (Putnam, 1935)

Williams, Harcourt, *Old Vic Saga* (Winchester Publications, 1949)

INDEX

Joke, 180; on *You Never Can Tell*, 205; on *Lloyd George Knew My Father*, 249–50; on RR in *John Gabriel Borkman*, 264
Hobson's Choice, 27
Hoggart, Richard, 275
Holland, Anthony, 246
Holly and the Ivy, The, 144
Hollywood, 119–22, 124, 132
Holst, Gustav, 329
Holtby, Winifred, 67
Home, 222, 223–3, 239, 242, 272, 276–7, 287, 307, 310, 313
Home at Seven, 140, 142–4, 145, 160
Hope-Wallace, Philip, 116, 162, 189, 198
Hopkins, Anthony, 122, 156–7, 171, 216–17, 255
Hordern, Sir Michael, 150, 156, 203, 340
Horner, Rosalie, 327
Howard, Alan, 191, 346
Howard, Leslie, 68
Howard, Trevor, 145
Howell, Gillian, 130, 133, 136
Howell, Peter, 85, 88–9
Hudd, Walter, 147
Hudson, Hugh, 119, 332–5
Hudson, W.H., 332–3
Hulbert, Jack, 63
Hunt, Martita, 36
Hunter, N.C., 161–2
Hutcheson, David, 120
Huth, Angela, 324–9

Ibsen, Henrik: *Peer Gynt*, 84, 88, 127, 263; *Brand*, 127; RR's work, 137, 155, 222, 254, 255; *When We Dead Awaken*, 220–1; *A Doll's House*, 254, 255; *John Gabriel*

Borkman, 257, 260–1, 263; *The Wild Duck*, 302
Importance of Being Earnest, The, 27
In Cold Blood, 222
Independent Broadcasting Authority, 276
Inner Voices, 336–41
Inspector Calls, An, 107, 108, 114, 128
International PEN, 274
Invitation to the Wedding, 332
IRA, 336
Irons, Jeremy, 329–30
Irving, Henry, 34
Irving, Laurence, 60

Jackson, Gordon, 220
Jackson, Sir Barry: Birmingham Rep, 26–7, 85, 283; Royal Court productions, 31, 32, 346; Malvern Festival, 50; *Marriage Is No Joke*, 54; Stratford, 150
James, Henry, 5, 101, 119
Jarvis, Martin, 215, 341
Java Head, 63
Jayston, Michael, 287–8
Jealous Wife, The, 39
Jefford, Barbara, 187–9, 191–3, 220
Jenkins, Megs, 161, 187, 189
John Gabriel Borkman, 106, 257–65, 266, 296
Johnson, Ben, 112, 345
Johnson, Celia: in *Three Sisters*, 147; in *Flowering Cherry*, 167–9, 172; in *Lloyd George Knew My Father*, 250, 252; in *The Kingfisher*, 280–2; *The Understanding*, 325–6; death, 326–8; Memorial Theatre, 329
Johnson, Richard, 173
Johnson over Jordan, 73, 74–5, 209
Jones, Dr Ernest, 71